RANGER

10/20/17

To CPT Jameson, Benjamin, a US Army
        Ranger

    Thank you for your service to this
great country in which we are privileged
to live.
    You are one of those who are
keeping us free!
    Rangers Lead the way!
    Ralph Puckett
Honorary Colonel, 75th Ranger Regiment
JAN 1996 — JAN 2008

AMERICAN WARRIORS

Throughout the nation's history, numerous men and women of all ranks
and branches of the U.S. military have served their country with honor and
distinction. During times of war and peace, there are individuals whose
exemplary achievements embody the highest standards of the U.S. armed
forces. The aim of the American Warriors series is to examine the unique
historical contributions of these individuals, whose legacies serve as enduring
examples for soldiers and citizens alike. The series will promote a deeper and
more comprehensive understanding of the U.S. armed forces.

SERIES EDITOR: Roger Cirillo

An AUSA Book

RANGER

A Soldier's Life

Colonel Ralph Puckett, USA (Ret.)

with D. K. R. Crosswell

Afterword by
General David H. Petraeus, USA (Ret.)

UNIVERSITY PRESS OF KENTUCKY

Scholarly publisher for the Commonwealth,
serving Bellarmine University, Berea College, Centre College of Kentucky, Eastern
Kentucky University, The Filson Historical Society, Georgetown College, Kentucky
Historical Society, Kentucky State University, Morehead State University, Murray State
University, Northern Kentucky University, Transylvania University, University
of Kentucky, University of Louisville, and Western Kentucky University.
All rights reserved.

Editorial and Sales Offices: The University Press of Kentucky
663 South Limestone Street, Lexington, Kentucky 40508-4008
www.kentuckypress.com

Photographs are from the author's personal collection.

Library of Congress Cataloging-in-Publication Data

Names: Puckett, Ralph, author. | Crosswell, D. K. R. (Daniel K. R.), author.
Title: Ranger : a soldier's life / Colonel Ralph Puckett, USA (Ret.) ; with
    D. K. R. Crosswell ; afterword by General David H. Petraeus, USA (Ret.).
Description: Lexington, Kentucky : The University Press of Kentucky, [2017] |
    Series: American warriors | Includes index.
Identifiers: LCCN 2016049879| ISBN 9780813169316 (hardcover : alk. paper) |
    ISBN 9780813169323 (pdf) | ISBN 9780813169330 (epub)
Subjects: LCSH: Puckett, Ralph. | United States. Army—Officers—Biography. |
    United States. Army. Eighth Army Ranger Company—Biography. | United
    States. Army. Ranger Regiment, 75th—Biography. | Korean War,
    1950–1953—Personal narratives, American. | Vietnam War,
    1961–1975—Personal narratives, American.
Classification: LCC U53.P84 A3 2017 | DDC 355.0092 [B] —dc23
LC record available at https://lccn.loc.gov/2016049879

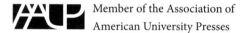

I owe every success to my soldiers, who carried me on their shoulders,
and the many friends who helped me along the way.
I would be nothing without the support of my wife
and the sacrifices of my children.

Humility must always be the portion of any man who receives acclaim earned in the blood of his followers and the sacrifices of his friends.

—Gen. Dwight D. Eisenhower

Contents

Photographs follow page 156

1

Georgia Boy

Early Influences

Tifton, Georgia, is not the typical Deep South county-seat town. It boasts no square with a historic courthouse and monument to the Lost Cause. The town, founded by Connecticut Yankees during Reconstruction, prospered owing to a newly constructed railway spur and the booming lumbering trade. Once the forests were gone, the rich soils yielded a variety of crops—peaches and pecans, cotton and tobacco. Because of the long growing season, Tifton, styling itself the "Plant City," produced truck-farm seedling for shipment north to places like New Jersey. The importance of agriculture spurred the influential Tift family to convince the state to found a two-year agricultural school, the Georgia State College for Men, in Tifton in 1908 (now the Abraham Baldwin Agricultural College) and the Coastal Plain Experimental Station in 1919. By 1920, Tifton had grown into a thriving little city of about eight thousand.

In other respects, Tifton was a typical south central Georgia town. The men would gather in one of the two restaurants on Main Street to play backgammon and share local gossip, news, and crop predictions, but mostly they talked about Tifton High's fortunes in football. Despite Tifton's opera house, most people's idea of culture involved coming into town on Saturday, doing trade, and going to the movie house. And naturally—given the Jim Crow times—the town possessed a definite dividing line between the races.

"Always Do the Right Thing"

I entered the world on 8 December 1926, the second child of Ralph and Clara Stedman Puckett. My parents met when both were about eight years old. As Mother told the story: "I was riding my bicycle when the chain came off—not an uncommon occurrence in those days. As I stood there wondering what I was going to do, this cute boy rode up on his bike, stopped, tipped his cap, and asked if he could help me. I, of course, asked him to put my chain onto my bike, which he quickly did." Daddy always interrupted at about this point in the story, interjecting, "She was the prettiest little girl I ever saw, with her long, blond pigtails and big, blue eyes." Love at first sight. When Daddy was old enough, he started riding his bicycle the twenty miles to Ocilla, where Mother lived. They were sweethearts for the rest of their lives.

Mother was a very self-sufficient, no-nonsense person. She had to be because her father died when she was twelve and her mother followed him six years later. An orphan at eighteen, she watched as all the family's possessions were burned because both parents had died from tuberculosis. She had nothing and was on her own. Since young single women did not live alone during the early 1900s, she moved into a boardinghouse until she married. These experiences produced the independent, self-reliant, and strong-willed woman I knew growing up—and those traits were instilled in her children. And there was something else. One glance at an old photograph of my maternal grandfather, Frank Stedman, that Mother kept on her dresser indicated which side of the family I most resembled.

Despite these setbacks, Mother acquired the cultural graces expected of a young southern lady. She mastered the piano and organ. One of my most pleasant family memories growing up was seeing the pleasure Daddy derived from sitting and listening to her play either instrument—our house boasted both. She devoted much of her free time to her crafts. Her "workroom" was crowded with works in progress. She painted china, applying gold leaf and a monogram, eventually giving a complete set to each of her children and grandchildren. Her work won local acclaim; many of the ladies in town apprenticed under her. She also collected old silver patterns and over time "found" a complete set for each grandchild. Mother also had a competitive side, especially when she played bridge. Although her crafts and hobbies were impressive, nothing compared to her skills in the kitchen. By universal acclaim—at least among family members—mother's culinary talents could not be matched.

Mother did her best to make a gentleman out of me. At the appropriate time, she would inject into our conversation some instruction on how a gentleman should act. One night she and I walked along the sidewalk coming home from a movie. "Junior," she said, "a gentleman always walks between the lady and the street." I asked why. "Because he will be in a position to protect her if a car comes from the street or if a car splashes mud," she responded. "The gentleman can block the mud, and it won't splash on the lady." At eight, this baffled me. I saw neither any reason to block the mud nor any car that might head our way. "Because that's what a gentleman is supposed to do," she insisted. If she said so, it was good enough for me. She also told me about opening doors, offering my chair, standing when a lady or an older person came into the room, holding the door for older people, and a host of other little niceties. Both parents had taught me earlier to say, "Yes, Sir," "No, Ma'am," "Please," and "Thank you." Those are rooted southern customs.

My father's full name was Ralph Atticus Puckett. Not much is known about the Pucketts. They were not among the "first families of Georgia," but they were definitely old stock. Unlike others who looked back on long bloodlines and heroic forebears in the Civil War, my sense of identity sprang from my parents. Although my mother exerted great influence on me, I hero-worshiped my father. From my earliest memories, I wanted to be like him in every way. He embodied integrity; his word was his bond. He never insisted on any contract; his handshake sealed the agreement.

Another reason for idolizing Daddy was his physical presence: he was about six-foot-three, handsome, and, at 185 pounds, strong and trim. A fine athlete in college, he made "All Southern" as a pitcher his two years at Georgia Tech. The Philadelphia Athletics, then in the process of rebuilding after Connie Mack sold off Home Run Baker, Eddie Collins, and Chief Bender, offered him a five-thousand-dollar signing bonus—huge money at that time. Mother kept him from signing, although he begged for her consent. He stressed the big bonus and, if he made it to the A's, the large salary. She never gave an inch, telling him that she knew he would blow it all. Easy come, easy go. Daddy never signed.

He had the good sense to succumb with grace. Mother could be pretty formidable. They would sometimes argue—both possessed strong independent streaks—but once a decision emerged, they both stuck by it. About signing with the A's, he always maintained, "Your mother was right. I wouldn't have saved any of it," but he would wistfully add, "I know I could have thrown that ball by those big-league batters!"

Instead of the bright lights of Philadelphia, he returned to Tifton, where he ran an independent casualty insurance agency. Like many people in the South at that time, he owned some low-rent houses that provided additional income. After the stock market crashed, he formed a partnership with two of the big money men in Tifton and bought a nearly bankrupt wholesale grocery operation and later a company, also in dire financial straits, that shelled and ground corn. For a very small salary, Daddy assumed responsibility as president to run and turn around the two ailing businesses. Knowing he lacked experience with either enterprise, he set about to learn their operations by working briefly in each position from warehouseman to salesman to shipping clerk. Mother would often get angry with him when he returned home covered with grime or meal. But he learned the ropes, and in a few years the two businesses were solidly in the black.

Daddy worked long and hard. For several years he arose before daybreak and worked until nine or ten o'clock at night. Mother put his supper in the oven so that it would be ready when he came home. She always apologized for it not being perfect, and he always responded, "This is fine, Honey. It's my fault I'm late." The long hours came from juggling the insurance agency, the rental properties, and trying to keep the grocery and mill afloat—which absorbed most of his time—during the deepening depression. His partners, each holding one-third interest in the two businesses, refused any salary increase. They sat back and enjoyed the fruits of Daddy's labor. He never complained, but I am sure it bothered him.

My parents were strict and loving. They wanted the best for their children and expected much from us in both character and performance. My sister, Clara, was my senior by eight years. Monkey, as we called her, spent a lot of her time looking after her boy siblings. Tommy entered the picture two-and-a-half years after me. She left for college when I was nine or ten. Obviously influenced by Mother's love of the piano, Clara studied music; talented and a hard worker, she earned two degrees in four years by going year-round to Wesleyan College, a woman's school in Macon, and Brenau in Gainesville, Georgia. After graduating, Monkey returned to Tifton and taught, building a reputation as an accomplished pianist. A sweet, caring, and thoughtful person, Clara was a great big sister.

Tommy and I could not have been more dissimilar had we tried. The age gap—which seemed large when we were young—offers one explanation. He followed me everywhere, but big brother did not want him tagging along. Aside from the usual sibling rivalry, our personalities differed. Junior was shy, serious, and the "responsible" child; Tommy was full of life, mischievous, and outgoing. Daddy often commented that he wished he could put us into a bottle and shake us up. He said he would have two perfect sons at that point. Both of us grew up thinking the other was the favorite; Ralph was the "achiever," and Tommy had the likeable personality. Not exactly rivals, we never were close until much later in life.

Like other middle-class families, the Pucketts had African American help. A housekeeper came each day and did the cleaning and some cooking, but

Mother always fixed breakfast and prepared the evening meal. Once a week, the clothes went to the black quarter of town for laundering. Nobody thought much about racial matters; strict separation of the races was considered perfectly normal. No integrationist—the idea would not have occurred to him—Daddy always treated African Americans fairly. To them he was Mr. Ralph.

Formal religion played no particular role in my growing up. That might seem a little unusual for a family living in the Bible Belt. Daddy objected to the hypocrisy of many of the clergy and parishioners, people who avowed their faith in church yet seldom in their daily lives practiced what they professed. One particular preacher often told dirty jokes in male company, supposedly to establish rapport. Another continually solicited money, often with tearful appeals mixed with his prayers. Our family more than tithed; Daddy just grew weary of being hit up for money during every sermon. Instead he and a friend directed their money into funding the building of a church in a poor neighborhood. Although my parents seldom talked about God or religion, they obviously were believers. We never ate without Daddy saying a blessing. What loomed larger was the answer to the question, "What is the right thing to do?" In the Puckett house, religion was lived, not preached.

I went to Sunday school only because the other boys my age did. One benefit of Sunday school was the outings. One teacher, Mr. Todd, was particularly good with us. We would go to some abandoned field "in the country" (wherever that was) and have a wiener roast and toast marshmallows. After eating our fill, we played hide-and-seek. What a great time we had. Mr. Todd never knew what a positive impact he made on his boys.

As a very young child, I said my prayers every night. "Now I lay me down to sleep. . . ." I added "Bless Mother, Daddy, Tommy, and Monkey." I included Tiancy, my pony, and Spot, our dog. Sometimes there were other special requests. When older, I repeated the Lord's Prayer but always included a supplication that became the goal of my existence: "Help me to grow up to be big and strong and make my Daddy proud of me."

As a child I believed if I were "big and strong" I would be like a knight in shining armor, fighting all evil no matter the risk. To understand my thinking, one must keep in mind the perspective of a very impressionable child whose heroes were King Arthur, Ivanhoe, Robin Hood, and Horatio Alger's characters. If I could be like them, I thought, I would be living the way God would want me to live. More important, if I grew up to be like those heroes, Daddy would be proud of me.

Actually, though, I did not have to look to books to discover a genuine hero. One night before I was born, a lynch mob assembled at the Tifton jail. Inside a black man was held accused of some heinous crime (in the eyes of the white men). The crowd planned on breaking in and lynching him. Knowing and respecting my dad as a man of integrity, some of the local African American leaders called on him for help. Daddy went to the jail, put himself in front of the crowd, and "stood them down." Since Daddy was physically imposing and in possession of a fearsome temper—he was a pugilist of some note, especially when his honesty was challenged—they decided he meant business and dispersed. Years later, when Mother told me the story, I asked Daddy why he had taken the risk of being injured or even killed by the hate-filled mob. "Son," he responded, "what those people wanted to do just wasn't right." That's all he said. Only later did the obvious parallel to Atticus Finch in the novel *To Kill a Mockingbird* occur to me—even down to the same name. His courage in doing the "right thing" left a deep imprint.

Although comfortably middle class by southern standards, as a child I knew times were tough. Money was tight, and Daddy's various business endeavors left him heavily in debt, which bothered him a great deal. After Tommy and I had gone to bed—with Monkey away at college—our parents talked about finances. I knew they were worried. Hoboes rode the boxcars, and men came by the house wanting work for a meal. We saw crowds of unemployed in the newsreels. One day, Daddy made mention of a schoolteacher to whom he had loaned money so she could buy a house. She had faithfully paid the mortgage month after month until some bad luck caused her to miss a couple of payments. As Daddy told the story, I piped up, "Daddy, why don't you foreclose on her? You can keep what she has paid and then sell the house to someone else. That would be legal, wouldn't it?" Everybody in those Depression years knew about foreclosures. He turned to me, looked me in the eye, and said, "It may be legal, son, but it isn't right."

Life's Little Lessons

Tifton was a safe place, so our parents pretty much let us run wild anywhere within a mile of the house. At age four, I developed a very dangerous notion of "fun." I would stand by the side of the dirt road near our house and wait until a car approached. At the last minute, I would dash across the street. Too young to appreciate the danger, I saw only the challenge. One day the inevitable happened. The driver, probably petrified he had killed me, got out of his car, picked me up, placed me in the ditch, pulled my cap over my head, and drove away.

All I recall was the cook next door picking me up and carrying me inside; I later regained consciousness in the hospital. My parents, hovering about me, broke into big smiles. Embarrassed, I apologized for the expense of the hospitalization and promised Daddy my piggy-bank savings would contribute to the costs. He laughed, gave me a hug, and told me not to worry. Other than a jagged scar on the side of my head—which would serve as the butt of many a joke over the years—I suffered no permanent damage.

Around the same time I started saddling and bridling my Shetland pony. Several boys and girls in the neighborhood also had ponies. We had a fenced, vacant lot behind our house with a shed for the ponies. I loved to ride and wanted to be a cowboy. Not as good a rider as I thought, I often got thrown from my mount. Once I was riding with a group of teenagers who decided to gallop as fast as they could. I tried to slow Tiancy down but could not. She was determined to keep up with the herd. All of a sudden, I lost my seat, my foot got caught in the stirrup, and I was dragged some distance before Tiancy stopped. More frightened than hurt, I burst into tears. Somehow I ended up in our living room, where Mother cuddled me, took off my shoes, and warmed my feet by the fire. When my tears dried, both my parents told me to get back on the pony immediately; otherwise, they said, I would never overcome my fright. After much urging and with some reluctance, I went outside, mounted Tiancy, and rode away.

I had lots of friends. Two of my closest were my classmates Charles Kent and Charles Massey, but I often palled around with boys two or three years older. Perhaps my best friend—certainly the one who had the most influence on me—was James Bowen. Although James was about four years older, he was always very patient with me and spent a lot of time teaching me things boys should know.

We often got to "tussling." Although James was never mean, being older and stronger, he always won. Getting whipped was no fun, and often I became angry and started lashing out at him. I remember one day he flipped me over his shoulders, causing me more embarrassment than pain. I broke into angry tears and started swinging wildly at him. After dodging and weaving, James grabbed my arms and pinned them to my side. "Junior, you shouldn't cry every time you get a little hurt," he said. "Be a man! Don't cry! Next time you get hurt, concentrate on not crying. It'll come easier each time." With that, he let me go, and I walked home—still crying.

A couple of days later, while playing in the house, I gave my noggin a tremendous blow that almost immediately brought forth a huge knot. As tears immediately began to rush to my eyes, I remembered what James had admonished me to do: "Be a man!" Somehow I managed to hold back my tears, finding that it was not so hard after all. As a very impressionable boy, I had learned a great lesson. It continued to come to mind as I fell victim to the many cuts and scrapes of boyhood. And it would influence me as an adult. While the adage "Grown men don't cry" appears passé, it epitomized what I considered a virtue.

The schools reinforced many of the values my parents taught at home. One of the advantages of growing up in a small town was that all the schools stood within walking distance from home. At Tifton Grammar School the teachers were generally good and enforced tight discipline in their large classes. Ms. Annabelle Clark was a strong woman and a tough principal. If you got a whipping at school, another awaited you at home. Junior high stretched from the fifth to the eighth grade. Each 11 November, the principal, Frank Kelly, came to every class and talked about World War I and the meaning of Armistice Day. The alarm would ring on the water tower precisely at 11:00 a.m., and everyone observed a minute's silence. That left a lasting impression on me.

As soon as the school bell rang, I made tracks. People in that part of the world do a lot of hunting and fishing. My father decided a gun should wait, but he let me buy a rod and reel. We went to Roddenberry Hardware, where Daddy and the salesman picked out a rod, a Pflueger "Akron" reel, a spool of line, and two artificial lures. The price came in at a staggering $10.80, but Daddy loaned me the money. It was winter—and unusually cold for Georgia—when I bought the rod and reel. Hurrying home from school day after day, I retrieved the rod and reel and went outside to practice casting. Actually, I spent more time untangling the backlashes. Finally it got warm enough for me to ride my bike the mile to Fulwood's Pond to try my luck. After what seemed weeks, I landed my first bass—a whopper of about three-quarters of a pound. I was so proud.

No doubt inspired by my father's work ethic—and it never hurt to have some walking-around money—I always had at least one job. I started selling magazines—the *Saturday Evening Post* and the *Ladies' Home Journal.* Going door-to-door a couple of afternoons each week soon built a few steady customers and probably cleared fifty cents or so weekly, a huge sum for a ten-year-old at the time. The money helped me repay the loan.

At twelve my horizons broadened. Hiram Goodman, a second cousin, let me operate the soft drink and candy concession at his service station during the summer. I managed the whole operation from buying the products and selling them at a healthy markup, making about ten dollars each week, a tremendous sum during the Depression, when the minimum hourly wage stood at twenty cents. A dollar went for "spending money," and I placed the rest in a savings account earmarked for college expenses.

During the school year I worked for Hiram a couple of afternoons each week and on Saturdays. Duties included collecting delinquent accounts, running errands, washing windshields, and performing the myriad other tasks that needed doing. Hiram, a positive influence, once offered very short and to-the-point counseling: "Junior, I noticed you were a little 'down' today. No matter how you feel or who it is, when a customer drives in I want you to run out there as fast as you can. Give him a big smile and ask, 'Can I fill it up, Sir?' No matter how that customer acts, you are to be as nice and polite as you can be. He is our customer. We appreciate his business."

Around this time my interests began to change. I began devouring the weekly editions of *G8 and His Battle Aces* and the *Lone Eagle*. These pulp magazines filled my thoughts with the heroic endeavors of World War I aces and great aviators like Lucky Lindy. Notions of becoming a cowboy faded; now my dream centered on being a fighter pilot.

If the air corps had to wait, the next best thing was the Boy Scouts. Desperately wanting to join, I had to wait; Tifton did not have any Cub Scouts. I looked forward to my twelfth birthday with great anticipation. Scouts did such interesting things and wore good-looking uniforms. Wismer Holland, a man who had a great influence on me, served as our scoutmaster. Although I had no way to know it at the time, the Boy Scouts would have a profound and long-term impact on me. Applying myself, I made Eagle Scout in two years, the minimum time permitted. The bronze and gold palms to the Eagle Badge soon followed. Along with that came my selection as patrol leader and then senior patrol leader. These responsibilities gave me my first taste of exercising leadership. The senior patrol leader conducted the meetings each week, formed the troop outside, checked attendance, and selected the neatest scout in the troop from those selected in each of our patrols. The Scout Oath was not taken lightly: "On my honor, I will do my best to do my duty to God and to my country. . . ." Repeating the oath at each meeting provided the first realization that I had a duty to my country. Doing my "best" meant that there was no room for slack. I never doubted what course to take. If my deeds fell short and had not been my best effort, I had not lived up to the oath. There were no excuses.

One example of falling short involved Tommy. He was almost always selected as the neatest in his patrol. He could have been a poster boy for scouting. Unfortunately, I sometimes passed him over for fear of someone accusing me of favoritism. Obviously, I did not do the right thing; I was more concerned about the derision I might receive from my peers. It was a lesson never forgotten—and learned at my brother's expense.

When I turned fourteen and Daddy thought I was old enough to learn to handle a gun, he gave me his beautiful Browning semi-automatic shotgun. Johnson Goodman, a second cousin who worked for Daddy, supervised on our several hunting forays. I enjoyed the physical test, the endurance it required, and the skills involved. The fieldcraft I learned in the Scouts also came in handy. In time I became a fair shot.

Daddy had very few conversations with me about the serious aspects of life. When he did talk to me, what he had to say was generally very brief and to the point. One bit of wisdom—which he learned the hard way—involved never "getting in debt . . . and don't buy something you cannot pay for." Poised to enter high school, I asked, "What do you think I ought to be when I grow up?" "Son, be a man!" he replied simply. That was all he said, but I knew exactly what he meant. To be a man, I must be a person of integrity who did his duty no matter the risk, no matter what ridicule he might receive from his friends. It was the way he lived that influenced me most.

Moving on to high school presented no particular anxiety. Although the academic curriculum left a good deal to be desired, I liked everything about Tifton High. Sports always played a big role in our family. Tifton High did not have a baseball team until my tenth-grade year. Naturally, Daddy tried to make a pitcher out of me. He caught me for hours. I had a fast ball and decent control but nothing else. When it became clear pitching was not in my future, he hit me hundreds of grounders. Those times with him were some of the happiest memories of my life. While never very good, I loved practicing. Also in the tenth grade I went out for football spring practice but was not destined for stardom. In fact, I was less than mediocre.

If organized team sports were not for me, maybe golf was. Daddy became an outstanding golfer, holding the course record on our home links for years. He gave me lessons every afternoon after school. Ray Raynor, a famous pro golfer, wintered in Tifton. Raynor taught me the fundamentals and urged me to concentrate on the short game. A couple of hours of practice every day, week after week, soon made a difference. Some knowledgeable golfers said that I had a perfect Bobby Jones swing. But golf just was not my thing, either. Tommy, on the other hand, loved the game and became a skilled player.

I was on the golf course, the ninth green, when news broke about the attack on Pearl Harbor. I immediately decided to get into the war. That would have to wait since I would only turn fifteen the next day. All of the experts in the club-house figured the United States would whip the Japanese in six weeks. The war would be over before I was of age. The war in Europe had been raging for two years. We listened to the war news on the radio—especially Edward R. Mur-row reporting from London during the Blitz—and followed the advance of the German forces. Daddy, turned down by the navy during World War I for being too tall, worried about the prospects of the United States being drawn into the European war. Reading *Mein Kampf* heightened his concerns.

Tifton resembled every other American town on the Home Front. The town had an air-raid observation tower manned by the Civil Air Patrol. The Boy Scouts felt pretty important making the rounds enforcing the practice blackouts. My mother and sister took Red Cross classes. Blue Star service flags sprouted on houses all over town. Tifton was shaken when the telegraph arrived announcing the death of Frank Autman, the first Tifton boy killed in the war. The Autmans were not the only ones to display the gold star flag before the war ended. The one thing that sticks in my mind was the intense sense of community and national unity that drew people together. Every-one pitched in: saving kitchen fats for ammunition, squashing tin cans for recycling, observing rationing, and cultivating victory gardens. The schools focused on collecting tin foil from cigarette packs. War news became the chief topic of conversation.

My childhood fascination with flying had not waned. The stories of the Luftwaffe battling the courageous RAF over England thrilled and intrigued me. In this country the exciting field of aviation was growing by leaps and bounds, and I wanted to be part of it. When I was fifteen, my parents let me begin flying lessons. Money earned working in the wholesale grocery warehouse—which meant getting up at 5:00 a.m. to load the trucks—let me pay for the lessons. It also helped that Wismer Holland, the scoutmaster, acted as my flight instruc-tor. He later joined the air corps and flew the Hump in the China-Burma the-ater. I loved everything about flying: the thrill of putting on a parachute for the required training in spins; the excitement of preflight checking the aircraft and spinning the propeller to start the engine; and finally the rush of getting into the air. All this conjured up fantasies of doing great things in the air: flying in combat and becoming an ace.

We flew a Piper Cub J2, a tail-dragger, with maybe 50 horsepower. To go into a spin, the pilot had to stall the aircraft, press the rudder, and move the stick. Once in a spin, you counted the rotations and had to come out exactly after two turns. The first few times made me dizzy and queasy in the stomach, but I managed to complete training without losing my lunch. I do not know which I liked more—the spin or wearing the parachute. Although regulations prohibited me from soloing—you had to be sixteen—Holland assured me not to worry.

2

Want to Be a Flyboy

Training with the U.S. Army Air Corps Enlisted Reserve

A military career never figured prominently in my calculations. One of my first memories was going to the drugstore after church one Sunday. Daddy wanted to buy a paper. We encountered a man on crutches selling red flowers. As we left the store, I asked my father about buying the flower. Daddy explained the man lost his leg in the Great War and the flower was a poppy like the ones that grew in France and Belgium where much of the fighting took place. Later, in school, we memorized John McRae's poem "In Flanders Fields." And each Armistice Day gave everyone pause to think about the costs of war. In the rush to war after Pearl Harbor, those cautionary notions were forgotten. Like most everybody else my age, I wanted into the war, and if I went into the services, it would be the U.S. Army Air Corps. That decision grew more from boyish enthusiasms than from careful consideration.

In my family, going on to university was a given, and my sights were firmly fixed on Georgia Tech. Although they were far from realistic, I entertained dreams of baseball and football success like Daddy had earned. Thoughts about becoming a pilot fused with my ambition to earn a degree in aeronautical engineering. Tech boasted an outstanding reputation as the place to get that engineering degree. Tifton High had some fine teachers. Miss Annabell Williams drilled us in grammar and ran a special literature class I was selected to attend. The math and science offerings were inadequate for admission into the rigorous engineering curriculum at Tech. After the tenth grade—Tifton High only had eleven—my father approached an old classmate and then a dean at Tech about the chances of me getting into the engineering program. He suggested sending me to Baylor School in Chattanooga to pass the necessary math classes. I entered the twelfth grade, skipping the eleventh.

Studying hard in the closely supervised environment of Baylor, I performed well academically, scored straight As, and made the honor roll in each grading period. All the teachers were superb. The classes were small, and most of the students bright and motivated. Attending Baylor became a great source of pride; I thanked my father for his foresight. In pursuits other than academics, I fared less well. Dreams of glory on the diamond and gridiron—and in the boxing ring—all quickly faded. My aspirations far exceeded my capabilities—but I tried. Whereas Tommy, with his winning personality, suffered no lack of girlfriends—another point of contention—I was tongue-tied around girls and very easily embarrassed. I always looked at myself as pretty square and of no interest to the opposite sex.

After graduating from Baylor, I entered Georgia Tech at age sixteen and selected aeronautical engineering as my major. With my dreams of designing and flight-testing aircraft, no one could say that I did not think big. A job as assistant concessions manager at Grant Field helped defray costs. The duties ate up all day Saturday, a half day on Sunday, and a couple afternoons during the week and brought in a respectable $125 for the football season, which covered about half of my tuition for the next semester.

Never a social animal, I joined Sigma Chi fraternity; without that, I would have had no social life at all. The big event was the "Sweetheart of Sigma Chi" competition and ball. All the sororities participated. With no prospects of a date, some of my fraternity brothers arranged for me to escort a young lady nobody else dared approach. Summoning up the courage, the call was made, the invitation accepted, the orchid bought, and the car and tuxedo rented. After testing the route so as not to arrive late—and the house was in the best part of Atlanta—I drove into the driveway of a large mansion. Greeted by her father, I nervously awaited the appearance of my date. In a scene right out of *Gone with the Wind,* she descended the balustered staircase, the very vision of the southern belle, complete with long blond hair and a strapless black velvet gown. Needless to say, I was scared to death. We made our way to the top floor of the Biltmore Hotel. The combination of fright and me being the worst dancer on the floor produced the expected disaster. The dancing featured me repeatedly stepping on the dress and her struggling to keep her bodice in place. Fortunately she disappeared during intermission, much to our mutual relief.

While at Tech, I continued flying and soloed without difficulty. Going to the airport on Saturdays and flying for thirty minutes whetted my appetite to be a military pilot. Always seeking the fast track, I wanted to earn my advanced qualifications as rapidly as possible. Since it was 1943–1944, the airport was crowded with military aircraft. I could identify them all and fully expected to fly one someday.

The military was everywhere. Tech had always been big in Naval ROTC. Now, with the war on, the campus swarmed with soldiers and sailors. Wanting to be a part of the biggest adventure out there, I set my sights on the U.S Army Air Corps. My goal became more focused. Immediately after turning seventeen, I went to the recruiting office in Atlanta and took the entrance examination for the Army Air Corps Enlisted Reserve. The recruiting sergeant complimented me on achieving the highest score he had seen. I was thrilled that one more step had been completed toward becoming a pilot. One Saturday shortly afterward, orders came through to report to Fort McPherson, near Atlanta. I left my room at Tech very early on a dreary, rainy morning, and after a couple of bus transfers, I made it to Fort Mac. Eager for active duty, I had to cool my heels for another year before entering aviation cadet training.

Hundreds of other men reported for their draft physicals. We formed an endless line of naked bodies shuffling from one station to another. Eyes, ears, nose, lungs, hearts, and every other part of our bodies were checked and probed, including the dreaded short-arm test. I worried about my feet; they were flat as pancakes. Flat feet were a cause for rejection, although for the life of me I did not understand what that minor complaint had to do with being in the air corps. Resolved on being a flyer, I had to get by the doctors. Someone told me that the examining physician would determine whether a person was flat-footed by looking at the bottom of his feet. If they were dirty all over (we were barefooted and had been since the beginning) he would know the individual was flat-footed. If the feet were dirty only on the outside edges it would indicate there was an arch. That bit of prior intelligence gave me an idea; I would walk on the outsides of my soles until reaching the examining physician. That I did. The dirt indicated that I was not flat-footed. One more hurdle was passed on my quest of achieving my dream. Still beaming about my little coup, a few days later I was sworn into the U.S. Army Air Corps Enlisted Reserve. We received a pair of lead wings with no clasp, but I figured out a way of attaching them to a coat or shirt and wore those wings everywhere, expecting one day soon to earn the real thing.

The army created a training program to accelerate the flow of technicians and specialists depending on the War Department's sliding manpower requirements. Selected participants in the Army Specialized Training Program (ASTP) attended universities and received appropriate instruction from academic faculty and limited military training. War Department personnel planners badly miscalculated the needs for combat infantrymen, and with the forces in Italy and training divisions earmarked for Europe facing serious combat manpower shortages, specialist training programs were curtailed from a high of 150,000 students to 60,000—the bulk of the surplus ended up in the despised infantry replacement system. Fortunately the army retained seventeen-year-olds in the Army Specialized Training Reserve Program (ASTRP); when they turned eighteen they would transfer from reserve to active-duty status. The army and air force still required engineers; with a high school diploma, high enough scores on the IQ tests, and two semesters at Tech, I gained entry into the program.

The ASTRP consisted of twelve-week blocs. Orders arrived directing me to the University of Florida. Daddy drove me down to Gainesville, where we stayed with one of his acquaintances in the wholesale grocery business. The next day, 12 June 1944, I joined a company of 200 soldiers: 150 active-duty men attached to the ASTRP; the rest were reservists, with a handful from the Army Air Force Reserve.

The student body consisted mostly of co-eds because so many men of military age were in the services. The classroom work focused mostly on engineering subjects, and the strictly military aspects consisted of only a modicum of military training. The course ended on 2 December. Six reservists, including myself and all army air force men, were sent to Pennsylvania State College for further training where we joined more than 100 other reservists. The three-month training stint started on 11 December, and for a southern boy the winter spent in State College, Pennsylvania, was tough. I looked forward to finishing the program on 3 March and moving on to real training somewhere warm.

That never happened. A few weeks later the army air force dashed the hopes of the pre-aviation cadets. With the war in Europe winding down and the pipeline already full of trained aviators, the air force disbanded the program. Because we had volunteered, the air force offered two options: discharge (and facing the draft) or continuing in the program with the prospect of becoming a navigator or bombardier. I opted for the latter, figuring that I could work my way into the pilot's seat. Shortly afterward the air force sent another letter. There would be no rated officer training. We could accept a discharge or become a gunner. I chose gunner, guessing that sooner or later I could get into flight training. However, another letter came offering the option of ground crew or discharge. I chose the latter.

3

A Soldier's Apprenticeship

West Point, Fort Riley, Kansas, and Fort Benning, Georgia

While I attended Georgia Tech, my father approached our congressman, Eugene Cox, enlisting his help obtaining an appointment to the United States Military Academy. Never having laid eyes on a West Pointer, the "long gray line" held no great attraction. Everybody knew the lore about plebe initiation in Beast Barracks, the hazing, and walking off petty demerits in the Area; and about the army football team under Red Blaik. Army featured Glenn Davis and Doc Blanchard and went undefeated in 1944 on the way to the first of three straight national championships. None of that provided any particular push to attend West Point. The Academy trained pilots (the air force remained part of the army until 1947), and my ambition remained set on becoming a flyer. Congressman Cox secured the appointment, and on 2 July 1945, I became a member of the class of 1949.

The Point

Immersion into the plebe system began the minute the aspirant cadet stepped through the portal of the Central Barracks area. Of all the recollections of West Point, the first day remains the most vibrant. A first classman confronted me and said only four responses existed for any question: "Yes, Sir!," "No, Sir!," "No excuse, Sir!," and "Sir, I do not understand!" Instead of being put off, "No excuse, Sir!" became sort of a personal axiom. It succinctly summed up all the life lessons I had learned growing up. No matter the circumstances, failure was a personal responsibility.

Beast Barracks initiated the process of instilling the foundation of "Duty, Honor, Country." More than a motto, it acts as a creed, a commandment. For eight weeks plebes received orientation and instruction on the Honor Code and what it meant. Aside from initial military training and physical conditioning, the initiates were proselytized, beginning the process of exorcising the civilian and building a soldier. A plebe must always display a soldierly bearing, maintaining an exaggerated posture at attention whether seated or walking. The old joke had it that plebes ranked only the superintendent's dog, the commandant's cat, and all the admirals in the U.S. Navy. They were assigned details like delivering mail and laundry and demeaning mess chores. They memorized military terms, regulations, and jargon and repeated them verbatim to a hectoring senior. Part of the rite of passage involved upperclassmen conducting a walking tour of the grounds: the Plain, the huge parade ground that would become so much a part of our lives at the Academy; the statues of some of the great heroes along its perimeter; and the cemetery with its Old Cadet chapel and the graves of fallen heroes. No surprise that the markers of Winfield Scott and George Custer particularly stood out.

A large percentage of the incoming cadets had served in World War II. Many had opted for West Point because it got them out of combat. In the middle of August, we had just finished hiking up a tough hill when somebody announced the Japanese surrender. With that, a number of cadets said, "That's it. I'm out of here." With the war over, they resigned and severed their commitment to the army. Other veterans could not handle the "Mickey Mouse" harassment of Beast Barracks and simply quit. A surprising number of those who remained graduated at the top of our class.

After Beast Barracks we marched on the Plain and rendered our oaths as members of the 707-strong fourth class (at West Point the numbers are reversed). During the war West Point went to a three-year cycle. The return to the four-year program left those who entered in 1944 in limbo. The army allowed half to graduate on schedule (1947); the rest became the new class of 1948. The postwar classes were much larger than in the interwar years, which created crowding. In response to the housing crunch, barrack rooms designed for two now roomed three. The initiation continued throughout the first year. Academic classes were followed in the afternoon with sessions in tactics, drill, and ceremonies. Plebes commit to memory procedures such as the five-paragraph operations order and "estimate of the situation" and must be able to "spout" them off on command as well as answer purely plebe questions such as "the days" (the number of days remaining for a series of significant events such as the army-navy game, the beginning of the holidays, June Week, and graduation).

The fourth and third class curriculum offered academic subjects like any university: math, English, a language (French, Spanish, German, or Russian), and in the second year, physics and chemistry. The only choice was which language to take. Supposedly the language would be determined by preference, prior exposure, and the results of a diagnostic test. Although I had had a year of Spanish and requested it, I was assigned to French. In addition to academic classes, we took and received grades in military subjects like military topography, aptitude for service, and tactics. Initially cadets were grouped alphabetically, but after six weeks placement depended on performance. I ended up in the upper sections in math and English but in the last section in French. With only sixty demerits, I finished number 129 in the class.

Being naturally competitive, everyone cared about class standing, the Order of Merit. Because daily recitations, tests, and exams received such close grading—down to two decimal points—the Byzantine scoring meant the difference between my average and that of the lowest-ranked distinguished cadet amounted to 6 percent. For upperclassmen much more was riding on class standing: privileges, weekend passes, and the most vital of all, selection of branch. At the other end, cadets competed for the honor of being the class "goat"—the lowest-ranked cadet who avoided flunking out or being found (deficient in a subject) and turned back to the next class.

Physical fitness played a big role in our lives. West Point candidates took medical and physical fitness exams. The medical exam was like any other, but the physical fitness tests were more demanding. The Academy used a series of physical tests designed to determine whether the individual had the physical fitness to withstand the rigors of cadet life and, subsequently, military service. Meeting the requirements for successful application was only the beginning. Specially designed tests and obstacle courses were scheduled throughout the academic year. Plebes had to complete successfully a program of boxing, wrestling, swimming, and gymnastics. Those who failed took remedial classes and had to meet the standard; for a very few, this extra training spread over years.

Physical training constituted a part of the curriculum for four years. Cadets participate in a corps squad sport or activity (representing the Academy at the intercollegiate level or in intramurals). Qualifying for the plebe squad in one of the corps teams was a prized goal. Not only did the successful fourth classman have an opportunity to compete at the intercollegiate level, but he also would sit on a corps squad table in the dining room, where he was free from the onerous tasks that befell his less fortunate classmates who had to endure the rigors of the fourth class system.

Varsity football was king. Football weekends were very big events. The whole corps went to the army-navy game. Army went undefeated in 1945, beat Navy in Philadelphia, and emerged as consensus national champions. The undefeated season brought delight to the plebes because when army won, we got to fall out in the mess hall. Boxing was my sport. I made the plebe team and won all four of my scheduled fights under the guidance of our coach, Billy Cavanagh, a former professional middleweight. I liked the physical demands, the camaraderie, and the adrenaline rush I got when stepping into the ring, and, yes, also the feeling of relief and accomplishment when the bout ended. In addition to the many required activities for plebes, there were what seemed innumerable extracurricular activities: language and glee clubs, choir, academic coaching, chess, *Pointer* (the cadet magazine), or *Howitzer* (cadet yearbook). I served on the *Howitzer* staff each of my four years.

Attendance at chapel was mandatory. Reflective of the "Old Army," it was High Church Episcopalian—even though members of other Protestant denominations predominated. The services were acceptable to me; I had no strong leanings toward any particular doctrine. The Cadet Prayer, like the Boy Scout Oath, did exert a strong sway. I remember some of the phrases: "Make us to choose the harder right instead of the easier wrong. . . . Help me to live above the common level of life. . . . Never to be content with the half-truth when the whole can be won." The prayer set forth ideals—the quest for perfection—as the standard to be met. I always derived guidance and inspiration from those words.

That which is difficult to obtain, in this case women and not grace, becomes an obsession. With such rigorous limits on our free time, on places you could escort a date, and the decorum that regulated social events, women became a hot topic of conversation that contained a good deal of wishful thinking and exaggeration. Given my track record in that area, I pretty much avoided contact with the gentler sex.

June Week marked the end of the school year and gave reason for general celebration, especially for those at the top and on the bottom of the pyramid. For first classmen, it meant graduation and posting to their first duty assignments; for plebes, it marked liberation from the rigor of the fourth class regime and a one-month leave to go home.

After the all-too-short leave we returned for an eight-week round of military training at Camp Buckner, a cantonment near the Academy. As in Plebe Year, academics dominated the next nine months. The curriculum closely resembled the first year except for the addition of courses in physics and chemistry. Now that I knew the ropes, my class standing improved except for a disastrous French final and a miserable score in military topography.

Many compare West Point to a monastery, and for me it felt like one. I remained tongue-tied around girls. During my Christmas leave in my second (sophomore) year, however, I did get up the courage to ask Lou Bowen, James Bowen's sister, to wear my "A" pin. (The "A" stood for army, and giving it to a girl was like asking her to wear your fraternity pin.) While not a formal engagement, it meant that to me. She was beautiful, very popular, talented, and poised. Most important, she was a fine young woman. She was everything I wanted—and everything I was not. I could not believe that she would be interested in me. In short order, I fell head-over-heels in love with her. Our courtship would last about eighteen months—a wonderful, joyous time—and then turned sour. I was broken-hearted, and it would be years before someone took her place. I will always be grateful to Lou for showing me how having someone special in your life could bring so much happiness.

Hopes for boxing success unraveled early in the season when a punch to the kidney sidelined me. The doctor warned another similar hit might cost me my commission. Since boxing played such a large role in my life at the Academy, the news was a real body blow. Although nobody confused me for the next Joe Louis, I enjoyed everything about boxing.

An uneventful Cow Year followed. Although my grades kept me in the top third of my cohort, they slipped across the board. I finally made corporal in the Second Regiment. Boxing provided the only highlight. Risking further injury and my commission, I made the team, lettered, and placed second in my weight division at the Eastern Intercollegiate Boxing Tournament. At season's end my teammates voted me captain for the next year.

During the summer before our last year, the army staged tours of Fort Bragg, the home of the Eighty-Second Airborne, together with five air force installations to help us decide on branch preference. The summer before we went on a "Combined Arms" trip to the traditional combat arms branches—infantry, armor, artillery, and engineers. At Fort Bragg we went through about two weeks of paratrooper ground training, flew in an aircraft, and watched jumpers exit the craft. Clearly they pulled all the stops to impress us. The training was perfect, and the paratroops assigned to guide us could not have been sharper. Everything went like clockwork. Col. William Westmoreland, division chief of staff, orchestrated it all. Maj. Gen. James Gavin, the commanding general, visited training and spoke informally to us as we clustered around him—just as he had done with his soldiers in World War II. Everyone left North Carolina very impressed.

Having wanted to be a fighter pilot seemingly forever, I greatly anticipated the air force trips, but after Fort Bragg, it all went downhill. We visited fighter, bomber, close-air support, reconnaissance, and troop carrier units. Unlike the airborne, where everything was laid on, our arrival at the air base meant waiting around until the escort officer could be retrieved from the officers' club or the golf course. The transport to the barracks usually showed up late. I was most interested in the fighter jocks. They regaled us with stories about heavy drinking: "See that pilot? We have to pour him into the cockpit, but he can fly that airplane!" They—and most of them were married—boasted of their philandering exploits. If they sought to convince me—with stories of wild living and their obvious lack of discipline—how great it would be to join the air force, they failed.

My first class year proved less than memorable. Except in tactics, my grades continued their retrograde movement. The grades in social sciences, military history, and ordnance told the story of a complacent cadet who had stopped applying himself. And my great expectations of leading army to boxing laurels never materialized. Another kidney shot, suffered in training in the lead-up to the first meet, ended my fighting career. Boxing bestowed my biggest morale boost and incentive, and suddenly it all evaporated. Coach Cavanagh understood and made me coach of the plebe squad. The plebe team won all its matches; that gave me some satisfaction, but it paled next to my dreams of what could have been.

During the winter of our last year, as graduation neared, we received additional branch orientations. Officers representing different branches briefed us, showed combat films, and oriented the class on equipment. The Infantry presentation especially stood out. They showed John Huston's *Battle for San Pietro*, about a failed attack on the stalemated Italian front in World War II. The gritty film captured real infantry combat: soldiers firing, running, being hit and falling, and dead on the ground. Leaves could be seen clipped from branches as bullets zinged through olive groves. Watching it prompted questions: Am I tough enough and smart enough to be an infantryman in combat? Do I have the guts and brains to be an infantryman?

One of my barracks mates in the second year was Doug Bush. A decorated lieutenant, Doug had served as a pathfinder in the famed 508th Parachute Infantry Regiment of the Eighty-Second Airborne Division. An impressive guy with Hollywood good looks and a self-confidence bred by being a veteran paratrooper, Bush did his best to sell me on airborne. Although impressed, I still wanted those pilot wings.

Despite the negative reaction to the air force tour, childhood dreams did not die easily. When it came time to fill out the branch wish list, I picked air force pilot. Cadets could select air force ground if they wanted to be in the air force in a nonrated capacity, but I wanted to fly. My next choices were infantry, armor, and artillery. I even had "United States Air Force" engraved inside my class ring. But when I reflected about the time at Fort Bragg and the air force tour, doubts mounted. Those questions prompted by viewing *San Pietro* flooded in. After much agonizing, I decided on the Infantry, but the paperwork was already filed. Then the "flat foot dodge" occurred to me: failure on the air force eye exam would disqualify me for my first choice. The eye exam duly "failed," I got Infantry.

The long-anticipated graduation ceremony marked our last muster on the Plain and the final metamorphosis from cadet to officer. Marching that day it occurred to me, of all the many influences over those four years, the greatest came from the tactical officers, or tacs. The tacs personified West Point and by extension the army—they prepared callow young men to lead soldiers into battle. While never expecting to bring glory and renown to the Academy, I vowed never to do anything that would bring dishonor on that great institution or the army.

My parents drove up from Georgia and took part in some of the social events that attended graduation. Like all parents they were very proud. If they thought about the prospect of me going off to war, they never mentioned it. In the afterglow of victory in World War II—despite the onset of the Cold War—war did not seem likely.

For many in my class, with better romantic skills or luck, another ceremony awaited them—marriage. Slots in the chapel were filled, and nuptials went off in rapid succession. With the rounds of weddings and parties complete, we said our good-byes and headed our separate ways, knowing we would always share that special bond of membership in the class of 1949.

Twenty of us took the opportunity to travel to Europe on free transportation aboard a hospital ship. The ten-day passage went by very quickly because a contingent of women from Special Services were on the same ship. Add young, just-graduated, and unattached men to young, equally unencumbered young ladies, and things will happen. Some of my awkwardness around the fairer sex eroded on that voyage.

After landing in Bremerhaven, eight of us bought Zundapp motorcycles and set off on our various itineraries. I paired with John Saxon, another Georgia boy, bound for Paris. Biking through the Low Countries and northeastern

France, we would arrive in a town late in the afternoon and secure a stay in a hotel or pension—always careful to wash off the road grime and dress properly as presentable American gentlemen. In Paris we met two girls from Oklahoma and treated them to some "real food"—burgers and shakes—at a U.S. armed forces snack bar. After discovering they were headed for the South of France and Rome, we observed the proprieties—they introduced us to their parents—and followed them to Nice and Italy.

The Poor Bloody Infantry

After returning home and a couple of weeks with my family, I made the trek out to Kansas and Fort Riley. Every newly minted second lieutenant—except products of the Officer Candidate Schools—attended the Officer Basic Course, Branch Immaterial. The course served as an eye-opener. It instructed us in areas only superficially handled in previous training. The Riley course threw us together with ROTC officers from colleges all around the country and with men from all branches of the service. Just as intended, this mix of officers broadened perspectives and produced lasting personal associations. Instruction included the organization and mission of each branch. Practical work sessions took us to the training areas, where we planned and participated in tactical exercises designed to require a basic understanding of the capabilities and limitations of the different branches. Some of the field training consisted of demonstrations involving artillery, armored vehicles, engineers, and support branches. Administration, supply, transportation, and other necessary activities were included in the instruction. Like the tactical instruction, these sessions introduced us to the many requirements that must be planned and implemented in any successful operation.

As is always the case, many valuable lessons came not from a field manual or the training program but from practical experience imparted by our instructors. Instructors described a situation and then asked for possible courses of action. Some of the problems seemed almost intractable. Among the instructors, Capt. Jack Null particularly stood out. After exhausting our ideas, someone would invariably turn to Null and ask, "Sir, what would you do?" He often answered, "I would turn to one of my outstanding assistants and ask him for his advice. Remember to surround yourself with capable subordinates." Null's advice—perhaps a truism but not always followed—was one of the best guides I ever received.

Fort Riley had long acted as a cavalry post: Custer served there as did, at various times, the Seventh Cavalry, and it housed the Cavalry School before the army finally retired its horses. About thirty retirees remained stabled on post. Several of us took the opportunity to go riding, and that sparked the interest of a couple of the old cavalrymen. One was retired Col. Hiram Tuttle, a legend in equestrian circles who rode the first American-bred horse to place in an Olympic dressage competition. Each Saturday morning he most graciously gave about a dozen of us instruction in the finer points of dressage. The other officer, Maj. Fred Jencks, a member of the school's staff, took anyone who appeared for rides each Sunday. He led us over all sorts of terrain and lectured on cavalry tactics and the care of mounts. He also set up a cross-country military stakes ride for us. Although both were dyed-in-the-wool horse cavalrymen, neither tried to convince us that the horse still had a place on the modern battlefield. Both were most gracious; I have never forgotten them and their charming wives for their courtesy and friendliness.

Together with a classmate and very close friend, Bruce Peters, I took advantage of the instruction every weekend. During the week, we rose each morning at five thirty to go to the stables, saddle a horse, and ride for an hour before having to brush down the mount, put the gear away, and hurry to class. We also went on a couple "hunts," consisting of officers—many old horse soldiers—and their wives, organized and conducted by the Riley Hunt Club. What an exciting experience it was riding to the hounds. A rider dragged a bag of chicken entrails over the landscape a few minutes before the hunt commenced. Afterward we assembled at the officers' club for a magnificent brunch. Those were some of my happiest times in the army.

The Riley course, focusing on the duties of company grade officers with emphasis on the platoon leader, provided good training. The program gave me a much better picture of what to expect when I assumed my first platoon command, a situation I eagerly anticipated. Our graduation speaker was Lt. Gen. Edward H. Brooks, who commanded a corps in Europe and then headed the Personnel and Administration Department of the army. During his remarks he told us we should feel free to write him whenever we wished. I remembered that offer.

As my first "active-duty" army experience, Fort Riley proved extremely valuable. The program of instruction taught me many basic skills, and the varied backgrounds of my Riley classmates—sources of commission, military experience, and education—helped me see the profession of arms from a much broader perspective. The training provided a good foundation for "branch school," where we would delve more deeply into the specific skills and knowledge required to be a qualified platoon leader. After Christmas leave we reported to our branch school. For me, that was Fort Benning, Georgia, home of the Infantry.

Everything about Fort Benning screamed Infantry. The Infantry School had existed there since 1919, and the post experienced an explosion during World War II as a training facility for infantry, armor, and airborne forces. The Infantry Officers Basic Course (IOBC) was well organized and fleshed out, in more specifically infantry terms, the basic leadership principles covered at Fort Riley. In common with all trainees who ever attended an army school, we complained about too much time spent in the classroom and not enough combat- and leadership-focused training. Better to learn the core requirements for a platoon leader than to be exposed to the many things that he might be called upon to know in the future. For those things about which I knew little or nothing, as experience later taught me, you could always find some NCO or officer who knew their stuff.

As at Riley, more practical knowledge—rather than doctrine and supposed theory—was acquired through personal contacts with seniors than in a classroom. Lt. Col. Louis G. Mendez, a member of the Infantry School staff, is a case in point. Mendez commanded an airborne battalion in the 508th Parachute Infantry Regiment. Doug Bush often talked of how much the men respected—even revered—Mendez and suggested that I look up the colonel when I got to Benning. After "checking in," I did just that. Colonel Mendez immediately invited me to his quarters. This outgoing friendliness was a characteristic of both him and his wife, Jean. On one occasion while talking to the colonel I confided my doubts about whether, under the test of combat, I could control my fear. "If you are thinking about your own safety," he replied, "you're not doing your job. You are supposed to be thinking about your men. Get up and go check on them when you come under fire. You'll be too busy to think about yourself." Colonel Mendez was right, and I never learned a more valuable lesson. Whenever I followed his advice, it worked. When I did not, the cold tentacles of fear began to clutch at my gut.

The Benning course could not end soon enough. Experiencing both eagerness and trepidation, I longed to put into practice all the theory and training received to date. At the same time I wrestled with self-doubt about failing to make the grade. That test had to wait. The idea of becoming an officer in the line Infantry never appealed; I wanted airborne. Jump qualification would not guarantee an airborne billet. Without combat experience, I had nothing that would confer any kind of status in the eyes of the men in my future platoon except being a West Point grad and paper certificates. Finagling a slot in jump school took some effort.

At that time, the army sent officers to jump school only if they had orders for an airborne posting. My orders had me slated for Okinawa. Remembering what General Brooks had said during the Fort Riley graduation ceremony, I wrote him expressing my desire to be a paratrooper. I dreamt up every conceivable argument to convince him that permitting me to go to jump school served the best interests of the army. The letter must have worked because the general commented, while talking to my IOBC class, that he had received a letter from a second lieutenant requesting assignment to jump school. He brought the matter up with Maj. Gen W. A. Burress, the Infantry School commandant, who agreed to accept all those in my class who wanted to attend jump school upon graduation from IOBC. This experience disabused me of ever again believing in the Old Army saw, "Never volunteer."

Officer basic ended on Friday, 17 June 1950, and I reported to jump school the following Monday. About fifty second lieutenants from IOBC took advantage of the offer to attend jump school. For the first time in five long years I was physically active all day with no studying at night. Jump school was rigorous, physically challenging, and fun. Although the "Frying Pan" (training area) was very hot in June and July, I had the time of my life. I now fixed my sights on becoming a paratrooper. The Black Hats (training NCOs) were top-notch. Everything they did seemed perfect. No slack. The tiniest infractions—real or contrived—earned a "gimme ten" (push-ups). Naturally officers got it worse. We knew that the push-ups served as reminders to do it right the next time. There is no room for error. Mistakes can end in serious injury or death.

The first week consisted of ground drills: how to hit the ground and roll with your momentum so that injuries would be prevented, or so we hoped. We rehearsed the jump commands on the aircraft, what to do when we exited the door, how to maneuver the chute in the air to avoid other jumpers, preparation for landing, and landing, how to roll up your chute and return to the assembly area. The hard, exciting training produced plenty of adrenalin. The biggest challenge awaited us at the end of the week, when the trainees made a mock jump from the thirty-four-foot tower. Most people wash out at this stage. The tower provided enough sensation of height to weed out those who could not take that first step. For the rest of us, the leap off the short tower provided one of the most enjoyable parts of the course.

Tower Week followed. Initially we made jumps off the low tower. Not dissuaded by the groin chafing caused by the harness when it jerked tight or the "gimme ten" that awaited us, we competed to see which among us could make the most vigorous door exit. The next step involved being released from the top of the 250-foot tower. We donned a parachute harness attached to a chute tethered and held in a fully inflated position to a ring that was attached by a cable through one of the arms of the high tower. Upon command of the Black Hat we were hauled to the top of the tower. After receiving last-minute instructions megaphoned to us from below, we were cut loose, and floated to the ground. As we descended, the instructor continually shouted instructions for a student to slip his chute in the desired direction away from the tower as another trooper cut loose from an adjoining tower arm. The high tower provided our first experience of freely floating through the air. During the second week we also learned how to pack our parachutes. We packed five main and one reserve chute for the next week when we would make the five qualifying jumps. Riggers instructed us and meticulously supervised as we packed those all-important five chutes. No room for error. Jump school dropped this requirement shortly after our class graduated; the rationale being why spend valuable training time teaching soldiers how to pack chutes when they would never do it again unless they became riggers. Another qualification for jump week was the five-event physical fitness test: pull-ups, push-ups, sit-ups, squat jumps, and a 300-yard run. You either met the tough standard or no jump. The rigorous everyday physical training prepared us well.

Finally, jump week arrived. We chuted up in the sheds and underwent close inspection by the riggers. Then, after what seemed an interminable wait, our two sticks (the troopers who would be loaded into one aircraft) executed the paratrooper shuffle into the waiting aircraft. Buckle in. Take off. And then, as we entered the final approach, our jumpmaster yelled the commands: "Get Ready! Stand up! Check equipment! Sound off for equipment check! Stand in the door!" Hearts pounded and adrenalin rushed. The first student stepped into the door awaiting the next command. "Go!" With that, and a slap on the thigh, he exited the door as the remainder of the stick rapidly followed. The stick in the other door of the aircraft had gone through the same drill and exited at the same time.

I remember vividly the exhilaration. I made a good exit and immediately went into the proper position: head tucked looking at my boots, hands flat against the reserve chute ready to pull the ripcord if needed. Then the count: "One thousand! Two thousand! Three thousand!" As I reached three, my chute blossomed with a terrific jolt as my canopy caught the blast of air and slowed my body that had been hurtling through the air at about 110 miles per hour (the speed of the aircraft) to zero forward motion. Although body-wrenching, the jolt was comforting. My chute had opened. The next requirement involved checking the canopy. Was it fully deployed? Were there twists in the risers (the lines that connect the trooper's harness to the chute skirt)? Mine was perfect. Now watch out for other troopers as we floated through a crowded sky. After only a few seconds it was time to prepare for landing. A quick check below. Nobody beneath me. Get ready to land! Slam! Go into the parachute landing fall. On my feet in an instant; roll up the chute, put it into the kit bag, and double-time to the assembly area. What a thrill! Jump stories filled the bus on the way back to the hangars and the sheds, where we shook out the leaves and other debris that may have gotten into the chute after the landing. We were through for the day.

The remaining four jumps were humdrum except for the third. Checking the canopy after it opened, I saw a huge hole (bigger than my helmet—the criterion for activating the reserve). I immediately pulled the ripcord of my reserve and yanked in the main canopy, tucking it under my arm so that it would not snarl with the reserve chute. I landed without injury. Unfortunately the weather was uncooperative on two of the days, so we made two jumps on Saturday morning followed by a quick cleanup and graduation. After our speaker concluded his remarks and pinned on our wings, an NCO walking behind us unobtrusively placed glider wings into our hand. At that time, the week of air transportability training and the glider ride we took during officer basic substituted for the same week of training in the airborne course. This class was the last to receive glider wings. Jump school lived up to all my imaginings. Those spit-shined jump boots were beautiful, and paratroops never tire of shining those boots.

During my first week in jump school, the North Koreans invaded the South. I heard the news while sitting on my bunk in a World War II wooden barracks spit-shining my jump boots. I vowed that I would not "miss out" on this war. Somehow I would get to Korea.

4

Korea

Eighth Army Ranger Company

After jump school and a great leave, I headed for Camp Stoneman, California, located outside San Francisco, the port of embarkation, with orders for Okinawa. Immediately upon arriving, I went to the personnel office and asked for a change in assignment to Korea. The personnel sergeant asked incredulously, "Don't you know there's a war going on?" I assured him I did and had not taken leave of my senses. "Okay! If that's what you want," he replied and filed the papers requesting a change in orders. With the situation in Korea growing worse each day, it did not take long before the new orders came through: destination Camp Drake, a replacement center in Japan. I was going to get my war.

The long three-stage flight across the Pacific—made longer by a malfunctioning engine on a Civil Reserve Air Fleet DC4 that required a return to base—proved forgettable. Except for me, all the passengers were captains, World War II Coast Artillery officers who had been recalled and reclassified as infantrymen. Although a totally green second lieutenant, I had more experience with infantry—albeit in schools—than these soon-to-be company commanders. At long last we arrived in Tokyo and, after a short ride, at Camp Drake.

Newspapers accounts—and Korea was the last of the print media wars—related the debacle that befell the Twenty-Fourth Infantry Division in its rear-guard actions as it fell back into the Pusan Perimeter. Not for the last time in the Korean War, a complete intelligence failure by the national security apparatus and Gen. Douglas MacArthur's headquarters in the Dai Ichi building in Tokyo produced a degrading defeat. American military history runs in circles: a woefully unprepared army suffers humiliating defeats; American resources in the end overwhelm the enemy; the demands to "bring the boys home" accelerate the dismantling of the wartime forces; the army slips back into its prewar routines and marginalized existence, starved of funding and manpower, overburdened with its many missions, and unable to preserve training and equipment

31

standards; only to repeat the cycle again in the next war. Only five years after victory in Europe and Asia/Pacific, the army had reached its nadir. The mushroom clouds over Hiroshima and Nagasaki, in the eyes of many, rendered the ground army superfluous. The Infantry appeared useless—except perhaps as an occupying force—as a cavalry lance. Nobody volunteered in the army with any idea he would be called upon to fight. American forces—understrength, untrained, physically soft, armed with outdated weapons, and psychologically ill-equipped—proved no match for highly trained, physically hardened, mostly veteran, and heavily indoctrinated North Korean troops. The situation in Korea looked very grim.

Replacement depots (repple deppels, in army jargon) bore a deserved unsavory reputation. During World War II, because of the foibles of the manpower replacement system, some men languished in replacement depots for months. That was not a problem for company-grade officers headed to Korea. Six weeks after the North Koreans smashed across the 38th parallel, the Eighth United States Army Korea (EUSAK), South Korean, and United Nations forces held a weakly defended perimeter around the port of Pusan in the southeastern tip of the peninsula. Scuttlebutt in Japan predicted another Dunkirk. The captains on the flight, the dreary replacement center, and rumors making the rounds in Japan all pointed to the deplorable state of the army. The life expectancy of an Infantry second lieutenant could not have been very long.

On my third and final day at Drake, I received assignment to the Twenty-Fourth Infantry Division with orders to ship out the next day. The Twenty-Fourth Division—one of four understrength, badly trained, and poorly equipped divisions detailed for occupation duty in Japan—drew the unhappy task of acting as the "shock absorber" of the North Korean blitzkrieg. Throughout July, the division took a pasting in a series of rearguard actions. In the middle of July, at Kun River and trying to hold Taejon, the units committed suffered 50 percent casualties. In seventeen days, the division lost 3,600 men. Junior officer replacements were in high demand. I heard an announcement on the public address system ordering me to report to an office in the post headquarters. Of all the replacement officers being processed through Camp Drake, why would I be summoned to headquarters? After being directed to the correct office, I checked and double-checked my uniform before knocking on the door. I received clearance to enter and gave my most military salute and reported to the lieutenant colonel sitting behind a folding field desk. When the colonel gave me "At ease," I assumed a very military "Parade Rest." In a low voice Lt. Col. John H. McGee said, "I am selecting volunteers for an extremely dangerous mission behind enemy lines." I said, "Sir, I volunteer!" Skeptical, the colonel asked, "Don't you want to know what the mission is?" "Yes, Sir! But I volunteer!" I replied. "I am selecting volunteers for a Ranger Company to operate behind enemy lines," McGee patiently continued. "Sir, I volunteer!" I restated. Puzzled, the colonel went on to say he had selected the platoon leaders but needed a captain as company commander. "Sir, I have wanted to be a Ranger all my life," I said, stretching the truth. "If you will take me into that company I volunteer to be a squad leader or a rifleman."

McGee spoke to me at length. Knowing I had no active-duty experience, he noted that I had captained the boxing team at West Point. He pointed to my recent completion of jump school and assumed I was in peak physical condition. Dismissing me, he said he would let me know his decision the next day. Reporting the following morning, I heard the news; McGee had selected me to command a yet-to-be-formed Ranger company.

Resurrection: Formation of the Ranger Company

Leaving his office, it suddenly dawned on me what I had volunteered for: command of the first Ranger unit activated since World War II. Suddenly very nervous, I thought about my liabilities: a new second lieutenant with no command experience, not even a single day of troop duty. I probably did not know enough to be the rifleman I volunteered to be. The challenge brought an adrenalin rush. I said a quick prayer that I repeated on many occasions: "Lord, I need your help. Please don't let me get a bunch of good guys killed."

One of the officers on McGee's staff told me later that my boxing experience had struck a responsive chord; the colonel boxed as a cadet at the Academy. Many years later McGee confirmed what his staffer said, adding that my eagerness and airborne training influenced the decision, as did his belief that an officer with no combat experience might prove more aggressive than a combat veteran from World War II. McGee had interviewed dozens of officers; he had rejected many volunteers, and others he had tabbed refused the assignment. The two platoon leaders were classmates of mine—Barney Cummings, the class goat, and Charles Bunn, one of those prior wartime service cadets. They had recommended that the colonel talk to me. While not clear why McGee chose me to command the company, I have always been grateful that he did.

McGee had been brought into the EUSAK Operations Section (G3) by Lt. Gen. Walton Walker, Eighth Army commander, to head the oddly named Miscellaneous Section. McGee's job involved raising and training an experimental unit for special operations behind the lines—initially behind friendly lines. The first phase of the Korean War predated the North Korean conventional offensive. The South Koreans confronted and suppressed a Communist-led insurrection, but pockets of guerrillas still operated in the South, including inside the Pusan Perimeter. The North Koreans fielded commando-like units, elements of which easily infiltrated through the porous lines and, linking with guerrilla bands, attacked soft targets in the American rear areas. The overstretched combat units had no manpower or training in combatting special forces and guerrillas. Since the army disbanded Ranger units after World War II, Army Chief of Staff Gen. Lawton Collins ordered one reconstituted. Walker had a more immediate concern. The North Koreans controlled a salient in the eastern end of the perimeter near the village of Pohang. Walker worried the North Koreans might mass forces and supplies in the Pohang Pocket for a major offensive thrust. In another example of the problems Walker confronted holding the perimeter defense, Eighth Army units proved incapable of mounting effective reconnaissance and combat patrols—normal infantry missions—into the salient. Walker wanted a special unit created to perform these vital roles. McGee was given no specified date for the unit's activation.

McGee knew something about operating behind enemy lines. Taken prisoner after the debacle in the Philippines and interned in the infamous Davao Penal Colony camp in Mindanao, he escaped by jumping overboard from a Japanese "hell ship" and made it to shore, eventually joining a guerrilla band. He fought in several actions with the Filipino resistance fighters against Japanese forces until evacuated by an American submarine.

The first order of business centered on organizing the unit. Initially McGee thought of the Alamo Scouts, a special reconnaissance unit organized by Sixth Army in the Southwest Pacific theater during World War II, but no table of organization and equipment (TO&E) could be located. McGee did find a TO&E for a World War II Ranger company, and that served as the immediate organizational template. The unit called for seventy-four enlisted men and three officers.

McGee and his three assistants perused hundreds of Form 20s (the enlisted man's service record) looking for possible candidates. Those selected were assembled and informed that Eighth Army needed volunteers to undertake hazardous missions behind enemy lines; they were briefed on the rigorous training and the special camaraderie unique to special operations units. Then they were told, "If you are not interested, you may leave now." Most did, and the rest ended up on our interview roster. The colonel arranged all the administration but left it to his company officers to flesh out the manpower requirements.

Cummings, Bunn, and I set up shop in an empty building and for the next three days conducted interviews to select the few needed to reach the authorized number. Working from before dawn to after midnight, we interviewed the men, considered their previous experience, and, since there was no time for physical training (PT) tests, made calculated guesses on their physical condition. We had little to go on and generally based the decision on the impression the interviewees made.

During the next week the selected soldiers reported to our company headquarters. Pfc. Billy Walls came to me and suggested we needed something distinctive to set us apart and proposed Mohawk haircuts. I agreed and told him to spread the word while I posted an order on the bulletin board. I then went to the closest barber for my Mohawk. It certainly set us apart, and we kept them until the temperatures plummeted in November.

I recall feeling real pride during the first company formation. The men provided a genuine snapshot of the United States. We had plenty of WASPs and so-called hyphenated whites—mostly of German and Italian extraction—but also Hispanics, Nisei Japanese from Hawaii, and African Americans. The army—not the best institution ever conceived to spearhead social reform—willfully went as slowly as possible executing Truman's executive order of July 1948 to integrate the armed forces and still maintained token all-black units. Wilbert Clanton and Allen Waters became the first African American Rangers and, as it turned out, two of my best soldiers. In my mind, race, ethnicity, religion, or region never counted for much; what mattered was what they had behind their belt buckles and between their ears. Did they have the guts and brains to be Infantrymen and Rangers?

All these men could have probably sat out the war in some safe rear-echelon billet. Almost all the enlisted men came from service and supply units in Japan—Transportation, Quartermaster, Signal, Engineer, Ordnance Corps—and they were all good soldiers but not qualified Infantrymen. Instead they volunteered and made the cut for the same reasons generations of American citizen-soldiers have answered the Republic's call. The obvious motive: they wanted a chance to fight and prove their manhood. For many, their relatives fought in World War I and their brothers in World War II; now it was their turn. The country found itself in another war—and few thought much about stemming the tide of communism—and it fell to them to get the job done as quickly as they could and go home to their families. They were young—mostly eighteen or nineteen; all under twenty-six and all but one unmarried—and not afraid to take risks. Two of them were only sixteen; one would die on his seventeenth birthday. They responded to the challenge of becoming Rangers, and most calculated that if they were going into combat, they wanted to fight with the best unit in the Eighth Army. Considering that our understrength company was led by three second lieutenants fresh from school in charge of a motley collection of GIs from every organization except the Infantry, we had a long road ahead of us if we meant to achieve those lofty aspirations.

Ranger Hill

The Eighth Army Ranger Company officially activated as a unit on 25 August at Camp Drake. We had three days to complete the assembly of our complement of men and allotment of equipment and put the unit into some semblance of organization. The TO&E called for two, not the standard three, platoons. Other than the three officers and three sergeants—two World War II infantryman and one engineer plucked from the replacement pipeline—no rank structure existed. On 28 August we moved to the port of Sasebo and three days later boarded the ferry bound for Pusan.

Pusan offered the first glimpse of mainland Asia. The port bustled with activity as manpower and materiel flooded in to reinforce Eighth Army. Hot, teeming with what seemed like very busy people, with a constant, not easily identified background clatter and an exotic and unpleasing smell—Pusan was like nothing I had experienced before. Met on the quay by a captain on McGee's staff, the unit mounted trucks and headed for the grandly named Eighth Army Ranger Training Center near Kijang on the east coast. The center, dubbed Ranger Hill, consisted of pup tents set up in the middle of rice paddies. It would be home for the next six weeks.

Obviously, we had our hands full converting our clerk-typists and cooks into Infantryman, let alone making them Rangers. Still suffering the ill effects of serious stomach complaints, thanks to his Japanese captors and life in the jungles of Mindanao, Colonel McGee was not very active. Other than fielding my nightly reports and acting as a sounding board for my suggestions, the colonel and his staff never issued any training requirements. You might not call it a philosophy, but I had some fixed ideas on what needed to be done.

After West Point, Forts Riley and Benning, and jump school, I entertained a mental picture of what a soldier should be; the brief stint at Camp Drake disabused me of that image. The performance of the Eighth Army made it obvious that the garrison army in Japan had forgotten about physical conditioning, teaching basic soldiering skills, and maintaining discipline; and the soldiers on the ground in Korea paid the price in blood. The isolation of Ranger Hill and the buffering provided by McGee granted me the almost unbelievable opportunity to form the unit according to that ideal prototype I brought in my head from the States. Reducing the problem to its essence, my job as a company commander of light infantry centered on physically hardening the men and training them in small-unit tactics for combat. Courses taught at Riley and Benning helped—although I recognized areas for improvement—but mostly my ideas derived more from the value system instilled by my parents and reinforced by West Point, informal discussions with experienced seniors, private reading and reflection, and osmosis.

First came defining the mission: develop a combat-ready unit that would succeed and survive on a lethal battlefield against an unforgiving and highly motivated enemy. To achieve our goal, we needed to build on the individual strengths of each soldier, whatever they might be, to help others perform. Our training program must identify and build on the few strengths we possessed, teach the required tactical skills, and develop the values and attitudes of warriors.

At the outset, I developed a vision for our company, setting out four training objectives:

Each Ranger would be in outstanding physical condition. Every Ranger
would be a Tiger.
Each Ranger would be highly skilled in the tactics and techniques of the
individual soldier.
Each squad, platoon, and the company as a whole would smoothly
function as an efficient fighting machine.
Each Ranger would exude confidence in himself, his fellow Rangers, and
his leaders, and exhibit the esprit that motivated him to volunteer
and work toward the aim of making his Ranger company the best
that the United States Army could produce.

If we achieved the first three in training, the fourth would take care of itself.

Physical training—conducted by platoons—permeated everything we did. Every morning began with thirty minutes of calisthenics, the "Army Dozen," followed by five to fifteen minutes of rapid-fire grass drills: "Turn! Hit the deck! Run! Hit the deck! Too slow; do it again!" The officers participated in all the conditioning, and since we had recently completed jump school and were in better physical condition than the troops, we set the standard. Any minor screw-up got the man twenty push-ups, with his officer doing the same. One platoon trained with the bayonet under my supervision while the other practiced hand-to-hand combat under Barney Cummings. The next day they switched. Incrementally the repetitions of the exercises increased for the first few days. Improvement was both rapid and obvious as the men executed the ever-increasing number of repetitions. We double-timed everywhere: through the rice paddies, up and down hills, in the mountains. As the training program progressed, the tactical problems became longer in both time and distance. Coupled with the daily PT, the tactical training began to develop the stamina absolutely required in a combat Infantryman. By the end of training, every Ranger vouched that he was in the best condition of his life.

The priority task that first week involved putting together some chain of command. The TO&E called for a company headquarters consisting of one officer and four enlisted men, and two identical platoons, each with an officer and thirty-five men. As special light infantry, the Ranger mission centered on moving fast on foot over distance and delivering concentrated firepower. Each platoon had two assault sections and one special weapons section. The assault sections fielded automatic rifle and light-machine-gun squads; the special weapons section possessed a Browning Automatic Rifle (BAR) squad in addition to 3.5-inch rocket launcher and mortar teams. Assigned no vehicles, mess facilities, or medical support (or Ranger designation or hazard pay), the company, once activated, would be attached to a battalion or higher formation.

The pool for noncommissioned officers looked pretty shallow: three sergeants and twenty-two corporals, with the remainder privates and privates first class. One of the sergeants, Charles Pitts, an experienced soldier from World War II, was made first sergeant—my "first Soldier" and strong right arm. After conducting lengthy interviews with each individual and comparing notes with Cummings and Bunn, we created an initial chain of command.

The company trained that way during the first week, working the selected cadre into leadership roles. The idea revolved around giving leadership training to as many men as possible and in the process finalizing the command structure. Cadre received a briefing on the task—it might be a work detail or a combat mission—and was held responsible for results. The officers coached them in the required skills and techniques, and at the end of the week we conducted a thorough one-on-one critique and made specific recommendations on how they could improve. Then we selected another chain of command and followed the same procedure during the succeeding three weeks of training. By the end every man had held a leader's position at least once, most two or three times. Based on our observation we had a good idea of each man's capability and potential and on that basis selected our final chain of command. This "fall out one" approach—basic to the training—meant every soldier had some training and experience as a leader and could move into a position of responsibility in the event of casualties.

With time compressed, we worked the men six days a week and a half day on Sunday. As emphasis passed from physical conditioning to tactical training, the platoons went on night patrols, prepared defensive positions, negotiated across paddies full of human excrement sometimes "face down," engaged in rough hand-to-hand fighting, and dealt with poisonous snakes and plagues of insects. Exercises simulated setting up ambushes and roadblocks, conducting raids, scouting and patrolling, map and compass exercises, and calling for and adjusting supporting fires. The presence of Communist guerrillas in the countryside always held out the prospect of real contact. Weapons training took place on improvised ranges, with the men firing rifles and automatic weapons at makeshift targets simulating combat in rough terrain, uplands, and in the paddies. Mortarmen lugged their weapon, base plates, and ammunition up hills and estimated distances because Rangers must master that skill in broken terrain and night actions. The men learned how to handle and fire all the company's weapons, demolitions, and techniques of camouflage and concealment. Rigorous physical conditioning remained central to the program, including cross-country runs with full loads, weapons, and ammunition, and even running in the surf on Sundays. When not in the field, the men sat for classes on leadership, personal hygiene, and military courtesy, endured what seemed to them pointless inspections, and paraded. The officers never sat around and supervised; they led by example, shared the hardships, taught the classes, and ran the company.

At the Fort Benning basic course, students went into the field, conducted supervised field exercises and tactical problems, and sat through the after-action debriefing when the tactical officers provided their critique. But because of the minutely timed training schedule, the school never repeated the exercise to correct the problems. In our training, the most dreaded and oft-repeated phrase was, "OK, let's do it again." Drills were practiced so many times that proper performance became reflexive. In the postexercise critiques, the men not only related what orders they received, what actions they took, and what difficulties they encountered in carrying out their orders, but they were encouraged to make suggestions on improving performance. We would attack the same hill, do it better, but still make errors. The exercise might be repeated a third time, even a fourth; each was followed by a detailed critique asking the same question: "How do we do it better?"

Generally, training proceeded according to the book. We published training schedules, followed the manual, obeyed regulations, enforced safety rules, and maintained strict discipline. With almost no time on their hands, the men were too exhausted to get into any real trouble. The platoon commanders, especially Charlie, and the NCOs accused me of making excessively high demands, shooting for perfection. Pleading guilty, I replied that no Ranger should die because he was not physically fit, could not shoot, lacked the discipline to follow orders, no matter how difficult, or did not know what to do amid the chaos of a firefight.

Although I always made sure to pat the troops on the back when they performed up to these exacting standards, most of the men probably hated my guts for my Regular Army punctiliousness, the Puckett 20s, and all the "OK, let's do it agains." While I could never show it, the fast pace and heavy physical demands took their toll on me. No matter how tired or overwrought, I always said my prayers before falling off to sleep. They always ended with "help me to be big and strong and make Daddy proud of me," and for the duration of my time in Korea I added, "Help me die like a man." I had no death wish; the prayer was my way of saying, "No matter how frightened I become, Lord, help me do my job. My Rangers are counting on me."

The opening months of the Korean War resembled a football game. The North Koreans drove over the fifty-yard line but ran out of steam as they approached the end zone. In a goal line stand, the United Nations defenses held in a series of bloody positional battles. Elements of Eighth Army reinforced X Corps for MacArthur's amphibious end-run at Inchon; the remainder, reinforced and with a decided numerical advantage, stood poised to break out of the perimeter. The high-risk Inchon operations succeeded beyond all expectations, and on 18 September Eighth Army's breakout turned into a pursuit. After a sluggish advance, X Corps liberated Seoul on 25 September but never entirely severed the North Korean line of retreat. Five days later, MacArthur got the green light and promptly moved in force across the demarcation line, opening the drive into North Korean territory. In possession of the initiative, MacArthur set his sights on advancing to the Yalu and completing the destruction of the Korean People's Army.

Clued in that Inchon was in the works, I wanted to expedite the company's training sequence. The dramatic reversal of battlefield fortunes ended the company's raison d'être and redoubled my determination to get into the fight.

After consulting with the platoon leaders and senior NCOs, I informed McGee the company would be ready in another two weeks and requested he recommend to Eighth Army that we be committed. Although more training would have been beneficial—and in hindsight problems emerged I had never envisioned—I believed that we were primed to go. Reviewing my list: the men were in peak physical condition and inured in the Ranger Way, going without sleep and putting one foot in front of the other; as individuals they knew their stuff as Infantrymen, and as a group they melded as squads as part of an assault team, platoon, and company. Since the officers accompanied them in every phase of training, the men trusted us, depended on each other, and as a collective acted and felt like a team.

Colonel McGee concurred and informed Eighth Army headquarters that after completing four of the authorized seven weeks of training, the company was prepared to undertake the following type missions: raids, reconnaissance, and combat patrolling, as a motorized detachment and as trail blocks. He noted that the company had received intensive training, with special emphasis on physical conditioning and patrolling, and had developed a chain of command; that the NCOs exhibited a high sense of duty; and that the unit possessed great firepower and a high degree of foot mobility over difficult terrain. He highlighted the company's potential for conducting special operations requiring tactical surprise but also emphasized the necessity for providing sufficient time to plan and rehearse missions. Finally, pointing to the lack of organic field kitchens, transportation, and medical support, he recommended that consideration be given either to expanding the company into a Ranger battalion or deactivating it.

The request made its way up the command chain to General Walker. After completing our training series on 1 October, orders finally came down the next week activating and designating the company as a provisional unit placed directly under Eighth Army command (we still wore no Eighth Army shoulder patches and no Ranger insignia). We were rechristened the 8213th Army Unit. Of the seventy-six men who had arrived on Ranger Hill, sixty-six marched out as Rangers.

Mopping Up the Rear

On 8 October we bid farewell to Ranger Hill and moved by truck to Taejon, headquarters of the Twenty-Fifth Infantry Division. The headquarters staff—chiefly the operations officer (G3) and his assistant and the G4 (chief of logistics)—provided a good briefing and explained the company would perform roles similar to those we had trained for: clearing the division's rear of guerrillas, stay-behind elements, and stragglers and generally protecting the rapidly lengthening line of communications. As a provisional unit without a staff or incorporated supply capability, we would be attached to a parent organization. Within a couple days the company was wedded to the Twenty-Fifth Reconnaissance Company.

Our troops immediately melded with the reconnaissance company. Bunn's First Platoon moved to a nearby village; the other platoon settled in Poun with the Recon Company. We patrolled east of Taejon for the next month. The Recon Company provided the vehicles—a couple of trucks and maybe a tank— and the Rangers debouched at a set location and moved over difficult terrain, establishing roadblocks and setting up ambushes along known and suspected routes of enemy movement. The Rangers operated independently and only once joined the Recon Company for a night trail block. Following the daylong patrol, we moved to a prearranged point to be retrieved by our transport. Many men in the Recon Company expressed their amazement at how much ground we could cover—a testament to our physical hardening. I led a patrol each day to set an example and lead from the front; Bunn and Cummings might have bristled at the intrusion, but I wanted to assess the effectiveness of our training. An after-action critique followed each patrol to help hone our technique and discover how the unit could improve. Basically daily patrols served as advanced training and conditioning for refining our teamwork and patrol methods that focused on immediate response to enemy contact.

Encounters with the enemy were rare; they were not nearly as active as expected. On 16 October, we came under fire for the first time. Our half platoon detected movement on an adjacent hill that dominated our position. Hurriedly deploying behind a series of large rocks, we received heavy small-arms fire. Bullets, ricochets, and rock fragments filled the air. Remembering the words of Lt. Col. Louis Mendez about thinking of my men's safety first—and fueled by a surge of adrenalin—I ran from one Ranger to another assisting in locating and placing fire on the opponent. At some point I took a number of superficial hits from rock fragments.

Suddenly the incoming fire ceased. I yelled to my Rangers to cease firing and shouted to the men on the hill. A clear American voice responded. He wanted proof, and I agreed to come up the hill, where an American captain greeted me. We had been exchanging shots with a South Korean police unit. Harutoku Kimura, not seriously wounded, was the first Ranger casualty in the Korean War.

It was not a particularly auspicious baptism of fire, and when Bunn suggested that night my wounds rated a Purple Heart, I could only demur with embarrassment. What would my men think of their commander putting himself up for a decoration for sustaining only superficial injuries from friendly fire? I liked Bunn a lot at West Point and during our shared stints in army schools, but unmistakable signs of friction developed soon after we joined the company. Relations became strained during the month we conducted patrols in the denied area east of Taejon. Not spending much time with Bunn, in hindsight, was a mistake. Toward the end of our time with the Recon Company, the commander, Capt. Charles Matthews, told me Maj. Gen. William Kean, the division commander, wanted to promote me to captain. The policy called for a promotion for any lieutenant who held a captain's billet for thirty days. Barney Cummings would be pleased with my success, but Bunn presented a different story. And I wondered if the lieutenants in the Recon Company would be jealous. Having weighed all these considerations and concluding the promotion would have a deleterious effect, I urged Matthews to ask Major General Kean not to promote me until my company had actually seen some real combat. Matthews agreed, and the promotion died. This "second-guess" decision ranks among my worst. Promotion to captain—and for each subsequent grade—was delayed for three-and-one-half years.

By the end of October the front had shifted far to the north. On 4 November, still attached to the Recon Company, we mounted trucks and moved 175 miles north to Kaesong. Although we moved forward, the mission remained the same: safeguard the line of communications and clear guerrillas and stragglers south of the 38th parallel in the area Uijŏngbu-Donghucheon-Shiny-ri along Route 3, one of the main corridors of escape for retreating North Korean forces. I took the opportunity to visit Maj. Robert Sadler, an experienced World War II veteran and the assistant operations officer I had met at the first briefing in Taejon. He ushered me in to see the division chief of staff, Col. George Childs. Like McGee, Childs entertained the same reservations about my orphan provisional company, by now short about a dozen men from when it left Ranger Hill. I talked with Colonel Childs, who thought the unit should be increased in rifle strength. I resisted because we had trained and worked together as a team, and the addition of unknown line infantry replacements—who had not undergone the rigors of training—could undermine unit morale and reduce our combat effectiveness. As I discovered later, this experienced officer knew better.

From 10 November, we were attached to Task Force Johnson. The division still tried to determine what to do with us and probably surmised that we might be useful to Major Johnson. Perhaps Johnson could have provided more direction and guidance to me, but he made us feel like a valuable contributor to his team and essentially gave me a free hand—what every commander wants. I continued my practice of going with a patrol each day and conducting the detailed debriefings afterward. Because of our mobility, we sometimes surprised enemy elements. Once, after a fruitless daylong sweep, the patrol halted just before dark for our only meal of the day. Just then four guerrillas leapt to their feet only a few feet away; Cpl. Allen Waters, my BAR man, immediately cut down three of them. On another sweep we encountered a half-dozen enemy. Showing more impetuosity than sense, I sprinted after them as they fled, and Pfc. Harland Morrissey, another BAR man, nearly shot me. Despite the lack of results, the platoons continually improved their patrolling techniques, and their long humps through difficult and broken terrain maintained their high levels of fitness. I knew every minute expended in what amounted to advanced training would make us more combat-effective and save lives.

About a week later, orders came through for the Recon and Rangers to move from the south of the Twenty-Fifth Division area to, as we discovered, the northern tip of the advance, beyond the Ch'ongch'on River. Travelling through Pyongyang, the North Korean capital, the city appeared eerily deserted, except for a few ragged civilians. As we were trucked north it became apparent—from the depth of the buildup—that the Eighth Army stood poised to renew the offensive.

The Big Push: Home by Christmas

Despite the Chinese signaling their intention of entering the war if UN forces drew too close to their frontier and ample evidence that elements of the People's Liberation Army had already deployed in North Korea, MacArthur willfully ignored all intelligence except that generated by his own staff, which told him exactly what he wanted to hear. Everybody knew about the drubbing taken by the First Republic of Korea Division and the Fifth and Eighth Cavalry Regiments at Unsan at the beginning of November. Other firefights took place against soldiers in strange quilted coats. But nothing would deflect MacArthur from his grandiose offensive to the Yalu.

On 22 November, I reported to the headquarters of our new command, Task Force Dolvin. During the briefing the intelligence officer (S2) reported at least twenty-five thousand Chinese had deployed opposite the Twenty-Fifth Division's sector. Even as a callow lieutenant I entertained grave misgivings. At

Benning we learned that doctrine called for at least a two-to-one and preferably a three-to-one manpower advantage in the attack. Clearly the enemy had
a paper strength of three-to-two in their favor. Armed Forces Radio reported
the existence of four Chinese corps between Eighth Army and the Yalu. It was
not known how many soldiers that amounted to, but one thing was certain:
they had not come to frigid Korea on vacation. The final "big push" would com-
mence on Thanksgiving, in two days. Nobody believed MacArthur's promise to
have us home by Christmas. Knowing my father would be worried, I sat down
and wrote a letter to reassure him things were not as bad as they appeared,
though I was fully expecting some very heavy going.

Task Force Dolvin consisted of elements of the Eighty-Ninth Medium Tank
Battalion with a tank company and assault gun and recon platoons; two companies of infantry; a company of engineers, and the Twenty-Fifth Recon and us,
the 8213th Ranger Company. The task force would serve as the connecting element covering the gap between the Thirty-Fifth Infantry Regiment on the left
and the Twenty-Fourth on the right in a general advance by the division. Dolvin had instructions to push northeast along the Yongbyon-Ipsok Road toward
Unsan on the east bank of the Kuryong River. While the rest of the division ate
Thanksgiving dinner with all the fixings, we moved forward into the point position of the advance. We ate cold turkey sandwiches and prepared for the next
day's advance. A strange apparition appeared in our lines; two exhausted and
bedraggled GIs captured at Unsan and curiously released by their Chinese captors. They reported others were out there in the dead zone, but patrols went forward about five thousand yards without seeing anything.

Thanksgiving dawned crystal clear and cold. The army never learns from
its mistakes. Just as in Europe in the autumn and winter of 1944, other logistical considerations trumped outfitting Eighth Army for winter operations. We
had field jackets and woolen long johns but no parkas. The army had just issued
what became dubbed new Mickey Mouse boots, great for standing guard but
terrible for patrolling. Standing from our position I could see the entire vista
of the Kuryong Valley with its paddy fields ringed by brown hills. In Korea,
everything looked brown. Dolvin briefly came forward accompanied by the
commander of the tank company to which the Rangers would be attached. We
walked into a frozen paddy together, and he pointed to a hill in the distance.
"That's your objective," he said. When I asked about suppressive artillery fire for
our assault, he replied in the negative. If we needed artillery support, he assured
me, he would provide it.

Just before we leaped off, the tank commander, who had just returned with Dolvin from task force headquarters, assigned us the mission of securing two hills to our front and gave me fifteen minutes to plan and disseminate orders to my platoon leaders. A couple minutes later he asked if we were ready to move out. Having had no time to issue my instructions to Bunn and Cummings, I refused. He brewed up, but I held my ground. The Rangers were ready in the allotted fifteen minutes. This exchange led me to believe he had not thoroughly briefed his subordinates on our role or emphasized the importance for his Bravo Company tankers providing the support fire. My premonitions proved correct.

I positioned myself with Cummings's platoon. Riding on the tanks, we encountered no opposition. Everyone was keyed up. We were the vanguard of a major offensive, yet we were entering into empty space. About four miles down the dirt road we encountered a small knot of American soldiers, those men in the dead zone we had heard about. After moving about seven miles up the road, our little convoy emerged from behind a hill and came under small-arms fire from our first objective, Hill 224. The Rangers immediately dismounted and formed an assault line, with Bunn's platoon on my left. According to doctrine, the tanks would provide a base of fire, but instead of returning fire, the tankers immediately buttoned up. About a football field distant from the hill, I led an assault section of ten Rangers from Cummings's platoon and, under fire, ran across the paddy field and ascended the hill. Pfc. Joe Romero, who outpaced the rest, took several hits but continued firing until he expired. The unit's first battlefield fatality, Romero received a Bronze Star for his actions. Arriving on the top of the hill, we found it deserted; I never knew where the enemy fire originated. No sooner had we crested the hill when four 76mm rounds smashed into our position, fired by our fire-support tankers. One round exploded about ten feet from where I stood without effect. Five of my Rangers were not as lucky (two died). At least the enemy was impressed enough to pull back. Incensed, I sprinted back across the frozen stubble field, and what I said to the tank commander could not be printed.

Fratricide happens in the fog of battle but should not have in this case if basic leadership principles had been observed. The tank company commander blamed me. In his view, my place was with him, in his command tank, coordinating the attack and fire support. "You may be able to command your company from a tank in the rear," I said calmly but with emphasis, "but I lead my Rangers from the front. That's where I belong. That's where I will be!"

Bunn's platoon never made the assault and remained hunkered down behind a low earthen wall of a rice paddy. Standing on the paddy, I yelled for them to move forward, and they proceeded to run up Hill 224. Despite the demoralizing loss of our comrades, the Rangers immediately went about their duties, evacuating the wounded and dead, reorganizing and manning a 180-degree defense, and digging into the frozen ground in anticipation of a counterattack.

We spent a hellish night up on that hill. The cloudless sky meant the temperatures plunged. The men took turns lodging their feet in their buddies' armpits to keep from freezing. Just as McGee and Childs foresaw, the lot of a provisional unit is never happy. Although the tankers showed no outward signs of hostility toward the Rangers, I sensed the armored company commander viewed us as a burden, which might help explain what happened that day. I also felt estranged from the task force headquarters. Since I was an inexperienced officer, I thought it would have been a big help if my superiors had spent some time with me or—if Dolvin was too busy—had sent forward a staff officer. Nothing came up from the task force, no intelligence or even our sleeping bags. We were alone up there with nothing more than what we carried on our backs.

The Fight on Hill 205

November 25 was another frigid, clear day. Our mission remained unchanged: supported by a tank platoon, we would attack across eight hundred yards of open, frozen rice paddy to seize Hill 205. Fifty-one Rangers and nine Korean enlisted men attached to the unit (KATUSAs—Korean Augmentation to the United States Army) were present for duty; it was just a reinforced platoon. The script remained ominously the same: at 1000 hours we crossed the departure line, again mounted on tanks; after clearing the cover of a masking hill, we received rifle and automatic weapons fire but this time accompanied by mortars; the Rangers scrambled off the tanks and took cover behind a ubiquitous dike; and the tankers buttoned up and never returned fire.

Running to the rear of the tank, I tried to open the box containing the telephone. Failing that, I climbed on the tank and starting banging on the hatch with my rifle. When finally the hatch opened a crack, I used some well-chosen words demanding he fire on the suspected enemy position. He responded that he had only three inches of steel between him and the enemy and needed to keep the hatch closed. In language laced with expletives, I informed him my Rangers had one-sixteenth of an inch of field jacket protecting them. He placed some desultory fire in the direction of the suspected enemy. Once again we were on our own.

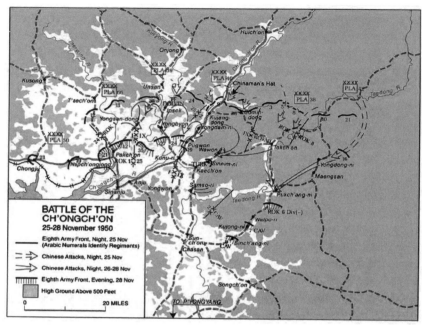

Task Force Dolvin, 25–26 November 1950. Hill 205 stood to the east of the Ipsok Road (*center of map*). From Billy Mossman, *Ebb and Flow: November 1950–July 1951,* United States Army in the Korean War series (Washington: Center of Military History, United States Army, 1990), 66.

Jumping off the tank, I yelled to Bunn's platoon, "Let's go, Rangers!" We moved across the paddy, maneuvering and firing as we went, seeking what little cover we could find. In one covered position, behind a small bank, Cpl. Barney Cronin was waving his patrol cap in the air, trying to entice the enemy machine gunner to reveal his location. Yelling to Cronin that I would run across the open space to draw fire, I took a deep breath and sprinted. The enemy fired, but no visual appeared. I jumped up and ran again with the same result. As the tension mounted, I yelled, "OK! This is the last time!" The third time proved the charm. Cronin zeroed on the enemy position and eliminated it with a burst of BAR fire. Like the proverbial Private Murphy says, "If it's stupid but works, it ain't stupid."

The advance continued with Cummings and his platoon moving forward on our left. Efforts to communicate on the radio failed. At one point air force planes strafed and napalmed a hill adjacent to our fight. As we ran across the stubble, a shower of spent caliber .50 gun cartridges rained down on us. I hit the ground, much to the amusement of my Rangers. Finally we reached the base of the hill—our assault position—followed soon after by the Second Platoon. When Barney inquired of the whereabouts of the rest of his squad, Sgt. Merle Simpson pointed back to the dike. Simpson dashed back and moved his men forward, later remarking he could never have imagined making that run without the tough physical conditioning. Crossing the paddy cost four casualties— three Rangers and one of our ROK soldiers.

Taking time to reorganize the platoon, the company fixed bayonets and started up the hill. After navigating the rubble we entered the wooded gradient. The trees—typical Korean scrub—were not dense but permitted no more than fifteen feet of visibility. Approaching the top of the hill, we discovered enemy defenses perfectly sighted to handle any assault on the approach just completed. Fortunately they were empty.

The Rangers began digging a 360-degree perimeter. We knew the nearest American ground unit was over a mile away, far beyond supporting range. The frozen, rocky soil made digging difficult, which was made worse by the fact we found ourselves in a small burial ground. We heard voices in the distance, and the KATUSAs said they were not Korean. Simpson heard a shout and reported a soldier in a strange uniform running down the hill. Nobody fired, but everyone began digging with renewed vigor.

After walking the perimeter with Cummings and siting the machine guns, I was satisfied the defenses were well positioned to command the likely approaches. I left Barney in command and returned to task force headquarters. With my radio malfunctioning, I needed to coordinate artillery fire support. Running back across the paddy and drawing sporadic fire, I arrived back where we left the tanks. I found Bunn lying facedown near a tank. Bunn yelled, "Get down; you're drawing fire!" Some small arms did come in our direction. I knelt by Bunn—he was clearly shaken—and quietly yet strongly entreated him to join his platoon on the hill. He said, "Puck, I just can't do it." "Charlie," I continued, "we need you." He responded again, "I can't do it." I felt sad, not angered, by his refusal and concluded the failure was mine.

Colonel Dolvin was not at his command post (CP), so I met Capt. Gordon Sumner, the artillery fire support coordinator. As I surveyed the S3's map overlay, the tactical situation did not look good. The task force was already under severe pressure. Company E, Thirty-Fifth Infantry had been hit hard, and a battalion was then in motion from the reserve to reinforce the task force. My Rangers sat isolated atop a hill, fully expecting a Chinese attack, and could only look to support from the artillery. Together we plotted expected coordinates for artillery concentrations. While waiting for the colonel, I disassembled, cleaned, and reassembled my rifle in the dark. Finally Dolvin arrived, and after a brief conversation about the current situation, he told me to return to my Rangers. I set off for the hill but not before checking with First Sergeant Pitts. Pitts was my total rear echelon; I relied upon him completely for resupply and food. He begged to go with me to the company defensive position, but since he was the only person I trusted to act without supervision, he had to remain.

Collecting a Ranger who fell out during the assault to care for one of the wounded, we each grabbed ammunition and a case of grenades and started back across the paddy and up the hill. It was dark by now, but the full moon provided enough illumination to enable us to find our way. Although the temperature plunged, we worked up plenty of sweat hauling the ammunition up the face of Hill 205. I gave a shout as we neared the position so no trigger-happy Ranger would shoot his commander. As we crossed the company perimeter, the piercing sound of bugles, whistles, and voices over a loudspeaker ("Tonight you die, Yankees!") shattered the silence. It was about 2200 hours.

I raced to the command foxhole and called for artillery support. Much to my relief, the radio worked for the first time in Korea. Well-directed Chinese mortar fire cascaded on our position, followed by a ground assault. The Chinese surged up the hill, and the Rangers poured a furious fusillade of small-arms and machine-gun fire against the unseen enemy. Soon well-directed artillery fell on the enemy. It was all over in about fifteen minutes. Faced by overwhelming firepower, the Chinese fell back.

During the first attack I was hit with a grenade fragment. As the Chinese closed on our perimeter they hurled grenades toward our positions. Running from foxhole to foxhole, checking on the perimeter, and handing out lots of "Atta boys!" to encourage my Rangers, I saw a grenade coming toward me. The primitive Chinese grenades emitted a trail of telltale sparks. The book said that if you hit the deck and hug the ground, the grenade will explode and the fragments will disperse harmlessly above you. I discovered the book was not always right. A shard tore into my thigh; it was painful but not a serious wound. After sprinting for cover in the foxhole shared with Barney, I explained my befuddlement. All we could do was laugh.

After the repulse of the initial attack, I again visited the foxholes. The Chinese had pulled back but remained just below the brow of the hill. Privates First Class Judy and Sarama held the foxhole directly in front of ours. Judy pointed to a tree about twenty yards in front and said a Chinese soldier was taking pot shots at him every few minutes, but he could never get off a clear shot. For the second time that day I played a game of high-stakes chicken, and, as in the first one, Judy nailed him on the third attempt.

For the next three hours the Chinese launched four assaults on the hill, each time in greater numbers but with the same result. The Chinese mortars, grenades, and burp guns took their toll. I instructed Simpson, who occupied a portion of our perimeter in the rear, to move some of his Rangers to fighting positions in the front. The hilltop was a bedlam of carbine, rifle, BAR, and machine-gun firing. The Rangers fought with remarkable valor. By sheer weight of numbers, the Chinese penetrated but never breached the defenses; at a couple points the Rangers threw them back in hand-to-hand fighting using the bayonet and their rifles as clubs.

The employment of flare shells after the first attack greatly contributed to the defense. With the aid of flares I could identify large knots of Chinese troops advancing well behind their lead squads. Adjusting fire, the artillery dropped the next high-explosive rounds from the 105mm and 155mm howitzers into their midst. With casualties mounting and ammunition running low, doctrine had to be abandoned—it prescribed an interval of six hundred yards—as I called in "danger close" artillery fire, erecting a wall of high explosives and steel in front of our position. Throughout I circulated along the contracting line, trying always to be at the main point of the attack. Everybody knew we were up there alone. The desire to be there for my Rangers energized me; I wanted them to know that we were in this fight together and that we would hold.

At approximately 0230 hours, the Chinese (later estimated at five-hundred-man strength) mustered for their sixth assault. The blare of the bugles announcing the next attack sent me rushing to the CP foxhole where I encountered Cummings and Beatty. Unbeknownst to us on that hill, the Chinese had launched a massive offensive all along the front; the artillery was occupied with a fire mission in support of another heavily engaged unit. I informed Sumner that we needed artillery badly; looking up, I saw the enemy had overwhelmed Second Platoon's defenses. I told Sumner we were being overrun.

The Chinese appeared everywhere, swarming over the position. As only a single example of many acts of valor, one of my two African American Rangers, Wilber Clanton, died while charging a swarm of Chinese. The air was thick with grenades. I still crouched on the radio when the foxhole churned with an explosion. Two grenades detonated, slamming fragments into my feet, buttocks, and arm. There were no signs of Barney or Beatty. Thinking it meant sure death if I remained in my hole, I struggled my way out. Now on my hands and knees, I saw the carnage all around me. The Chinese were bayoneting my wounded Rangers only fifteen yards away, but I could do nothing. I experienced a strange sense of floating, watching all this from twenty or thirty feet in the air; I even saw myself on the ground. Despite the maelstrom and noise, I felt at peace and totally helpless.

Ranger Judy ran up and asked if I were okay. I replied in the negative and told him to leave me behind. Unable to move me, he ran for help. Some elements of the First Platoon still held positions on the backward slope of the hill. Pfc. Billy G. Walls and Pfc. David L. Pollock moved over the crest in the direction indicated by Judy, killing at least three Chinese who were bayoneting and shooting my wounded Rangers. Finding me in a hump, Walls asked the same question, and I gave the identical reply. I asked him to check the foxhole for Cummings and Beatty. Walls assured me that there was no one in the foxhole. Walls handed Pollock his rifle and picked me up. As Walls staggered down the hill with me over his shoulder, Pollock provided covering fire. Walls began to run out of steam, but fortuitously we happened upon a heavily wooded draw. Pollock caught up to us and asked if I was still with them. "I'm still with you," I answered. "I'm not going to leave you." Pollock responded, "We're not going to leave you either, Sir."

Exhausted and unable to negotiate the tricky descent, they decided to drag me. At one point, Walls asked me if I was hanging in there, and I replied, "Yes. I'm a Ranger." After the men hauled me unceremoniously on my shot-up backside for about one hundred yards, we emerged at the base of the hill within hailing distance of the tanks (which had not fired a round in our support all night as they were in no position to assist). After a challenge and reply, a tanker sergeant joined us, picked me up, and carried me to a tank. I asked the tank commander to report to task force headquarters that we had been knocked off the hill and requested artillery fire on our former position. In short order the gunners pounded the hill with a major concentration of Willie Peter (white phosphorous). Beginning to take small-arms fire, the tankers loaded up the wounded and raced to the rear. My Korean War was over.

5

Back on Track

Convalescence, Marriage, and the Ranger Department

My evacuation went without mishap. The tanks conveyed the Ranger casualties to the rear. At the aid station my shredded boots were cut away. Capt. John Vann, who would take command of the Ranger Company, told me months later that the doctor who first examined my feet thought I would never walk again. After the battalion S3 (Operations) queried me about the battle, I was moved first to a major collecting point farther back and later to a schoolhouse near Sinanju and finally to Kimpo Airfield and evacuation to Japan.

Rather than worry about my condition, I felt embarrassed arriving at the hospital in Japan. Filthy and unshaven, I looked like Willie or Joe in a Bill Mauldin cartoon. The nurses appeared so neat and clean in their uniforms. After spending about a week in the hospital, on my birthday I boarded a plane for the States. When we crossed the International Date Line suddenly I became twenty-three again. It was not the best way to celebrate a birthday—even twice. After an overnight stop in Hawaii the aircraft continued to California.

I telephoned my parents at the first opportunity. They had received no word from the army but had read an *Atlanta Journal* article describing the fight for Hill 205 that mentioned no names but stated a young lieutenant from Georgia was the Ranger commander. My parents guessed I was that company commander. Naturally, they were extremely worried and overjoyed when they heard my voice.

Several celebrities, including Jane Russell of *The Outlaw* movie fame, visited the hospital. Ms. Russell came by herself and seemed ill at ease. She made her way through our ward, chatting with a few of the men. She must have had a hard night because she stretched out on an unoccupied bed. The bed's usual occupant was sitting in a chair. After she left, he exclaimed excitedly, "I'm going to tell everyone that Jane Russell was in my bed!" Of course, no one would believe him anyway. The next day, along with many others, I was flown to Montgomery, Alabama, for an overnight stay, prior to proceeding to Benning and Martin Army Hospital. I felt at home.

Silver Lining: Convalescence and Fortunes Told

The doctors—Capt. David Vesley and Lt. S. A. Harrison—immediately examined me and reported, after they patched me up, that I would be discharged from the army. I emphatically told them there would be no discharge; I intended on staying in the army. Then they said that they would fix a transfer to a service branch so I would not have to serve in the Infantry. I stated unequivocally, "I am Infantry" and would stay Infantry. "You patch up my feet," I said, "and I'll make them work." That remained my refrain for the next eleven months in the hospital and for the rest of my service years.

The doctors told me what they thought I wanted to hear. I was appreciative of their concern, but they read me totally wrong. They also expressed what they considered my likely prognosis. Obviously my right foot was damaged severely, and the doctors believed there was no way they could make it usable again. What their charts and tests could not gauge was my determination, which I never missed an opportunity to express whenever the doctors examined my foot. Over and over I said, "You stop the bleeding, and I'll make it work." This attitude proved crucial.

Shortly after arriving at Benning, just as in Japan, I wrote 1st Sgt. Charles Pitts expressing my great pride in what my Rangers accomplished. After providing my description of the action, I requested a list of the casualties and the names and addresses of the next of kin, especially any KIA (killed in action). I wanted to write their parents. Although I did not know many of the details, obviously many of our Rangers never made it off Hill 205. I also wanted statements from any of the Rangers that could be used in support of recommendations for awards. I had firsthand knowledge of what some had done but remained in the dark concerning others. Impatiently I awaited the information that never arrived; I wrote Pitts again asking for his assistance. When he and I next met years later, he told me that he had sent the information twice. For some reason it never reached me. Many of the Rangers wrote me, and I responded to each. In mid-January 1951, Capt. John Vann assembled the Rangers and had them prepare written statements describing what they and their comrades-in-arms had done during the battle; he forwarded those statements shortly thereafter. A few months intervened before I returned to duty and had someone type recommendations for awards. When completed, they were mailed to Headquarters, Eighth United States Army in Korea. All the recommendations won approval, and I received a copy of the orders for each award.

Barney Cummings's girlfriend, Benning Burgard—a descendant of Confederate Gen. Henry L. Benning—came to visit me several times. Naturally she wanted to know what happened on that hill in Korea. Did I think that he might be a prisoner of war? Did I think that he might have been killed? Joyous Mahaffey, one of Barney's sisters who lived with her husband, Joe, a civilian instructor at the Air University in Montgomery, Alabama, also came by. She asked the same questions. Unfortunately, I could give them no information. Was Barney in the foxhole? I thought so but could not be sure. I had asked Walls to check the foxhole before he dragged me off the hill. He reported it was empty. What had happened to Jim Beatty, my radio operator? I remembered him in the foxhole at the time. Beatty had made it off the hill but knew nothing of Barney. No one could shed any light on what might have happened to him. They were persistent, but Benning and Joyous never lost patience with me and could imagine the confusion as the Chinese overran our defensive position and my mental and physical state after receiving three wounds. Although they remained most supportive, I never forgave myself for not being able to tell them something about what might have happened to Barney. I certainly described his heroism and the regard in which we Rangers held him. I wrote Barney's mother and told her how proud she should be of him. Effusive in my praise without exaggerating, I merely told the truth. Barney was a courageous platoon leader, a great asset to our company and to me; his demise was a great loss to the army. Certainly my comments offered scant solace for a grieving mother, but it was the best that I could do.

A few days after I arrived at the hospital, the ward nurse told me of a young soldier in the psychiatric ward who claimed that he could tell fortunes. She asked if I would let him tell me mine since this activity seemed to calm him. Eager for some comic relief, I told her to bring him over. The nurse soon reappeared with the clairvoyant soldier in tow. As he gazed at my hand he said, "You have been on a long voyage." Since all of us in the ward had just returned from Korea, that hardly qualified as any great insight. "You will soon meet two girls," he continued. "One will be a brunette; the other will be blond. You will marry one of them!" Now that really got my attention. "Which one will I marry?" He did not know but averred, "You will marry one of them. One of them has a lot of money." More interested now, I inquired if I would marry the wealthy one.

That he could not foretell, but he prophesized I would do a great deal of traveling for the army. Although it burned a half hour and provided a good chuckle, I put no store in what the would-be Nostradamus predicted.

My parents and brother drove over from Tifton the first weekend I was at Benning. Needless to say, the reunion was a happy one. I told them about the fortune-teller's premonition. No sooner had I finished recounting the story when there was a knock on the door. When it opened, two very attractive girls stuck their heads inside; one a blonde and the other a brunette! Before a word was spoken, my dad, always a big kidder, pointed toward them and said, pointing to me, "He's going to marry one of you." I felt my face flush red as a beet. Who could guess what the two girls might be thinking? When I explained why Daddy had said what he did, everyone had a big laugh.

The blonde was Jeannie Martin, a high school senior, and the other was Peggy Ashworth, a freshman at the University of Georgia and the daughter of the publisher of the local newspaper (the rich one). Their coming resulted from an unusual happenstance. Jeannie's typing teacher had seen my picture in the paper. She recognized my name because she had been my seventh-grade English teacher in Tifton. As she showed Jeannie the photo, Ms. Nan Strickland asked Jeannie to visit me, saying, "I know this boy. He comes from a nice family. I know he is lonely and would appreciate a visit." Jeannie took the picture, stuck it into one of her schoolbooks, and promptly forgot all about it. Later Jeannie encountered Peggy, who asked her to come along on a visit to a soldier in the Fort Benning hospital. Peggy had seen my picture and remembered we had double-dated once while I attended the basic course before going to Korea. Although hesitant, Jeannie agreed. There is a busy intersection in Columbus that features a figure of a young woman, her hand cupped over her eyes as she peers into the distance. The locals joke the statue represents a local belle looking for an officer to marry. Actually, good Columbus girls were not supposed to date Fort Benning soldiers. Fortunately for many of us, a lot of girls—good and otherwise—defied that rule. Jeannie showed Peggy my picture. They were surprised that they were going to visit the same person. Needless to say, I was flabbergasted. Two beautiful girls coming to visit me! Maybe that fortune-teller knew something after all. Of course, none of us placed any credence in the prediction that I would marry one of them; we dismissed the visit as just a funny coincidence.

I was really taken by Jeannie, the most attractive, vivacious, and outgoing person I had ever met. Although surely wishing to get to know her, I expected never to see her again. Happily, I was mistaken. Jeannie visited me often, always with another girl. She did wonders for my morale as I underwent several operations on my feet. She visited two or three times each week and always came the day following an operation. She constantly presented a bright, happy, smiling face. After a few months, I finally got out of the hospital on pass. We began to date. However, she still came with another girl. We usually went to the movies—always a drive-in—with me on the backseat in my casts and Jeannie and a friend up front.

Inevitably, the time arrived to meet the parents, Jean and Frank Martin. The Martins were most gracious, often inviting me to dinner at their home or taking me to the Columbus Country Club. Naturally Jeannie's parents grew quite worried about our growing relationship. I was a soldier; worse—a paratrooper; worse yet—a Ranger. Since World War II, Columbus residents heard tales of paratroopers running amok, drinking, fighting, and generally raising hell. In truth, that all happened but mostly across the Chattahoochee in Phenix City, Alabama, known in the 1950s as the "wickedest town in America." At the time the Martins indicated no outward signs of disapproval, but years later Mr. Martin (nicknamed "Admiral" because he served in the navy during World War II) explained that his deep concerns developed because I was older than Jeannie, had graduated from college, earned a salary, and was in a position to ask his daughter to marry.

I liked Jeannie's twelve-year-old brother Butch, a very bright youngster. When I graduated to dating Jeannie without a girl chaperone, I always asked Butch to come along, knowing the Martins would be more comfortable with that arrangement. Jeannie thought I would never stop including her brother. When we began excluding Butch, he was amazed I preferred Jeannie's company to his. He claims that he was sure that we brought Jeannie along to make his parents happy. Butch got over his disappointment; he went on to become a successful lawyer and popular mayor of Columbus. Instrumental in many urban improvements—including luring the Olympic softball competition to Columbus—the city named a pedestrian bridge over the Chattahoochee River in his honor.

After about six months in the hospital, my petitioning worked and the doctors allowed me to return to duty on the condition that I got a desk job that gave my feet more time to heal. At one point they had considered amputating my right foot but persisted in treatment because of my attitude. They told me to give my foot a try and if I had trouble to return and they would execute a two-stage graft procedure. They explained that, while much more involved than the pinch grafts and single-thickness grafts they had already tried, this approach, if successful, would provide a much thicker pad for ambulation.

Effective 24 May 1951, I received assignment to Fort Benning and the Ranger Training Command (RTC). John Vann, returned from Korea and assigned to the Ranger Training Battalion, had me assigned to the battalion as the assistant S1—a curious appointment since the table of organization had no S1 slot. The commander, Maj. William R. Bond, had served in the First Ranger Battalion in World War II. The RTC trained Airborne Ranger companies for assignment, primarily to Korea. These companies differed from mine. They had three identical platoons with a total strength of five officers and 110 enlisted men. There was another, more significant difference. Each company came from a division, such as the Eighty-Second Airborne, and had experienced officers and noncommissioned officers when training began. That was a far cry from the seventy-three low-ranking service troops led and trained by three green second lieutenants. They also had a mess and cooks, medics, some vehicles, and other support.

After welcoming me and exchanging a few pleasantries, Vann asked, "Why aren't you wearing the CIB [Combat Infantryman Badge]?" "Sir," I responded, "I have never been awarded the badge." "I'll write Colonel Dolvin and have you put on orders," he replied, and in his usual take-charge manner, Vann did exactly that. I soon received orders awarding the CIB.

Never having held an assignment as a platoon leader, I needed basic remedial work. Vann provided it, showing me how to inspect a mess hall, barracks, and a company area. I made reveille with one company each morning, conducted an inspection of one barracks and mess hall each day, and reviewed all the paperwork that came to the headquarters and took appropriate action. Bond and Vann spent every day—and many a night—in the field observing training. When Bond returned to the headquarters each afternoon, usually about 1800 hours (6:00 p.m.), I briefed him on the memoranda that had arrived and what actions I had taken or recommended. He was very easy to work for; he generally approved my recommendations.

The RTC boasted some top-notch people. Col. John Van Houten commanded, and his deputy was Col. Edwin Walker, who had served in the renowned First Special Service Force during World War II. Both became major generals. Maj. John Singlaub, a future three-star, had served in the Office of Strategic Services, the forerunner of the CIA. Col. William "Coal Bin Willie" Wilson, a legend in the Airborne, was also a member of the command. I considered myself fortunate to be among them even though my administrative duties—and my all-too short tenure—kept me from having much contact. After only three weeks with the command, Bond gave me the task of selecting a headquarters area for the next field training exercise. After a little walking, my foot began bleeding profusely. Although I dreaded a return to the hospital, I knew it had to be done.

On 24 June 1951, I entered Martin Army Hospital and almost immediately saw Captain Vesley. Even though recently discharged from the army, he insisted on staying on my case. He explained he would slice a thick slab of flesh from my left calf, leaving one end of the slice attached to the donor site on my left leg. He would then sew the flap over the bottom of my right foot and put both legs in a cast, stabilizing the connection between the right foot and left leg. If all went well, the right foot would develop a blood-supply system with the slab that would continue after the flap was cut from my left calf. The procedure left me in the cast for several weeks, with the doctors coming each day to sniff the area of the wound, the odor indicating whether the blood supply was developing or becoming infected. The cast caused me a good deal of discomfort.

Satisfied the connection to my leg had "taken," the doctors performed the second stage of the process. This time, they cut the flap loose from the left-leg donor site and sewed it completely to my right foot. They expressed confidence that all would progress as hoped. Months would pass before I would be able to walk on that foot. I decided to view these difficulties as a challenge. After all, I counted myself lucky to be alive and not a double amputee. There was one very big upside to all this: if I had never been seriously wounded, I never would have met Jeannie.

Naturally, I saw Jeannie as much as I could for those three weeks with the RTC, usually on crutches. Now with me confined to the hospital ward, she visited me every afternoon. Without a doubt, her visits—always the high point of each day—made my recovery easier to bear. By the middle of summer we both saw our future as being together. Her parents intuitively knew what we had in mind. The topic did come up once when her father met me at her door as I came to take her out for the evening. Stepping abruptly in front of her just as Jeannie moved to open the door, Mr. Martin said to me, "I understand you want to marry my daughter. She's much too young to get married. You and I need to go for a ride." With that, he "guided" me toward his car, saying to Jeannie, "You stay home."

We rode for perhaps a half hour or so with the Admiral trying to convince me that we should wait until Jeannie graduated from college. She was about to enter Mary Baldwin College in Staunton, Virginia, in the fall. I was not prepared to wait four years. We had spent time together almost every day since we had met, but that had only been about eight months, and I had been in the hospital much of that time. I expected to return to "full duty" as the Headquarters Company commander with the Ranger Department. My days and nights would be almost totally comprised of work—not a good way to start a marriage. I offered an alternative: I was willing to wait until Jeannie finished her first year at college. It might be good for both of us. The Admiral agreed, probably hoping that Jeannie would meet somebody else up in Virginia.

When the Admiral and I returned to the Martin residence and told Jeannie and her mother about the bargain, Jeannie was surprised and obviously not pleased. Later, when we had some time alone, we discussed her parents' valid objections. Jeannie was young; I had a long way to go to be back "on my feet." Her parents wanted to be sure that it was not sympathy that Jeannie felt for me. Both of us wanted her family's approval. Family was important to both of us, so we made the "mature" decision to wait a year—but not without great disappointment.

Shortly before Jeannie left for college, we had another private tête-à-tête. I wanted her to be sure that she knew what she would be in for if she married me: the constant moving, the uprooting of children in the middle of school years, the barely adequate or nonexistent quarters. As an Infantryman I could expect to be in other wars that our country would surely fight. She would have to face the possibility of my being wounded or killed. Even without a war, we would still often face long separations during "hardship" tours (assignments unaccompanied by family). This litany of army wife sorrows prompted Jeannie to think I was not too subtly providing the rationale for a break-up. I asked her to think about all these things while in Virginia because I would have a question for her when she returned. We both knew the meaning of that.

When Jeannie departed in September 1951, she left a major void in my life. I had looked forward to seeing her smiling face each day. As we said our goodbyes on our last night, I burst into tears and sobbed uncontrollably. At that moment I recognized what she meant to me. She was the center of my life. How was I going to get along without her for a year?

Ranger Department

Early in October, I finally left the hospital with orders for the Ranger Department, U.S. Army Infantry School, Fort Benning. Almost eleven months had elapsed since my wounding. The Ranger Department had replaced the Ranger

Training Command on 1 September 1950. The director, Col. Henry G. Learnard, formerly headed the staff department of the Infantry School.

When I reported on 14 October 1951, Colonel Learnard sat me down in his office and spent at least an hour explaining the whys and wherefores of the Ranger Department. The training focused on developing small-unit leadership skills in those who had already proven themselves: the top 10 percent of Infantry company, platoon, and squad leaders. A decision had not yet been made whether Infantry company executive officers would be accepted; they were not commanders. Graduates would return to their units and raise them to a higher standard of combat readiness. Learnard envisioned that some graduates might be called upon by division commanders to establish division-level special training programs patterned after the Ranger Course. Ranger training would serve as a bootstrap for the Infantry.

Colonel Learnard told me that initially the award of the Ranger tab was a matter of discussion. The course had not been established to train soldiers for Ranger units, since none existed, but to develop the capabilities of leaders with the goal of improving the combat readiness of line Infantry units. Finally the brass decided on awarding the tab to graduates. Seeing a soldier with a Ranger tab in the early days was extremely rare. Learnard went into detail about what he expected of me: command the Headquarters and Headquarters Company for the Department until I recovered from my wounds. At that time I would become an instructor. Until then, my job centered on ensuring the cadre met the highest standards of appearance and discipline; determining what equipment we needed for training and getting it; having the barracks, mess hall, and supply room ready for the arrival of the cadre. Giving me complete authority in determining and filling requirements, he told me not to trouble him unless I had gone "all the way to the top." He just wanted relief from the details, but I took the instruction literally—as I always did.

The first students would arrive in January 1952 and graduate in March. We were in business. I kept very busy as the headquarters commandant. My cadre consisted of an experienced first sergeant, Dewey M. Denson, whom Colonel Learnard had personally selected, a company clerk, and an experienced supply sergeant, Master Sergeant Hoffman. I also had a full complement of cooks for my mess hall.

During World War II, the army threw up wooden barracks with no attention paid to the amenities. The mess hall had the ten-man "picnic" table-bench combination. I managed to locate some four-man tables on post and have them issued to us. The new décor consisted of tablecloths, artificial flowers, salt-and-pepper shakers for each table, and a few airborne pictures for the wall. Today those little things do not sound like much, but they were significant improvements in 1951–1952.

Very shortly after our activation, I held a meeting with my cadre to solicit suggestions. None were offered until finally one soldier said, "Why should we? It won't make any difference." "Try it and see," I responded. "Give me a chance. I certainly may not do everything you ask, but I will listen. If I don't produce, you will have been right." With that, he asked, "Can we get individual pitchers for coffee at breakfast so we don't have to get up and go through the line for another cup?" I replied, "Let me see what I can do." The supply sergeant requisitioned the pitchers, and they were on the tables in a couple of weeks. It was as simple as that. I had passed the first "test." Nothing spectacular—just some little things that made barracks life a little more enjoyable.

Sergeant Hoffman and I were starting from zero. What equipment did we need? An old-hand supply sergeant is a very valuable commodity. We—sometimes together, sometimes separately—made many trips to the Main Post supply point with requisitions. The people there, primarily civilians who had been on the job for years and knew their business backward and forward, possessed no sense of urgency. That the Ranger Department was in its gestation stage, with a student arrival deadline on the calendar, meant nothing to them. They would do their job as they always had, unhurried by a new company commander. Once, near the beginning of the Christmas holidays, I appeared on the scheduled day for submitting requisitions and requested help, only to be told the supply section was having a party. I firmly responded that I had a job to do and that was prepare for the first Ranger course that would begin immediately after the first of the year. They resisted. I insisted. I wanted to see the boss. When he finally appeared, obviously disgruntled, he greeted me with, "We're having a staff party and I resent your being here." I reminded him that the day was a regular workday and that I had complied with his published schedule and needed his help. Finally he relented and put my request in motion. I sprinkled my arguments with a heavy dose of "Sirs" and "Thank yous" in the hope that they would soothe his anger. For one of the few times in my life, I was not confrontational with a senior officer with whom I differed. I wish I had adopted that tone as my usual attitude for the rest of my career.

On another occasion, I met resistance at each level in the logistics chain. When met with a roadblock, I went to the next-higher level and ended up at the post G4 (Supply) office. As I waited to see the G4, Colonel Learnard walked in. Surprised to see me, he asked what I was doing there. "Sir, I have been unable to get the equipment that we need," I replied. "You told me to go all the way to the top if necessary. If I were still unable to get cooperation only then should I come to see you." He said, "OK. If you need help come see me." Fortunately, the G4 agreed the requests met regulations and procedures and directed his staff to see that I received what I needed.

The Ranger Department cadre, the assistant instructors (AIs), did not pull details. For them there was no kitchen police, fire guard, furnace stokers, interior guard—none of the numerous, sometimes onerous, details that must be accomplished behind the scenes for a unit to function. I had six badly overworked privates assigned to those details. I prepared a report showing how each of these soldiers required about eighty hours each week just to complete the scheduled chores required by regulations and took it to my next-higher headquarters in the Infantry School Detachment (ISD) in the Infantry School. This channel did not go through Learnard and the Ranger Department. In a few days, a lieutenant colonel appeared in my office. He asked if I had requested additional detail soldiers. After I replied in the affirmative, he said very smugly, "Well, you are not going to get them." Obviously, he came with a closed mind. After reviewing my requirements with him and explaining the memorandum he held in his hands, there was no disputing how many soldiers were needed for us to perform required functions within a regular workload. My chart showed that to accomplish functions directed by regulations would require each of the six duty soldiers to work more than seventy hours per week. After about an hour, the officer left. I was angry but held my temper. Regardless of what my charts said, he was sure I did not need any more soldiers.

To my surprise, in about a week, twenty-two men arrived at the orderly room without notice. Denson came to me with the news. I went outside to greet them. After expressing my pleasure to see them in a few welcoming remarks— and they were a motley-looking crew—I returned to my office while Denson and the clerk processed them. When Denson had completed his work, he came to me and told me with a wry smile that all of our new soldiers had been in some sort of disciplinary trouble. Several had been court-martialed, some more than once. It was obvious what had happened. The other companies in the Infantry School Detachment had taken the opportunity to fill the levy with their miscreants. Denson also told me that all of them had pay problems; some had not received pay for several months. While they had brought much of the trouble onto themselves through AWOLs (absent without leave) and other transgressions, the army still had the responsibility to pay them whatever was due.

The first sergeant had our clerk take the necessary data for the pay actions and hand-carry that information to the administrative center. My clerk received a promise these troops would be paid that Friday. We followed administrative procedures and did things according to schedule and requested no faster action than standard. I informed them that if the pay was not in my hands by Friday. I would be in the office of the inspector general when he arrived the following Monday morning.

Friday arrived, but the payroll for the new soldiers did not. As promised, I was at the inspector general's office the following Monday before he arrived. When he appeared, he invited me into his office. After explaining the situation, stressing we had done everything according to policy, he expressed his surprise that I was there for my soldiers—not for some real or imagined injustice visited on me personally. After a few minutes, he dismissed me, saying he would take care of my problem. The next day, I picked up the payroll and paid my men. Like the post G4, the inspector general was a very competent officer whose focus rested on the troops' welfare.

That day, my commander at the Infantry School Detachment called me into his office and made it very clear he and his staff had been admonished by the inspector general. In similar terms—my usual modus operandi—I repeated what I told the inspector general: procedures set by the administrative center had been followed and my men deserved their pay. I reminded him that even if the soldiers were castoffs and hard cases, they deserved proper treatment. Having them paid on time was my obligation, and I had taken the actions required to meet that responsibility. Rule #1: Do not aggravate superior officers—particularly your rating officer. But that is exactly what I had done.

Going to the inspector general was certainly not conducive to good relations with my commander and his staff. I had gone to my commander with this problem, and he never looked after it with any sense of urgency. All my future dealings with the administrative center would have to be correct because the inspector general came down on their heads. While the issue could have been handled more diplomatically, the solution would have taken much longer. The fault lay with personnel in administration, not with me. My zealous desire to take care of my soldiers would continue to get me into hot water, but with me the troops came first.

Keeping my promise indicated to the new levies I was a man of my word. No doubt they reserved judgment; they had been shuffled around too many times. I had to work with them and talked to them collectively and individually. I wanted to convince them that I was on their side—that I needed them and would treat them fairly. Each of them would receive a three-day pass if they stayed straight for that month. "Do not go AWOL," I told them. "Do your job. You will have an opportunity to better yourself and move into a better job and possible assignment to the Ranger Department if you wish." The experiment met with some success. Two or three of them went AWOL. One or two others went to sleep on guard. However, most of them performed satisfactorily.

The World War II barracks had a furnace on the ground floor. Keeping it stoked in the winter fell to the fire guard. The heat from the furnace did not warm the building evenly, and the furnace often filled the barracks with smoke and soot. As poor as it was, it beat going without heat during the winter. On one occasion, during a holiday period, we ran low on coal. A request for more coal was met with the explanation they were on holiday and would not make a delivery for several days. I explained our plight; the answer remained the same. Back I went to the inspector general, and we had coal that day.

All this makes Puckett sound like a quarrelsome young lieutenant with a death wish. One bad officer efficiency report will sidetrack a career very quickly, and there exists no better path to that sad end than alienating senior leadership. In a short period my name became well known in the personnel, administration, and logistics headquarters as well as to the inspector general—all due to the disapproval of one of my rating officers. One old axiom held, "There's the right way; the wrong way; and the army way." Another bit of advice for garnering favor in high places—and max scores on the all-important officer evaluations—was "to get along you have to go along." Obviously I was not going along. I simply acted on the colonel's enjoinder not to come to him with problems until all other avenues were exhausted—even "going to the top." When I did, the problem got solved. I also discovered the top people and their staffs recognized and accepted their responsibility for looking after the troops. I reckoned that was one of the reasons they held those positions. The lesson: although taking problems topside should not be practiced as a general rule, it was worth doing when necessary.

I worked steadily, regaining my fitness after my extended hospital stays. I took the five-event physical training (PT) test with the students, except in my case there were four parts. My feet were still not up for the run component. Scoring about 350 out of a possible 400 points, I emerged pleased, if not satisfied, with my performance. Returning to jump status as soon as possible remained the focus. In addition to regaining physical strength after a long downtime, my feet needed to be able to stand the shock of landing. Completing the Airborne Department refresher course, I made my first jump on 7 January 1952. All parachutists had to complete this training if they had been off jump status for any length of time. All went well. By pushing myself, I completed the required jumps and qualified as a senior parachutist by 16 October 1953.

At the end of the annual medical exam, the reviewing doctor threatened to give me a profile because of my injuries. I wanted no administrative action taken that might keep me from staying with the Rangers or inhibit my assignment to combat units. Following a brush with the doctor, I challenged him to a push-up contest. Push-ups, of course, had absolutely nothing to do with the condition of my feet. The doctor, a lieutenant colonel, was startled. Col. Edwin Briggs, the Ranger Department deputy director, chimed in, "Go ahead, Doc, and give him the picket fence [straight 1 grades for the six areas that the army used to categorize medical fitness]. He can do the work." The doctor took the challenge. Colonel Briggs really went to bat for me.

My feet, far from satisfactory, did not dim my determination to "make do." After all, no other option presented itself. Jeannie and my folks were concerned, but I made light of the recurring bleeding, infections, and swelling. In addition to my feet, I had taken fragments in my buttocks, thigh, and arm. Daddy often kidded me about the wounds on my backside. He said I could never tell anybody where they were: "If you tell them you were attacking the enemy, it must have been your own Rangers who shot you. If you say that the enemy shot you, you had to be running away." We had a lot of laughs over his comments.

For a number of reasons, the Ranger Department had difficulty drawing volunteers for the course. Ranger training was a new and unheard-of concept to most in the army. What was its purpose? What benefit would accrue to the student himself and to his unit commander who sent him to the course? Many soldiers did not want to volunteer to undergo anything as arduous as Ranger training. Another disincentive stemmed from the fact that the army did not return all graduating students to their unit. As a consequence, some unit commanders never sent their better troops to the course because there was no guarantee that the graduate would return.

The Department initiated several actions. First, it sent recruiting teams to basic training centers. In May 1953, Maj. Charles Kuhn and I went to Fort Jackson, South Carolina, and Fort Lewis, Washington. We showed a recently produced Ranger training film and spoke to hundreds of recruits. Our efforts mostly miscarried because the recruits were the least-experienced men struggling with the vicissitudes of basic training. We spoke to only a few NCOs and commissioned officers.

The Department tried another approach. It invited division commanders, G3s (Operations), and S1s (Personnel) to attend an orientation on Ranger training. The orientation generally lasted three to five days and consisted of a briefing, the presentation of the Ranger training film, and a visit to either the Mountain or Florida Ranger Camps. There the invitees glimpsed the technical and tactical aspects of the course. This approach proved more successful; our visitors went away favorably impressed, grasping the benefits not only to the individual soldier but also to the sponsoring unit. The problem of the graduate being reassigned was easily corrected. The Department of the Army simply changed its procedures requiring graduates return to their units.

Strict attention to regulations and established procedures—and my imperious approach to both—won few friends. As I saw it, my duty involved enforcing the rules. One regulation I rigorously policed was the limit on a three-day pass. It said seventy-two hours. The same applied with the start and end of a leave. No soldier could sign out before the official start of his pass or leave. What other officers did never concerned me.

Another responsibility Learnard stressed and one that I knew was mine as company commander consisted of always ensuring the barracks met the highest standards in appearance. The wooden World War II barracks had open bays with latrines at the end. Ranger cadre became lax in keeping their clothing and equipment straight. In addition to his footlocker, each soldier had a wall locker—something still rare in those days. If they kept their bunks straight and stowed and secured their stuff in the lockers, they met my standard. They were required to keep them locked as a theft-prevention measure. Simple enough. I never considered it important to explain these requirements to the company. The cadre objected, and many filed grievances with their committee chairman, who reported to the colonel. My obstinate enforcement of regulations precipitated my transfer, on 24 April 1952, as an instructor to the Florida Camp in the panhandle.

Unlike the current Ranger Training Brigade "break-in," or staff certification, program, I received a "vault file" and an assignment as principal instructor for a reconnaissance patrol problem. I read the file, talked with my assistant instructors, scouted the objectives, and studied and rehearsed my presentation several times. When the scheduled time for the class arrived, I was more than prepped. Although very nervous, my class proceeded satisfactorily, and the practical exercise went without a hitch. I sat in on the critiques of a couple of student patrols and made notes for use during the next cycle. Lane graders—officers who accompanied the patrols—presented their critiques. I presented the class the next day to the other half of the cohort. For the remainder of the cycle, I served either as lane grader or assistant instructor on different problems. If the students benefited as much as I did, they were doing well.

On 24 June 1952, in my second cycle in Florida, I was hurriedly appointed as commander of the Ranger Mountain Camp south of Dahlonega in north Georgia. The previous commander and executive officer had been relieved for improperly accounting for meal money in the mess hall. On the way to the mountains, I reported to Col. Edwin Briggs, the Ranger Department executive officer, who explained why Colonel Learnard had made the move. Not only had the previous commander failed as an accountant, but he had never maintained the proper standards of appearance and discipline. The Mountain Camp needed exactly the medicine I prescribed at Benning. "Get up there and straighten things out," Briggs said. The assignment vindicated my actions in Headquarters Company if not the approach. Another lesson learned and scrupulously followed: always keep in touch with the cadre.

The Ranger Mountain Camp was aptly named: a "tent city" in the wilds of the Georgia Appalachians. After a cursory inventory of equipment, I signed the property book. Considering the previous commander and XO (executive officer) had been sacked for misappropriation of funds, I should have exercised more diligence. As it turned out, some of the kitchen equipment was missing. Never having been a platoon leader, I missed much of the seasoning I would have gotten from a platoon sergeant and company commander. I learned the hard way—by making mistakes. Chalk it up as another lesson: be careful about what you sign, something the sergeants at West Point had stressed in the pregraduation classes.

Briggs gave me the mission of "tightening up" discipline in the Mountain Camp. The squad tents where the cadre lived were not maintained to specifications. In order to get the troops "squared away," the cadre—some of the same men who complained about my enforcing regulations at Benning—had to set the examples. I assembled them the first day and expressed my pleasure at being assigned to the Mountain Camp, talked of my pride in them and their skills in the vital training that lay ahead, and explained in a benign manner what was expected. Getting them up to standards proved none too difficult because of the caliber of the cadre and because they knew me. Soldiers generally are willing to do all that is asked if they see that the requests are reasonable and fair, a ground rule I had not followed in Headquarters Company at Benning.

In these early days of the Ranger Department, the cadre went back and forth from Benning to the Mountain Camp for each cycle with no permanent change of station. Consequently, we had a major convoy move a few days before and after each training cycle. Fortunately, they proceeded without mishap.

During my second cycle, Col. Stanley N. Lonning from the Infantry School arrived to inspect and make recommendations to the commanding general for what was needed at the Mountain Camp to meet minimum acceptable living standards. We lived in squad tents; the kitchen was a field kitchen; the dining hall, a big "circus" tent; the toilets, field latrines. The showers only worked when the gasoline motor powered the pump, and the water had to be heated. Not unbearable facilities for field operations but inadequate for a semi-permanent training facility.

Just a few days after the colonel completed his inspection, a reticent lieutenant arrived in command of a Combat Engineer platoon. From the start he tackled the job with a determination to accomplish all his platoon could within the constraints of time and available supplies. Despite their best efforts, the Combat Engineers could accomplish only so much. The necessary improvements required command action at the top level.

In 1952, the director of the Ranger Department made a wise decision about the organization of the two outlying camps. The Florida and Mountain committee chiefs—both majors—were placed in command of the camps. The current commanders—both lieutenants—would become executive officers. Although my actual duties did not change appreciably, the new arrangement worked because the ranking officer commanded. No longer would I be placed in the awkward position of trying to correct or overrule officers who ranked me. Maj. Robert Sadler assumed command. He had served as assistant G3 in the Twenty-Fifth Division in Korea, and although our contacts were few, I was pleased that Sadler would be my boss. I knew him as a very competent and likable officer.

Jeannie's year was up, and the Admiral kept his part of the deal. On 26 November 1952, the marriage took place in Columbus. It was a joyous occasion for all concerned: for our families who had come to know and like each other and for Jeannie and me. We spent our month-long honeymoon on St. Simons Island, Georgia, where my parents owned a beach cottage. It was a wonderful time for us. We dined in many of the fine eating establishments in the area, the best being the Cloister on Sea Island. At night we took many memorable walks on the beach. Although the weather was cool in November, we had our love to keep us warm.

We returned to Dahlonega to find our first home together. Before the change of command, I had stayed at the camp because an officer should be on-site twenty-four hours a day, and as commander that was my responsibility. Accommodations were very scarce. One possibility led us to an apartment in a large Victorian home near the town square. The lady owner perfectly matched the Victorian décor. She repeated several times her description of this "wonderful apartment" we would just love. The apartment was upstairs. We entered the apartment from the hall into a bedroom; next came the living room, followed by the kitchen and then the bathroom. As we completed our inspection, the lady said, "There's just one thing I need to tell you. The editor of the *Dahlonega Nugget* [the local newspaper] lives down the hall from you. He has no bathroom and uses yours. That won't cause a problem, though, because he works late, and you'll be in bed when he comes home. He'll come in very quietly, use the bathroom, and be out in no time. He sleeps late. In the morning, you'll be up and out of the bath before he gets up. He won't cause you any trouble at all." I thanked the lady sincerely for showing us the apartment and told her we might be back. Until then, Jeannie held her breath. We continued our search and hit it lucky. We found a three-bedroom house complete with living and dining rooms, kitchen, bath, and screened porch one block from the town square for fifty dollars a month. We had no furniture. Two army cots served as beds, a steamer trunk for a table, and we bought two chairs. The cots sufficed until a bed arrived from Columbus.

Welcome to army life, Mrs. Puckett. Rudely awakened between three thirty and four thirty in the morning to fix breakfast, Jeannie had to amuse herself until I returned after dark for supper. With the Ranger Department still very much in the developmental stage, we worked seven days a week, and students trained every day and night. My mother visited us a couple weeks after we moved into the house. Despite the Spartan conditions, we invited the Sadlers for dinner served on our steamer truck table. Mother slept on one cot, and after Jeannie and I experimented with sleeping on the other, I ended up on the floor. When Mother returned home she broke into tears, exclaiming to Daddy, "I know that little girl is going to leave him!" About a week later, a truck from a department store in Atlanta arrived, and the driver told Jeannie that he had furniture for a Mrs. Puckett. Jeannie told him there must be a mistake; she had ordered no furniture. The driver insisted. Mother had stopped on the way home and ordered two single beds, a small cherry table with four chairs, a braided rug, and café curtains. Jeannie knew she had a mother-in-law on her side.

Our time in Dahlonega was brief. We never even unpacked our wedding gifts. I was sent to Benning as the tactical officer for a new Ranger class for officers. No doubt with great relief, Jeannie returned to Columbus while I traveled with the class from camp to camp. All of this served as Jeannie's basic training in being an army wife; she soon learned to uncomplainingly make the best of any situation.

The tactical officer maintained records on each student and organized the buddy teams into a different patrol for each tactical problem. He kept himself appraised of the performance record of each student and discussed the class as a whole and each individual student with the leadership of the Florida and Mountain Camps. The tactical officer also made the daily inspections of barracks and equipment and ensured that all students attended every class. It was an important job that kept me busy.

Being tactical officer and accompanying a class through the course provided a valuable experience that proved very beneficial in subsequent assignments. I saw the complete course as a composite and developed a greater understanding of the difficulties of evaluating leadership while learning some approaches that might alleviate observed shortcomings. When the class graduated, I asked for and received reassignment to the Benning Committee. I taught map reading, mines and booby traps, leadership, drill and ceremonies, and assisted on all other classes taught at Benning. All this broadened my experience. It also afforded the opportunity of earning "constructive credit" for the Ranger course. The requirements included participating in two reconnaissance and two combat patrols in both the mountains and swamps; passing map reading to include the ten-hour land navigation course; passing the PT; completing the "slide for life," "suspension traverse," and rappels; completing stream-crossing expedients and a few other requirements; and obtaining the recommendation of the Ranger Department director. I received the certificate on 1 June 1953.

I had mixed emotions about the constructive credit. Glad to get it, I always felt that route was a lot easier than the Ranger course. The six-and-one-half weeks my company in Korea trained and our combat experience were a lot tougher than the requirements for constructive credit and certainly equivalent to the Benning Ranger course itself. The Department of the Army published a regulation authorizing the Ranger tab for any individual who had earned the Combat Infantryman or the Combat Medic Badge while serving in a Ranger Company in Korea. I was also eligible for the tab under that regulation.

While enjoying my relationships with the officers and cadre, I took an immediate dislike to the second department director, Col. Gerald Kelleher. Although a highly decorated World War II combat veteran, a mustang who rose from private to regimental commander in the same First Infantry Division regiment, his personality irritated me. Besides, he described my dog, an Alaskan malamute, as "funny-looking." Again my immaturity showed.

Kelleher was a stickler for "the little things." He said, "If you take care of the little things you won't have any big problems." He required the instructors to ensure the desks in the classrooms were aligned, the window shades hung even with one another, the floors properly swept, and the latrines clean. When instructors and staff from other Infantry School departments inspected one of our classes—staff from one department inspected other classes as a means to raise standards—they often commented favorably on our operation. Even though housed in temporary buildings, we met or exceeded the standards in Infantry Hall with its permanent facilities where most of the indoor classes were taught. This emphasis on "the little things" was one of the most important lessons I learned from this experienced leader. It is vital in combat. I would not forget it.

Immediately after assuming his position, Kelleher mandated that all students and cadre, when in a tactical mode, must wear the cartridge belt with suspenders, full canteen, and first aid packet. Until I discovered his rationale, the order rankled. Kelleher had served in North Africa, where many soldiers, taking a break, routinely unhooked their cartridge belt. If called upon to move out rapidly, they often forgot to rehook their belts and would not notice their loss until they needed ammunition or water. The suspenders kept the belt with the soldier even if he forgot to hook it. The benefits were obvious.

The department held a going-away party in one of the senior officer's homes for some of us rotating out of Benning. Kelleher, of course, attended. After taking a few belts he spied me across the living room, filled with officers and their wives, preparing to leave. He looked straight at me and in a loud voice said, "Puckett, you don't like me, do you?" A hush fell over the room. I responded with an outward calmness that belied my churning emotions: "No, Sir, I do not." Now the room felt like a vacuum as all eyes and ears focused on the colonel awaiting his response to my brassiness (or stupidity). "That's okay," he rejoined. "You respect me, don't you?" "Yes, Sir, I sure do," I replied honestly. "That's all right," Kelleher continued. "You don't have to have people like you as long as they respect you."

Jeannie and I left immediately. Jeannie knew of my animosity toward the colonel but was dumbfounded by my response and wondered if I had any sense. "I believe I like that man," I proclaimed. My feelings toward Colonel Kelleher changed 180 degrees. "Anybody with his combat record who can have some first lieutenant who is still wet behind his ears say what I said and not get mad has to be a great guy." An exasperated Jeannie blurted, "Tell him! Don't tell me!"

In any large stratified organization, personality conflicts are inevitable; but in the army, rank takes precedence in all things. Kelleher was a stickler for regulations; so was Puckett. Kelleher's insistence on the suspenders made eminently good sense and was the first thing I established on assuming my next company command. Kelleher's emphasis on taking care of "the little things" to avoid big problems became fundamental to my approach to all my assigned tasks. In short, I learned many lessons from Colonel Kelleher; whether holding my tongue ranked among them remained to be seen.

The Ranger Department offered a great learning experience during my slightly more than two years in that assignment. I commanded Headquarters Company and had been an instructor in Florida, the commander and later the executive officer of the Mountain Camp, a tactical officer, and an instructor in the Benning phase, where I taught or assisted in every class. I worked with outstanding officers and noncommissioned officers and hardworking students. My capability to evaluate and critique tactical exercises improved as did core skills such as map reading, demolitions, field expedients, and tactical movement. I relearned the necessity of maintaining communication with my soldiers. Command time emphasized and reinforced my recognition of the vital importance of company administrative and support personnel that I had learned in Korea. And I knew "what right looks like" when it came to individual and small-unit training. The Ranger Department emphasized and sharpened everything I had learned as a Ranger company commander in Korea and would be invaluable down the career path.

6

Latin Sojourn

U.S. Army Caribbean Command and Forming the Colombian Ranger School

In December 1953, orders came through for me to report to the U.S. Army Caribbean Command in Puerto Rico. Wanting troop experience at the lowest level, I requested and received assignment to the 296th Regimental Combat Team. I looked forward to a three-year tour in Caribbean Command and life in the tropics. The best thing about going to Puerto Rico was the likelihood of spending time with the troops. Although I had commanded a Ranger Company in combat and a Ranger Company at Fort Benning and the Ranger Mountain Camp, I felt that every lieutenant needed at least a year of seasoning as a platoon leader under a mature and experienced platoon sergeant who could teach him the ropes. Jeannie probably did not share my enthusiasm, especially since she was three months pregnant.

Jeannie and I would embark from New York through the staging facility at Camp Kilmer in New Jersey. I was lucky enough to avoid performing some tedious "make work" duty as I awaited departure, since my friend John Vann had secured permission for me to work with him in the ROTC detachment at Rutgers University. John had me teach a few classes, which I enjoyed doing. Jeannie and I joined John and Mary Jane for a few evenings in New York City. It was great reacquainting ourselves with the Vanns.

In the middle of December, we made our way to the quay and boarded the misnamed USS *Comfort*. The captain greeted us and provided a brief orientation, which included instructions in how to combat seasickness. He advised us to fight the urge to surrender to the first feeling of queasiness. Already suffering from bouts of morning sickness, Jeannie promptly ignored the advice and immediately crawled into her bunk when we entered our allotted room. She complained the ship's motion made her feel nauseated—a bad portent for the trip since the ship was still in its berth. Five days at sea almost did her in. When we arrived in San Juan, Jeannie looked as if she had spent the trip in the hold.

Puerto Rico

The political climate in Puerto Rico was tense. In October 1950, the Nationalist Party, calling for Puerto Rican independence, orchestrated uprisings in a number of cities. A couple of Puerto Ricans living in New York attempted to assassinate President Harry Truman. In the face of the Nationalist Party revolt, the governor called out the national guard. Relations between the Puerto Rico National Guard and the Regular Army were strained by the controversy over the army's handling of the failure of the Sixty-Fifth Infantry Regiment to hold and retake a hill in Korea. The Puerto Rican regiment fought in Korea from the Pusan Perimeter through the bitter winter fighting in 1952–1953 and won a Navy Unit Commendation for its role in the fighting withdrawal with the marines from the Chosin Reservoir. The Sixty-Fifth's failure at Outpost Kelly in September 1952 was a product of many factors: shortages of trained officers and NCOs produced by heavy casualties; the rotation system that extracted combat-experienced leaders and soldiers; and language and cultural differences between "Continental"—white and English-speaking—officers and Spanish-speaking "Insular" Puerto Rican enlisted men. Plunging morale lay at the root of the problem. A Continental colonel ordered the unit to desist calling itself the Borinqueneers, eliminated their special rations of rice and beans, forced the men to shave off their mustaches, and had one soldier wear a sign reading, "I am a coward." In the largest mass court-martial of the Korean War, 162 Puerto Ricans were arrested, ninety-five tried, ninety-one found guilty and sentenced to prison terms with hard labor. For obvious reasons, Puerto Rican resentment toward the United States ran deep, even if not openly manifested.

Headquartered at Camp Losey near Ponce on the southern side of the island, the 296th Regiment, Puerto Rico National Guard, had formed in 1936. The regiment had provided replacements to its sister companies in the Sixty-Fifth Regiment in Korea. Instead of a rifle platoon, I drew assignment to the regimental heavy mortar company at Henry Barracks, located near Cayey in the Cordillera Central about forty miles from Ponce. Among the more curious aspects of the Regular Army is the predisposition to revert, after a major war involving the infusion of masses of citizen-soldiers, to the living or working styles of the "Old Army" that preceded the conflict. In Puerto Rico, I had a sense of having been teleported back to the 1920s and 1930s, perhaps to the

Philippines. Training ended at noon. Afternoons were given over to sports, performing details, or siesta. Socializing in the evenings involved heavy drinking. Officers allowed the sergeants to run the show because "they have been doing it for years"—many had been with the regiment for two decades.

Capt. Patrick McDonnell commanded the company. We had only one other officer, Lt. Manuel Acevedo, who was the troubleshooter. Captain Mac made me his executive officer. I chafed at the lack of responsibility and wanted to command a platoon, but McDonnell refused because none of the other platoons had an officer. Acevedo was away on some special duty. The message was, "Don't rock the boat." I managed to gain some experience with mortars when the unit went to the training area at Camp Salinas.

On 27 April 1954, I received promotion to captain, which meant a move to Camp Losey and a company command. Because Jeannie was expecting, headquarters suspended the move until after the baby's birth. Jean Martin flew in to preside over the birth of her first grandchild. Everything was in readiness for the big event, but the baby refused to come. For a month, Jean and I monitored Jeannie's every move, which only heightened the anxiety levels, especially for my poor wife. The doctor decided on our last visit to Rodriguez Army Hospital in San Juan that since Jeannie was two weeks overdue he would admit her. Jean and I drove the hour back to Cayey. Early the next morning, Jeannie went into labor. She asked a hard-bitten army nurse, a colonel, to call me. The nurse looked at Jeannie like she was demented and asked, "Why should he lose a good night's sleep when he can't help you now?" The delivery traumatized Jeannie, not only because it was her first child but because the room was full of Puerto Rican women pleading loudly to their saints each time a contraction hit. Finally Jeannie was wheeled into the delivery room, and nature took its course. Only then did the nurse consent to call the father and nervous grandmother.

The day Jeannie and Jean Martin—named after her grandmother and her mother—arrived home, they confronted a house swarming with packers. Their *jefe* squatted like Yogi Berra on top of my desk issuing orders. Jeannie took to her bed, pulled the covers over her head, and tried to assure her mother that marrying Ralph Puckett was not a huge mistake. Admittedly, I might have been more gallant, but I was preoccupied with getting my company command. Matters did not much improve when we moved into the new quarters—an apartment with concrete walls, cement floors, no glass or screens on the windows, with some loose chickens running around. The contractor was then living at government expense in prison for misappropriation of funds. Things regained a measure of normalcy after Jean left, no doubt with many stories to tell the Admiral about poor Jeannie and her soldier husband.

No company awaited me at Camp Losey. Col. Frank Harrison, the regimental commander, slotted me as the supply officer (S4) in First Battalion under Lt. Col. Bert Perrin. The lot of a supply officer is not a happy one. Deskbound, the closest I got to training was reading observation reports. I spent time in the motor pool trying to ensure the vehicles were in tip-top order and visited company supply rooms trying to help with a multitude of administrative details. One of my primary duties involved personally checking soldiers before they were sent overseas to ensure each one had a complete issue of clothing. If not, he could not be sent to the port. I then placed the clothes under lock and key so that he could not remove items and wheedle out of getting shipped out. Given the fallout over the mass conviction of men from the Sixty-Fifth, Puerto Ricans had no desire for overseas duty.

After about four months as the S4, on 10 September 1954, I finally got command of Company B, First Battalion. The previous commander, Capt. Tommy Thompson, was described by Perrin as the best company commander he had ever seen. While inventorying equipment, I repeated the compliment to Tommy, and he admitted the company needed plenty of work—things Perrin never knew about. At the time I thought he was just being modest. It did not take long to discover what he meant.

About a month into my command, I submitted my appraisal of the company's combat readiness. The unit was significantly understrength, most of the crew-served weapons were in Ordnance for repair, and only a few of the gunners held qualifications on their weapons. I rated the company as 30 percent combat ready. As soon as the report hit battalion headquarters, I was called in and informed by the operations sergeant that Thompson's last appraisal was 95 percent. He indicated that my appraisal needed changing because the battalion commander would never accept my assessment. "That's my best estimate," I said. "I will not change it." In hindsight, I should have discussed my rationale for the appraisal with Perrin before turning in the report, but, with my "take it or leave it" attitude, I concluded he needed to know about the readiness of my company and his battalion. After all, the chief factor explaining the abysmal performance of the army in the opening stages of the Korean War rested with the slack, "business as usual" attitude toward training and conditioning that typified the occupation army in Japan. Evaluating combat readiness is no exact science—many of the calculations are subjective—but unless Thompson had been seriously padding the results, it was difficult to explain a difference of 65 percent. Perrin never raised the issue with me but probably did raise my appraisal to make it more in line with Thompson's.

My subsequent monthly reports substantiated real, not "pencil," improvements. The first assessment acted as a template. Afternoons remained untouchable, but training became a priority. We conducted qualification programs in all crew-served weapons. Over time, the number of crew-served weapons and qualified gunners, crewmen, and leaders increased.

I held company PT each morning. I always participated and usually led. In those days, there was a reveille formation. I "made" reveille every day and took the company on a run. Our chants caused dismay as we disturbed families trying to sleep. Harrison called me in for some "counseling" on this matter. He told me never to put "Airborne" or "Ranger" into the chants. (I never had.) After reveille and the run, we had breakfast. I could obtain a better feel for my company by attending reveille and breakfast than at almost any other time. If we could do those two functions properly at the beginning of the day and begin training on time, we could probably accomplish the rest of our responsibilities. After a couple of weeks Harrison called me to his office for an explanation. Why was I eating in my company mess? Did I not know that the officers' club needed the revenue? Suppose other officers ate with their companies and not in the club? I explained what I was doing and why and commented that perhaps other officers ought to attend reveille and breakfast. Not impressed, Harrison made sure I "got the word" not to eat in the mess hall.

Post details always detract from readiness. I suggested companies be tasked with specific details instead of levying many NCOs and enlisted men directed and supervised by the regiment, thus saving manpower, building unit integrity, and requiring less oversight. My idea was ignored. One afternoon Perrin and I walked near the parade ground and observed soldiers trimming grass using machetes. When I asked why, Perrin looked at me in surprise and replied it had always been done that way.

Perrin was a very bright and knowledgeable officer. At the time I chalked it up to him having, as the British say, "gone tropo." Life was good, and he enjoyed the pace. Later I decided Perrin represented the "weathervane" type officer—move in the direction of the prevailing wind, never create any waves, change nothing, get favorable efficiency reports, and move on to the next billet and do the same—all too common in the army in that period.

About a month after taking command, 2nd Lt. John B. Tower was assigned to Company B. An ex–first sergeant and recent Officer Candidate School graduate, John helped me chart my way. The Pucketts developed a warm relationship with John and his wife, Rita. They named their second daughter, born in Puerto Rico, Jean after Jeannie—even though John and Rita took some flak from the priest for not naming her after a saint. Jeannie and I returned to Georgia for the Christmas holidays. Both sets of grandparents were excited about the new granddaughter. While we were at home, a cryptic message arrived from John Tower saying that the colonel had removed me from company command and my replacement was already in my orderly and supply rooms. John urged me to return as soon as feasible. Harrison had named me as the commander of a yet-to-be-formed noncommissioned officer academy.

Upon my return, I tried to determine what was happening. My friend, the regimental S3, Maj. Roy Lunsford, told me that Harrison wanted a regimental NCO academy, and I was to be the commandant. Harrison thought the regiment needed to orient, train, and develop NCOs. The Sixty-Fifth Infantry Regiment colors were slated to return to Puerto Rico; the 296th would be deactivated and returned to national guard status. The furor over Outpost Kelly prompted the army to end Puerto Ricans "homesteading" in units like the 296th Regimental Combat Team and instead spread them throughout the army. In addition to the academy, I was tasked with developing and conducting a rotating two-week "orientation" training program for the privates and privates first class to ensure they had the fundamental skills that they should have learned in Basic. Continentals replaced the Insulars, who would then be transferred to units throughout the army.

Lunsford and the three battalion commanders urged me to dissuade Harrison from establishing an NCO academy. Judging from their comments, they not only opposed the scheme but might obstruct my efforts to create the school. Shortly thereafter, Harrison summoned me to his office. The regimental executive officer, the three battalion commanders, and the regimental staff were already there. I felt cornered because nobody in the room would cover my back. Harrison explained briefly what he wanted—a first-rate NCO academy and an orientation school. I weighed in with vigor, explaining that the battalion commanders opposed and would not support the plan, never mentioning that that equally applied to his staff. I crossed the line into insubordination.

Making no progress except in increasing the colonel's evident ire, I made my parting shot: "Sir, I request that you ensure that when your staff visits my command, they check in and out with my headquarters." In hindsight, it was a silly thing to say because, as Harrison angrily pointed out, that was normal procedure. My blood up, I replied, "They aren't doing it now." Harrison had heard enough and curtly told me as much. I came to attention, saluted, and responded that he could count on me doing my best to implement his wishes. With that, he brusquely dismissed me. West Point taught us when a junior officer believes his commander's decision inappropriate or wrongheaded, the subordinate stood duty bound to express his counter arguments even to the point of insubordination. What I thought might be viewed as a display of moral courage was not seen that way by the colonel. As endorsing officer, he took his revenge by making very caustic comments not only on my efficiency report for that rating period but, against regulations, on the following two.

After the contretemps in Harrison's office, I set to work trying to make the academy work. I visited the battalion commanders and asked them to complete a questionnaire concerning the desired training. I put together a projected organization with staffing that, obviously, would come out of the hides of the battalions, which is one reason why they objected to the programs. Afterward I discussed the subject with several company commanders, tapping their experience. Finally I made my decisions on training objectives, the program of instruction, and staffing and submitted the package. A couple days later, Harrison approved the program of instruction and staffing.

Camp Salinas housed the NCO Academy and Orientation School. I needed some very capable help and convinced the colonel to give me Tower. The organization and operation were based on the Ranger course. My two-plus years of varied experiences with the Ranger Department had given me a solid foundation in all aspects of establishing and conducting a small leadership development course. All I needed was good cadre, and Tower gave me a head start.

The Academy course lasted five weeks, with three weeks of classroom studies focused on theory and two weeks for tactical problems. The orientation course was relatively simple to establish. Training consisted of two weeks of basic, individual skills, including a lot of physical training. Some soldiers in the orientation program whined to influential fathers about "Captain Puckett's inhuman treatment." The fathers wrote their congressman or senator. These elected representatives forwarded the complaints to the Department of the Army through the Office of Legislative Liaison and, in due time, they boomeranged back on the regiment. Once again I got called down on Harrison's mat. My explanation was simple and straightforward: "Sir, everything we do is on the training schedule that I submit to your headquarters. We teach everything by the book [field manual]. I take PT with the trainees." The colonel responded, "I want you to know that if you get into trouble I won't help you." I was on my own and figured that if I were investigated fairly, I would be okay.

Both programs proceeded more rapidly than I expected. We conducted an orientation course every two weeks. The Academy ran on a six-week cycle. To prepare the cadre, John and I put them through the program of instruction. Both programs went well. John Tower and the cadre deserved the credit. When we followed up with some of the graduates, we learned what I had expected would be the case. While we taught everything "by the book," as soon as the men returned to their units, their commanders greeted them with, "I don't care what they said at the Academy. This is the way we do it here, and this is the way you will do it." I had heard it before and would hear it again.

As a tour of duty, Puerto Rico was no place for a temperance man. Each month saw a boozy *Bienvenida Despedida* (Hello Goodbye) party for newcomers and those departing. As command affairs, attendance was required. There was always a charge made to our officers' club bill to pay for the all-you-can-drink open bar. A nondrinker, I disliked having to pay for the booze, but I resented Perrin and his executive officer badgering me about not drinking. Finally, I told them in forthright terms that I did not drink and would not drink and would appreciate it if they desisted. They stopped, but I am sure Perrin looked forward to preparing my next efficiency report.

After completing the second NCO course, I received an alert for a six-month temporary duty assignment to kick-start the development of a Ranger school in Colombia. My first reaction: where exactly is Colombia? The selection criteria called for a captain with combat Ranger experience, and being the only Ranger-qualified captain in the Caribbean Command at the time, I was tabbed for the duty. Harrison had likely offered no resistance.

My eighteen months in Puerto Rico had not been happy ones save for the birth of baby Jean. I was very much the square peg in an environment of round holes. The other officers probably saw me as a ring-knocking gung-ho Ranger troublemaker, and I stood guilty as charged (though I never wore my class ring). It was disheartening to see the army—or at least this outpost of the army—lapse back into sloth so soon after Korea. When I left West Point, people wondered why, with the advent of the atomic bomb, I would branch Infantry. The day of the foot soldier was over. The air force and navy had gone nuclear, but the army still thought and acted like it was 1939. What I experienced in Puerto Rico was symptomatic of a larger malaise.

As I soon discovered, my time in Puerto Rico provided preparation—the formation and conduct of the NCO Academy in particular but also dealing with the Latin temperament—for what confronted me in Colombia. I was happy to face a new challenge; the downside was that Jeannie and Jean would not accompany me to Colombia.

The Escuela de Lanceros

Jeannie and I hurriedly cleared quarters. The army being the army, we could not keep them even though the new orders read "temporary duty" and I expected to return to Puerto Rico in six months. Colonel Harrison told me that he needed the quarters for incoming officers. Since my orders took immediate effect (18 June 1955), I hustled off to Ramey Air Force Base after hurriedly leaving Jeannie as she loaded on her flight to Columbus, where she would stay with her family.

While still assigned to Camp Losey, I had received a short communication from Col. Robert G. Turner, chief of the U.S. Army Mission to Colombia, welcoming me and telling me to stop at the Jungle Warfare Training Center in Panama on the way down to check out a newly recommended treatment for snakebites. The "new" part was that the two fang punctures should not be incised—standard Red Cross procedure—but instead, if intact, they would serve as "tubes" through which the venom could be withdrawn by suction. All very cheery news.

I arrived in Bogotá and was met by most of the officers, NCOs, and wives of the mission, which was customary for welcoming newcomers. Lt. Col. Joe Koontz, the Infantry advisor and instructor at the Colombian War College, arranged a room for me at the college, where I would stay for the next several months. Colonel Turner's driver ferried me most days. Other times I took a taxi. Koontz and his wife, Mickey, would become the most supportive and friendliest members of the mission that included the chief, about five officers, a few NCOs, and a Colombian driver and secretary. All the married Americans had their families with them and enjoyed the "good life" living in a *mañana* world. Food, furniture, and most other household goods were very cheap if grown or made in Colombia. In addition, an allowance permitted housing probably better than anything they had experienced.

Turner gave me a thorough briefing. Colombia was suffering from la Violencia, the carnage that had rocked the country since 1948. During that period as many as three hundred thousand Colombians had died in the cycle of violence. Our major concern focused on the Communist-inspired insurgents.

The Colombian Army, modeled on the German Wehrmacht and influenced after the war by Americans, was road bound. The insurgents controlled everything off road because the army lacked the capacity for fighting in the mountains and jungles. The U.S. Army Mission concluded that the Colombians needed their version of the U.S. Army Ranger School to develop officers and

NCOs with the confidence, capability, and desire to find, fix, and destroy the enemy no matter his location. As the Ranger advisor, my mission was to establish that school, and I was entirely on my own. I saw the assignment as part challenge, part adventure, and a great opportunity.

As a preparatory step, five Colombian lieutenants attended the U.S. Army Airborne and Ranger Schools. Those officers were due to return in a few weeks. Meanwhile, I had to select a site, develop a program of instruction, prepare a list of equipment requirements, and set up a multitude of administrative and logistical procedures. My experience in the different jobs in the Ranger Department and in developing the orientation course and NCO Academy in Puerto Rico stood me in good stead. Much of what we had prepared for the NCO Academy served as the bases for our policies in Colombia.

During the first few months I traveled to several locations to find a place suitable for the school, usually accompanied by Lt. Col. Mathew Santino, the artillery officer assigned to the mission. He spoke Spanish and knew his way around Colombia, having been on station for a couple of years. My Spanish was very rudimentary, and the rapid transfer from Puerto Rico to Colombia had not permitted me to attend a language course, the normal procedure for military assigned to an overseas advisory mission. The battalion located at Florencia, which the mission considered the best trained in the Colombian army, was one of the first places we visited. The highly regarded battalion commander wanted the school located in Florencia, and his unit provided a combat capability that would be highly desirable, but the location—across the Andes from Bogotá and difficult or impossible to access in bad weather—ruled it out. Another option was Tres Esquinas, a village situated in the Putumayo District on the southern border with Ecuador. Turner nixed Tres Esquinas because it was too remote and distant from the capital. Finally President Rojas Pinilla, whom I had briefed in my halting present-tense-only Spanish, directed that the school be established at Melgar, a small village a little over two hours by road south of Bogotá. It was much closer to Bogotá than anything I had considered. His reason was obvious: the president owned a *finca* (country estate) nearby and ordered the construction of a division-size post at Melgar that would house the school. While primarily political and personal, the decision was not a bad one. The Colombian army was expanding, and the base at Melgar would provide an airstrip, combat and service units, housing, and other facilities.

To assist in the planning and supervision of this major project, the U.S. Army sent an engineer colonel. He was very knowledgeable and experienced and soon had the Colombians eating out of his hands. Whatever he advised was accepted and implemented almost without question. His wife and daughter, Jackie Beamer, a "geographical widow" married to an army officer on an unaccompanied tour in Korea, came with the colonel. Jackie and her parents lived in a rented apartment in Bogotá. The colonel often went on "inspection trips" to various projects throughout Colombia, often accompanied by his wife. Left alone for a couple weeks in violence-prone Bogotá, Jackie wanted the security of a man in the house in her parents' absence. I jumped at the chance. It reduced my commute and guaranteed a well-prepared breakfast and supper each day. Like all expatriate Americans, the family employed servants.

Jackie laughingly confided to me that the maids were whispering that she and I were sleeping together since my bed appeared not to have been slept in each morning. Like the good soldier, I dutifully made the bed each morning upon arising. After overhearing the maids, Jackie went to my room each morning and "unmade" my bed. We both had a good laugh, as did the members of the mission.

After three months in Colombia, and making little progress in establishing the school, I brought Jeannie and our daughter down to stay in Bogotá. I sublet an apartment in a very nice building. Jean was beautiful, like her mother, and had the blondest, curliest hair I had ever seen. Naturally I wanted to keep our little family together, so we went to Melgar to see if we could find a suitable place to rent. Melgar was extremely primitive. Only a couple of houses were available: dirt floors, no indoor plumbing or running water, and the windows had no screens to keep out the flies and mosquitoes. And there was no medical care available if needed for our baby. While we could have rented something in Bogotá, we both knew that I would be training almost every day, including the weekends, with visits to Bogotá few and far between. We concluded that Jeannie and Jean should return home.

Four of the five Colombian lieutenants—Moises Patino Umana, Cesar Negret Velazco, Jose Moros Contreras, and Roberto Fernandez Guzman— finally returned from Benning. After getting acquainted, we moved to Melgar and began preparation of the site, where we were soon joined by two very sharp and industrious captains and future generals, Jorge Robledo Pulido and Eliodoro Narvaez Guevara. After some delay, Maj. Hernando Bernal Duran was selected as the commandant.

Colonel Turner believed that the selection of a major as commandant, when all other schools were commanded by more senior officers, indicated that Ranger training would not receive the support it demanded. He also knew Bernal was not held in high regard by other Colombian officers. I went to Bogotá and met Bernal and rode with him to Melgar. During the trip I oriented him on Ranger training. By now, my Spanish had progressed to the point where I could speak simple sentences clearly and without hesitation. I stressed the great opportunity he had, as a major, to shape the future Colombian army. At one of my earlier meetings with Maj. Gen. Rafael Navas Pardo, the commanding general of the school brigades, and soon member of the ruling junta, I convinced him that requiring all second lieutenants to attend Ranger school would significantly improve the combat effectiveness of his army. With only eight battalions, Ranger-trained officers and NCOs would soon permeate the entire army. Bernal gave the distinct impression that he was not buying any of it.

Initially the school consisted of three structures: a farmhouse that became the officers' club, another building for officers' quarters, and a newly completed barracks. Despite the limited facilities, we dedicated ourselves to creating a world-class school. Together we planned every hour of instruction: each tactical problem and objective; every class, including patrolling techniques, estimate of the situation, operations orders, map reading, hand-to-hand combat, bayonet and physical training, weapons, leadership; every bit of training that would comprise our program of instruction. In addition, we had to determine and obtain all the required logistical and administrative support. I made suggestions or commented on everything concerning requirements including the program of instruction, course objectives, tactical exercises, policies and procedures, and equipment and expendables ranging from machine guns to toilet paper. My "decisions" were only recommendations; the Colombians did the deciding. Surprisingly, very few disagreements arose, but implementing the decisions would pose difficulties.

Progress proved infuriatingly slow. It became obvious that not much could get accomplished in my six-month attachment, so I agreed to an extension. I hated the thought of another six-month separation from Jeannie and our little girl, but knew I had to stay if the school was ever going to take shape. Getting any kind of a decision from Bernal proved almost impossible. Each Thursday he left for Bogotá and returned the following Monday or Tuesday. He wanted none of the austere life at Melgar. He demonstrated no sense of urgency. Although I tried to get decisions from or through the lieutenants and captains, their hands were tied. In the Colombian army, junior officers never disagreed with seniors and rarely made recommendations. My weekly, lengthy, and laboriously two-finger-typed reports to Col. Daniel M. Cheston III, the new mission chief, expressed my frustration. I always gave

Bernal a copy. Obviously, he knew that I considered him a major obstacle to our success.

Finally, I confronted him in front of the four lieutenants. I did not choose my time well. I told Bernal that if he did not make decisions and recognize the potential importance of the training, the school would never be established. In my usual straightforward, confrontational manner, I placed the culpability squarely on him. Incensed, he responded by saying that he was leaving for Bogotá immediately. The next day, Lt. Mel Storey, the mission adjutant, called and instructed me to report immediately to Colonel Cheston. I did not have to be told why. Arriving at the mission office before the appointed time, I asked Storey the rhetorical question, "Am I in trouble?" I already knew the answer. Storey answered laconically, "I think so."

Cheston arrived and directed me into his office. I gave a very military salute and report. I stood at rigid attention with sweat pouring down my face and soaking through my shirt. My conduct with Bernal had been inappropriate, and I knew it. Cheston chewed me out unmercifully. After what seemed an eternity, he said, "Sit down, Ralph." With that we both sat on the sofa in his office. He repeated his earlier comments but in a much softer tone. Basically, he told me that I had been unprofessional, rude, and insubordinate to Bernal. The colonel recognized my frustration and agreed with the validity of all my criticisms but said that did not excuse my comportment. Making those comments in front of Bernal's subordinates compounded the problem. As he continued, he recounted that he had been called to Major General Pardo's office. The general made it plain that my behavior was inexcusable and unacceptable. Cheston explained that should I be recalled to the States because of this incident, my career as an officer would be over. He directed me to return to Melgar, assemble Bernal and the officers who had been present during my outburst, and apologize profusely and then use every bit of diplomacy I could muster to win over the major.

Colonel Cheston called for an appointment with Maj. Gen. Navas Pardo. I met with the general and apologized, stating it would not happen again. Fortunately, the general had seen me on several occasions and had been favorably impressed. While I knew that he was dismayed, he accepted my remorseful apology. Before leaving, I thanked the colonel. Without him going to bat for me with the Colombian general, convincing him that he should not request my reassignment, I would have been finished. My conduct had been totally unprofessional. And I surely had not learned anything from the incident with Colonel Harrison. Why could I not keep my hot temper under control? I knew the answer to that question: "No excuse, Sir!" I had no excuse for failure. That lesson from West Point had stuck.

I returned to Melgar, and at the first opportunity assembled the officers and spoke to Major Bernal. I apologized profusely saying all the things the colonel had directed. As I spoke, I looked Bernal straight in the eyes. Finished, I extended my hand. He hesitated and said nothing as he gingerly grasped my hand. I had my work cut out for me.

Over time our relations improved, but slowly. My outburst may have been partially responsible for the improvement. Perhaps it was my apology. Or maybe the recognition by all that we had a momentous task ahead of us. One of the biggest obstacles was psychological; the ingrained sense of inferiority the Colombians felt in relation to the U.S. Army. The four lieutenants had been to Benning and seen the lavish training facilities and aids in use. They knew that they could not equal those. I worked hard at convincing them that we did not need the state-of-the-art facilities, that we could improvise using what we had locally. I wanted them to believe they could be just as good as Benning. They had to believe in themselves.

Somehow those words of encouragement worked. A seeming transformation occurred right in front of my eyes. They built bleachers by mounding dirt, terracing it into steps and seats, and covering it with sod to prevent erosion. They constructed an elevated PT and hand-to-hand demonstration stand using logs cut from the nearby jungle and covered it with bed mattresses. They dug and tilled the soil in the practice area with shovels and filled the area with grain husks to soften the falls. For a tactical exercise involving a lengthy river trip, they obtained native dugouts in lieu of expensive inflatable boats. There were no bulldozers or ditchdiggers to construct defensive positions to be used as training objectives. Sweat equity made up for a lack of technology and funds. I expressed the delight I felt, complimenting them at every opportunity. More important, they were proud, too.

Our first course consisted of combined "cadre training" and "dress rehearsal." The four lieutenants taught all the classes. They asked me to teach a couple, but I declined, using the rationale that this course was a rehearsal; they needed to teach the class. I instructed the teachers working on improving their knowledge and capabilities but refused to teach the students. The results were gratifying. The lieutenants performed well. I often critiqued their rehearsals, evaluated almost all the classes, and accompanied a patrol on every tactical problem. No other cadre did that. I was very demanding and wanted things done not just "right" but in an outstanding fashion. While they could do better—and did improve as they gained experience—they needed that feeling of accomplishment: "Be proud but don't be satisfied."

We were creating a unit, but it still lacked a name. We discussed that problem. Some of the cadre recommended "Rangers" but rejected that as being too American and without meaning in Colombia. Others suggested "commandos," but that was British and in Spanish meant headquarters. I asked about Colombian military history and whether there existed a formation similar to the Rangers. Was there a small, highly disciplined, courageous unit that used hit-and-run tactics, stealth, speed, and ferocity to attack and defeat larger conventional opponents? They could think of none. Then one day, while receiving one of my very rare Spanish lessons from a local professor, I broached the subject. He responded immediately with the Lanceros, who had fought for independence under Simón Bolívar. Their tactics and characteristics exactly corresponded to what I had described. When I suggested Lanceros to Bernal and others, they agreed immediately. We would be the Escuela de Lanceros, and the graduates would be Lanceros.

We needed a shoulder patch, and the cadre immediately suggested an outline map of Colombia with a crouching figure ready to throw a spear with a scroll inscribed with the words *Lealtad, Valor y Sacrificio* (Loyalty, Valor and Sacrifice). I had nothing to do with the draft and was pleased with the design. Next we turned our attention to fashioning a qualification badge. I consulted our regulations and adapted and changed several of our badges—jump wings, pathfinder, Combat Infantryman Badge (CIB), and others—and asked the cadre for suggestions. They selected a badge similar to our CIB with a red background and gold scroll with an embossed "Lancero."

This first class graduated in a very simple ceremony on 14 April 1956. Navas Pardo, the ranking officer in attendance, pinned the Lancero badge on every graduate. I was both surprised and flattered that I was placed first in the rank to receive the badge.

On 21 May, the Colombian government presented me with the Orden Militar for my work at the Escuela. In accordance with army regulations at the time, I submitted the medal and citation through channels to the Department of the Army, requesting permission to keep it. It would take months for the approval to come through.

Frequent letters and infrequent telephone calls did not assuage the loneliness I felt for Jeannie and Jean. On one occasion, when Lieutenant Fernandez was going to Bogotá, I asked him to order via wire a dozen roses for Jeannie. She described her excitement and joy when she opened the box and found only eleven roses. Inside a note read: "Here are 11 roses. You make the dozen!" Jeannie was taken aback by this uncharacteristic display of sentimentality. She could not believe it, and she was right. When Jeannie wrote me about the note, I asked Fernandez about it. Looking at me with both a smile and a trace of disgust, he stated, "Only a gringo would send roses to his wife without some words of love."

The second cycle—the first for students—began shortly before my return to the States. Bernal and the other officers begged me to extend for another six months, but I refused. After a year in Colombia I was more than ready to go home to my wife and daughter. Besides, it was time for the Colombians to take charge. I did not leave the Escuela high and dry. Before leaving Puerto Rico, I had spoken briefly with Lt. John R. Galvin, who had worked with me at the Sixty-Fifth NCO Academy and who expressed a desire to come to Colombia. In our continued correspondence, Jack stated that he had put in for becoming my replacement. I strongly recommended to Colonel Cheston that the school needed an American advisor and Jack Galvin was the perfect choice, an outstanding officer and fluent in Spanish. He arrived for a two-year permanent change of station a few months after I left. His assignment was fortuitous for the Colombians. Under his leadership, the school steadily improved. Jack ended his career with four stars.

Although a lonely time for me and sometimes extremely frustrating, the twelve months in Colombia proved very beneficial to my professional development. I had planned the organizational, administrative, and logistical support; the program of instruction; cadre training; and student evaluation—every detail of establishing an individual leadership and small-unit combat training program. Much of the inspiration came from my experience in forming, training, and commanding the Eighth Army Ranger Company during the Korean War. Ultimately, the Escuela de Lanceros was founded on the hard work and dedication of the Colombians with whom I was privileged to work. We were a team.

I was pleased with what the Colombians had accomplished. They had overcome significant obstacles to establish the Escuela de Lanceros, which would significantly enhance the combat readiness of the Colombian Army. From its very modest origins, the school developed into a very influential entity in that army and served as model for other South American countries. The names of Major Bernal, Captains Robledo and Narvaez, Lieutenants Fernandez, Negret, Moros, and Patino and the NCOs are inscribed on a plaque beside the entrance to the headquarters commemorating the foundation. So, too, is Ralph Puckett.

Reflecting on the experience, I could see that my leadership philosophy remained—as it had in Korea—rooted in a vision of the outcome I wanted: a clear statement of mission; clearly defined, specific supporting objectives; mission-type instructions to staff; continual supervision as broad as appropriate; and hard work. And, of course, always striving for improvement.

7

Climbing the Army School Ladder

Infantry Advanced Course, USMAPS, and the
Command and General Staff College

After a year in Colombia I returned to Puerto Rico in the summer of 1956 and stayed with John and Rita Tower, expecting immediate orders to return to the States, most likely to the Infantry advanced course at Fort Benning. The regiment I left no longer existed, and in the normal progression of things I was due to attend the advanced class, and it made sense to go to Benning between duty stations. Maybe the six-month extension in Colombia threw off the career planners in the Office of Personnel Operations. And I wanted to be reunited with Jeannie and the baby.

Finally the orders arrived for the advanced course, and I got to Atlanta as fast as I could and spent a glorious homecoming weekend with Jeannie. In the Infantry School, we drew our housing assignment in an area just outside the main gate. In high school Jeannie had dated a schoolmate who worked a summer job on the construction of the units. When he showed them to Jeannie, she responded by saying something like, "You would never find me living in a place like that." But now we were really pleased to draw that housing.

Baby Jean, now two, was aware enough to know she did not like this intruder stealing the attention of her mother. Jeannie had often taken out my picture and talked about me in an effort to prevent Jean from forgetting me. However, for a while, she pointed to the picture and said, "Daddy." This new man was an impostor. Moving slowly and letting her set the pace, we connected over time.

Infantry Advanced Course

The ten-month course began with a student cohort of slightly more than two hundred, almost all captains with a few lieutenant "promotables." Most had been in Korea. The student company commander, Maj. Sid Berry, the rank-ing student—a fine officer and future lieutenant general—was an acquain-tance from West Point. At first the school presented a welcome change of pace. Instruction offered new and sometimes challenging material. In common with all army schools, the advanced infantry course lacked a firm center of gravity. Did the army want infantry officers competent to hold staff positions or com-pany command slots? With no firm direction from above, the advanced course tried to do both, and as a consequence the teaching cadre and the students were overburdened. Much of the staff instruction could not be conducted other than in the lecture hall and classrooms. Instruction was canned, based on rote mem-orization with students allowed no real input. Sometimes, at the end of exhaus-tive, all-day classes, the faculty, unable to plod through all the course content, passed out maps and overlays of material not covered in the lecture in the hope, rather than expectation, that the attendees would work the problem on their own. Although much of the material could not be covered in the field, I grew frustrated and bored with the eight-hour classroom presentations and innu-merable handouts. We went to the field often—sometimes well beyond mid-night—but never spent an entire night. Driven by the constraints of too much content and not enough time, the field training proved pretty unrealistic. Most students, though reasonably interested, never overexerted themselves.

Often Infantry School instructors bore the reputation of being fuzzy-cheeked products of the preceding class with no real experience, including ser-vice in Korea. That was not the case during my time in the advanced course. The Tactical Department, especially the operations committee, stood out. The committee boasted two Medal of Honor recipients, and one instructor offered some of the best-prepared and -delivered presentations I ever encountered in the army. As impressive as the officers charged with teaching the courses might have been, the doctrine they taught came straight out of operations in north-west Europe in World War II: "Two up and one back" and "Hey diddle-diddle, straight up the middle." Apparently the war in Korea never happened. Hav-ing experienced firsthand the work of the Medical Corps in Korea, the section dealing with the logistics of medical evacuations caught my attention as did some of the instruction on supply. Combat line officers always disparage logis-ticians, but the course demonstrated the army's newfound accent upon the sup-ply side of operations.

As the course wound down, everybody's attention shifted to guessing their next assignment. Despite the course's weight on staff instruction, most assumed they would draw time in company command. I wanted to return to troops, another company command preferably in an airborne division, and I was amazed when I found that only one other student, a lieutenant without company command time, expressed a desire to get a company. Many wanted no part of company command because of the problems associated with property accounting. Company commanders signed for all government-issued property down to mess cutlery and bore liability in the event of loss or theft. That policy exacerbated the age-old practice of scavenging and swapping. A story made the rounds of a company-grade officer who buried his unlicensed surplus; the inspector general got wind of the subterfuge, dug up the evidence, and the captain was relieved. Why would an officer inexperienced in handling the minutiae of property accounting hazard his career over something as picayune as purloined spoons? I possessed a certain amount of sympathy for that point of view since as a company commander I had to use an ordnance lock to stow ordnance equipment and an engineer lock for engineer stocks.

Another concern centered on the recent decree of Army Chief of Staff Matthew Ridgway that all Infantry captains must attend either the Ranger course or Airborne School. Most of the students had done neither. Several asked for advice, saying, "I'm not eager to jump out of an airplane, but I don't want to go through Ranger Training, either. That's a long, unpleasant experience." Trying to allay their concerns, I assured them that they could handle either and recommended they attend both.

The Infantry School assigned students the task of critiquing different portions of the program. I was required to comment on three subjects, one being physical training. The PT program was totally inadequate. Classroom time consumed most of the schedule. We learned all about physiology, but physical exercise sessions were rare and not challenging. Since many would progress to company command, I deemed it vital we should leave Benning in top physical condition. The army paid no attention to the lessons of Korea, where we suffered heavy losses in casualties and POWs, especially in the early days of the conflict, because so many officers and men lacked physical conditioning. My critique made specific suggestions based on experience establishing physical training programs for schools, companies including my Rangers, and a foreign army. In the next course the physical training program changed drastically along lines consistent with my recommendations.

An officer from the Office of Personnel Operations (OPO), Infantry Branch, informed us of our next posting. We termed Pentagon efforts at career management as "career manglement." OPO charted an officer's path, making sure all the correct boxes were checked as he moved up the rank ladder. The system was intended to raise the standards of professionalism, but it had the opposite effect, instead fostering the worst sort of "ticket-punching" careerism that already had infected the officer corps in Korea. The system may have changed, but attitudes proved more resistant. The officer corps remained as segregated as it had always been between line, staff, and technical services. Combat arms officers wanted to remain in the tactical/operational chain. Staff and training assignments meant time away from troops—in our view, divorced from the "real" army—and lost command time, which reduced promotion prospects. Instead of a company command, I drew West Point, presumably in the Tactical Department. A few weeks after the initial notifications, we received orders. Mine had me going to a university of my choice to obtain a master's degree in chemistry en route to West Point to teach. Supremely disappointed, I saw the next five years as sheer drudgery: two years in graduate school and three years teaching a subject that held no attraction; five years as a captain and major wasted when I should be learning my trade in a battalion.

I decided to request a change of assignment and hurriedly drafted a letter and asked Col. Robert York, the head of the tactics department, to review it and advise me. A highly respected tactical officer at West Point when I was a cadet, surely he would see my point of view. Although I interrupted him in the middle of a shower, he very graciously reviewed my letter. Neither advising me one way or the other, he recommended that if I genuinely felt that way about becoming an instructor at West Point, I needed to make the point clear.

Motivated by what the colonel said, I typed and mailed my letter to Col. E. C. Gillette Jr., the professor of chemistry and physics at West Point. After thanking him for the compliment of being asked to teach at West Point and for the opportunity for civilian schooling, I explained in my usual direct manner that I did not want to go to school and become an instructor at West Point. I qualified that by saying that if I were not released from this assignment, he could count on me doing the best I could as a chemistry instructor. He never responded. However, in a very short time a letter arrived from OPO stating that my nomination for graduate school had been withdrawn along with my assignment to West Point. The letter closed on an ominous note: "We will inform you as to what your assignment will be."

After a few weeks had passed, orders arrived assigning me to the United States Military Academy Preparatory School (USMAPS). OPO was "rubbing my nose in it." According to their calculations, my promotion possibilities would be enhanced by acquiring a graduate degree, and the army would pay tuition and costs as a bond in exchange for a three-year commitment to teach at

West Point. USMAPS held little enticement, but there was no chance of having that assignment changed, so I resigned myself to it. From my perspective, the USMAPS assignment was a lot better than what I had just escaped.

One supposed benefit of a posting to Benning was the ability to spend more time with my family; and Jeannie could be close to her family. Instead, the course proved very demanding on my time; though we did find the opportunity to have our second child, Martha Lane. Jeannie had a tough delivery finally completed by caesarean section. The special bond established the first time I saw Martha Lane lasts to this day, and as the family can attest, she had me wrapped around her little finger from the beginning. We named her Martha after Jeannie's great-aunt Martha Cooke, and Lane from a "way back" family name we liked. Our family was growing.

United States Military Academy Prep School

After graduation from the advanced course, I made a trip to Stewart Field, the home of USMAPS, about thirty miles from West Point, and checked in with Capt. Thomas Callagy, the commandant. Stewart Field had been the base where cadets received their initial flight training prior to graduation and entry into the U.S. Army Air Force. A very erudite and competent officer, Callagy was not a graduate of the Military Academy but had held the job for several years and knew more about the ins and outs of getting into West Point than anyone save perhaps the civilian responsible for that action in the Pentagon. Callagy told me that I would act as the "advance party" for the school's move to a former hospital complex at Fort Belvoir, Virginia. When Callagy and a few of the senior staff arrived at Belvoir, we began preparations for receiving the cadet candidates. Although most came with army backgrounds, the student body also consisted of students aspiring to attend Annapolis and Colorado Springs since neither the navy nor the air force had a prep school.

Capt. Ed Ross, a classmate of mine, and Lt. Howard Matson rounded out the four USMAPS officers. The first sergeant was M.Sgt. William D. Massey, a steady, mature NCO. He spent eight years at USMAPS and retired as a sergeant major with twenty-three years of service. Raymond M. Coolidge, the academic director, Robert O. Barnum and William D. Williams, heads of the math and English departments, and almost all of their instructors moved to Belvoir.

Although ranking Ross, I asked Callagy for the training officer slot rather than the executive officer (XO) position because I wanted direct contact with the candidates. I made a trip to Benning and selected four noncommissioned officers as the training or tactical NCOs. Except for academics, the training section conducted the military and physical training and bore responsibility for discipline. The training NCOs were excellent; M.Sgt. Lloyd "Tom" Thomas was a great assistant who always provided good advice.

During this period, ROTC graduates were commissioned as second lieutenants, and under one program, after completion of their basic branch qualification school, they served until they had accrued a total of six months on active duty; they were then transferred to the active reserve. Callagy immediately saw a great opportunity and convinced the commandant of the Engineer School, located at Belvoir, to assign several volunteer graduates from each basic Engineer officer basic course to USMAPS for their remaining six months on active duty. We used them as assistant training officers. The army and the lieutenants benefited because they had a real job with real responsibilities albeit for a short period. USMAPS benefited from these motivated second lieutenants assisting in our development of the candidates.

I enjoyed being the training officer with daily—and often nightly—contact with the candidates and the hardworking and dedicated NCOs. Working together we oriented our weekly competition, based on barracks inspections and physical training primarily, with the academic schedule, combining all activities to determine which candidates earned a weekend pass. The instructors shifted their weekly testing to coincide with our scheduling. Being proficient—posting a passing average—was a prerequisite for the pass.

Passing the Physical Aptitude Test (PAT) for entry into West Point became a focus of our formal daily PT training. Not knowing which of the five events would be used in the test, we prepared for all twenty-five on the list. Each day for a week we concentrated on five of those events before participating in intramurals. Lt. Col. James E. Kelleher, Department of Tactics, USMA, observed the testing and said that he had never seen candidates perform so well. Every candidate passed.

Following my first year at USMAPS, in the summer of 1958, I attended the Jungle Warfare Course in Panama. The training lasted three weeks and, in some respects, resembled Ranger School in the concentration on individual and small-unit skills in a jungle environment. The wet climate—since it was the rainy season, we were soaked most of the time—was rough on the feet, but they managed to carry me through the course. I qualified as a "Jungle Expert," certainly an exaggeration if there ever was one.

During my second year at USMAPS, I was selected "below the zone" for promotion to major. My good luck caused some embarrassment to Captains

Callagy and Ross. Callagy directed that Ross and I exchange jobs; he became the training officer, and I became the XO. Offering little to do, the job was very boring and should have been abolished. The academic department and training section did all the real work.

The cadet candidates were a mixed bunch: some showed real dedication to earning a coveted appointment to West Point or the other service academies; others saw USMAPS as an easy way to spend nine months away from their unit. The ones who applied themselves and adhered to the disciplinary standards were outstanding young men with real potential as officers. The others, who were just trying to find an easy assignment, returned to their branch of service. As with previous assignments, the great capability and potential of many of our young people impressed me. The slackers who tried to beat the system reinforced the notion that a good leader must motivate the apathetic and indifferent for the good of the team.

Once when I served as acting commandant, a cadet candidate who bore a reputation for insubordination threw his weight around because his dad was in the rating chain for both Callagy and me. After hearing about the incident, I asked the first sergeant to pull the candidate into my office. With Massey standing by, I recited the standard Article 15 procedure to the recalcitrant candidate, and after hearing his side and asking a few questions, I had him leave my office. Soliciting Massey's advice—he recommended one week of restriction to the barracks—I called the candidate back, explained the punishment, and dismissed him after ensuring he understood the limits of his restriction.

Knowing what would transpire, I immediately tried to get in touch with Callagy's rater and my endorser because I knew that the cadet candidate's father, a colonel assigned to the Pentagon, would be livid. The rating officer never responded, and when the inevitable happened that officer blamed me. I responded by stating that no candidate—whatever his connections—would demonstrate any insubordination to one of my NCOs. This occasion was not the first, or last, time in my experience that senior officers were not professional enough to permit their sons to be treated like everyone else. My next efficiency report commented, "I would fight to get this officer assigned to me in any position requiring extraordinary heroism but I would not want him for an assignment calling for diplomacy." In the "zero defects" army of the period, a negative comment on an efficiency report, even one couched in these terms, could sidetrack a career.

Because of my promotion on 18 June 1959, I outranked Callagy—who certainly deserved a promotion. This produced my temporary reassignment to

Headquarters, the Engineer Center, for about three weeks, where I performed some mindless administrative tasks. Earlier word came through of my appointment to attend the Command and General Staff College at Fort Leavenworth, Kansas. The nick on my efficiency report and defying OPO had not cost me.

The Road to the Top Goes through Leavenworth

After leave, our family made the long trek to Kansas. Fort Leavenworth enjoyed a deserved reputation as a "good family post." The army finally began putting money into the physical plant of the school. The gleaming new academic building, Bell Hall, opened in January. New family and bachelor quarters, schools for dependents, a hospital, and other improvements were added, under construction or in the pipeline. Modernization of the facilities went together with efforts to update the curriculum, methods of instruction, and how students were assessed.

The army had sleepwalked through the fifteen years since the end of World War II; intellectually it had not kept pace. By the mid-1950s, the army was grappling with an ongoing and accelerating technological revolution. Technology involved not only atomic rockets and guided munitions but also advances in air and ground mobility, surveillance, air defense, and the dawning of the electronic age in communications and data processing. The new chief of staff, Gen. Maxwell Taylor, embarked on an ambitious effort to revitalize the army and transform its conceptualization of war (together with legitimatizing its place in the national defense structure) and its warfighting doctrine and force structures. He also believed the army required a fundamentally new type of officer to face the challenges of the present and future. Leavenworth would play a focal role in that resurgence.

Before the 1957–1958 academic year, the whole curriculum centered on World War II–type operations in central Europe; afterward, instead of viewing the nuclear battlefield as the exception, it became the rule. All these changes—which called for complete reversals of long-held orthodoxies—produced radical alterations in concept, doctrine, and organization such as the army had never experienced in peacetime. Predictably, the sweeping reforms undertaken by the commandant, Maj. Gen. Lionel McGarr, set off an army-wide firestorm of resistance, but by the time my class arrived, the new program was already firmly in place.

Having been in Puerto Rico and Colombia and then at USMAPS during this period, I possessed only a dim awareness of all the turmoil. All officers sought admission to the Command and General Staff College (C&GSC) because attending Leavenworth more than graduating—since everyone did—represented the single-biggest ticket chop on the "road to the top." Leavenworth meant promotion to at least lieutenant colonel. Everybody war-gamed their punches aided by their branch OPO advisors: Leavenworth led to a Department of the Army punch, and then admission to the War College and for many a civilian graduate degree. In the STRAC (Skilled Tough Ready Around the Clock, which translated into military perfection) army of the period, officers curried the favor of their raters and endorsers to max their efficiency reports and score high on their Officer Efficiency Index to gain accelerated admission to Leavenworth. A good percentage of the officers encountered at Leavenworth had been promoted "below the zone" as captains and majors; many had been aides to senior officers.

I was not good at those games. For starters, service with the Sixty-Fifth Infantry, a year in Colombia, and being sidetracked to USMAPS took me out of the loop. I was never in a position to play politics. Instead I avoided contact with senior officers so as not to appear a "boot-licker." I never considered myself a "comer," and my goal remained fixed on becoming the best regimental combat team commander I could be. Leavenworth would help me achieve that. Because of the sheer size of the branch, Infantry officers were overrepresented at C&GSC. The office of the chief of Infantry made the decision on appointments, and I expected the selection board would be conscientious in their choices, figuring the best would go to Leavenworth. The vast majority of officers selected came from the Regular Army combat arms, mostly majors in their mid-thirties, and so I was not surprised when informed of my appointment. Although Colombia and USMAPs cost me "command time," and Leavenworth would add another year, I felt the school would better prepare me for higher command and more senior staff positions.

The regular course enrolled more than six hundred students; about eighty were foreign officers, around twenty from the other services, and the rest were army. As the senior tactical school of the combined arms and services, Leavenworth emphasized command but also prepared us to perform staff duties for the division and above. The thirty-eight-week course divided into four phases. The first, called "familiarization," contained segments introducing us to staff procedures and tactical and logistical principles followed by the "application" stage, where we learned by doing in staff exercises and solving basic tactical and supply problems. Then, toward the end of the academic year, we solved progressively more complicated problems in the "advanced application" module. A "general education" component was interspersed throughout the year. About two-thirds of the course centered on operations (intelligence and operations), with the rest given over to administrative support (logistics and personnel) and civil affairs. The course covered an introduction to basic nuclear weapons through work on infantry, armored, and airborne divisions, army aviation, unconventional warfare, and a segment on dealing with larger units (corps and army), joint operations, and communications zone-level support. It also differed from the pre-1957 curriculum in many important respects: aside from the introduction of the use of atomic weapons on the battlefield and the new Pentomic force structure, it shifted from the preoccupation with a general war in central Europe to a shared emphasis on limited war with attention paid to situations short of war in Eastern Europe, the Middle East and Africa, and Asia.

Another McGarr initiative featured a shift away from teaching the "school solution" and learning by rote. The six-hour day was broken into two lesson blocs. Faculty were assigned to basic work groups of about twenty students, with the emphasis on shifting the focus from the podium to discussion groups; there was less instruction and more student-centered learning activities. The army proceeded on the notion you had to be proficient in a staff position to be a good commander. We had lively discussions in our work group on the qualities of leadership. In the application phases we solved problems by role playing; everybody took their turn in command or acting as head of a general staff division (personnel, intelligence, operations, and logistics). We learned how staffs were organized and experienced how they operated. Never having held a real staff appointment—which I always avoided—Leavenworth made me grasp for the first time the complexity and importance of staff work. This was particularly true of operational logistics. Commanders and "operators"—and that was what I aspired to be—disdain the lowly logistician, but the quality of the logistics instructors—and, more important, their message—impressed me. Basically, that message underscored the validity of the truism "for want of a nail the battle was lost." This was an important lesson.

Another thing I took from the course involved the importance of having the right people in the right positions, or training and developing the people you have in your organization. One module compared how the general staffs in other armies functioned—the British, German, French, and Russian. A German staff officer attended the course, and we marveled, given our swollen staffs, at the small size of a Bundeswehr operational headquarters. While each had advantages, we concluded the organizational wire chart mattered less than getting good people into the right slots. Good people could make any organization work; incompetent people would founder no matter the organization.

We sat through a number of secret and top-secret classes on atomic warfare. Very few of us bought what the army was selling. It all seemed too mathematical and mechanical, like Buck Rogers stuff. You could probably fight on the atomic battlefield, but nobody had any real knowledge or experience that it was possible. I never had much confidence that it would work.

The same applied for the new ROCID (Reorganization of Combat Infantry Division) force structure. The Pentomic division killed the traditional regimental system, with its long histories that contributed to unit cohesion, replacing the triangular regiment and battalion with battle groups of five rifle companies. Under the old system, a lieutenant colonel or major commanded a battalion; a full colonel commanded a regiment of three battalions. Instead of three to five maneuver elements, the battle group commander had to oversee at least nine elements. And his zone of control expanded because, in the interest of dispersion on the nuclear battlefield, companies were expected to cover frontages as wide as an old regiment. The new structure left a gulf between the battle group commander and his company commanders because, with the disappearance of the battalion, its command assignments at the major and lieutenant colonel levels also vanished. After the experienced officers from World War II and Korea retired, officers would assume battle group command without assignments to maneuver units. For me, who aimed for a battalion command, the new structure was very disheartening. Almost without exception, the other officers in the course shared my skepticism.

The course introduced the army's newfound interest in unconventional operations, "situations short of war," and air transportable operations. Some of the instruction on tactics on the nuclear battlefield, fighting forward and winning against a numerically superior enemy, foreshadowed the later development of Land-Air doctrine. The air assault sections were taught by experts. Many discussions centered on the practicality of heliborne air assaults. Could forces be inserted by air against ground forces possessing adequate anti-aircraft capabilities? Many thought not, remembering the failure of Market Garden in 1944 and the experience of the French at Dien Bien Phu.

Under the new grading system, we were evaluated not only on examinations, tests and quizzes, and solutions to map and maneuver problems but also on effective writing and speaking, and class participation. Legends held that the stress of the "old Leavenworth competition" for class standing drove officers (and spouses) to suicide. I had no sense of that. To me, Leavenworth was another "gentleman's course"—six hours in class allowed for plenty of time for a round of golf, some tennis, and drinks in the officers' club. I participated in none of those activities but used the time for family. Weekends were free. You were left to do as much or little homework as you chose. Nobody failed, and few seemed obsessed with making the distinguished and honor roll or the "general staff eligible" list. Everybody, including me, wanted to get something out of the course, do some creditable work, and not waste the year.

McGarr saw Leavenworth as occupying a central role in raising the professional standards and quality of the officer corps. That meant more than improved military problem-solving, working as a member of a team, and effective communication skills. Being an officer was a calling, not a career choice. Personal leadership derived from character based upon high moral and ethical values. Careerism ate at the foundations of professionalism. Whether character—or command ability, for that matter—could be imparted to midcareer officers in a one-year course is debatable, but the army's senior leadership recognized the problem, and Leavenworth tried to address it. Imparting character at the major or lieutenant colonel level was late in the career progression, as the many incidents of misbehavior of midlevel and senior commanders indicated. Battalion or brigade command was sought after by many solely because they were steps to flag rank. They knew they needed command time to move up the ladder, but troop duty carried too many potential booby traps; too many things could go wrong and derail promotion. Far safer, most calculated, was to get appointed to a bloated staff and be looked after by some senior officer.

I never fit into that mold. Nor did I require any prodding in my already firmly implanted belief that being an officer in the United States Army constituted a profession of faith in serving and defending the Republic. Although by no means unique, I saw myself as different and plotted my own course. Not a club guy—always an abstainer—I seldom engaged in idle conversation. In the beginning I joined a night-study group to G2 the course but soon left. Working from the premise of isolating, in army parlance, the Essential Element of Information (EEI), I concentrated on what I needed to know and hoped to employ that knowledge down the road.

As advertised, Leavenworth turned out to be a good family post. Social demands—courtesy visits and the like—were not too high. Most notable about our stay in Leavenworth was the birth of our son, Thomas, in November. With two young kids and an infant, Jeannie and I had little time for fun and games. We visited Kansas City a couple of times—went to some of their famous steak houses—but mostly stayed at home. We lived in the ground floor of one of the older and unrefurbished family units. With our young family we liked to keep the heat up—and that winter we dealt with an outbreak of mumps—which, as we later found out, turned the apartment upstairs into a sauna. On the whole we spent a very enjoyable ten months at Leavenworth.

With no real sense of the "old Leavenworth" as the "make-or-break" year of my career, I graduated in June 1960 with a genuine feeling of accomplishment. I came with the typical line officer's bias about staff officers and their craft and left with a greater appreciation for the vital importance of staff and line operating in tandem. The course provided a number of intrinsic benefits. For the first time I enjoyed close associations with a wide array of army officers from the other branches—connections that stood me in good stead in the future—and with officers and perspectives of the other services and those of our allies. All this broadened my horizons and deepened my competencies as a professional officer. Leavenworth left me with the conviction that I had acquired sufficient training and education to hold any command and staff position that came my way. And I was eager to be on my way.

8

Tenth Special Forces Group

Three-Year Idyll in Bavaria

Again, to my disappointment, the army personnel managers put me on the West Point faculty track, including two years in graduate school. I contacted my good friend from Colombia, Lt. Col. Joe Koontz, now in the Office of the Deputy Chief of Staff for Personnel (DCSPERS) in the Pentagon. The Leavenworth course included a discussion of the role of Special Forces. The prescribed DCSPERS career path held no more attraction to me now than it had before. I wanted assignment to the Tenth Special Forces Group in Germany and asked for Joe's help. He contacted Lt. Col. Beverly M. Read, chief of the assignment section for Infantry Branch, who telephoned me and explained the importance of the proposed assignment and what my request meant. At that time—the summer of 1960—regular officers viewed duty with Special Forces as a career-ender. I understood and insisted on my preference for Special Forces (my paperwork was already submitted). Read said he would look after it and did. My orders arrived, directing me to the Special Forces course at Fort Bragg en route to the Tenth Special Forces Group in Germany.

Many friends expressed disbelief at my choice and urged me to reconsider, pointing to the pitfalls of placing myself outside the career-building mainstream. Special Forces offered everything I desired: working with young people in physically demanding circumstances in a mission I deemed important (even if the army leadership did not share that view). The assignment would make high professional, physical, and emotional demands. When Jeannie supported my choice, I knew it was the right decision. Not only did it turn out to be my best tour, but the timing was good. The new Kennedy administration would abandon the "New Look" and "massive retaliation" as the fulcrum of defense policy, instead embracing "flexible response." The conventional ground forces benefited because the new policy focused on forming an army—and ground forces would play the central role—possessing the capability to fight and win a midintensity war in central Europe consistent with the army's traditional concept of its chief mission. More vital, the army's enhanced role meant escape from the budgetary cleaver. But the new president would expand "flexible response" to include those "brush-fire wars" in emerging Third World countries that Taylor had talked about but, as it turned out, had no real intention of fighting. Kennedy and his secretary of defense, Robert McNamara, pushed hard for a shift in doctrine, army education, and training. But all that lay in the future.

The success of units like my Rangers in Korea produced a brief flowering of interest in unconventional operations. In the summer of 1952 the army formed the Tenth Special Forces Group at Fort Bragg. The preoccupation with the nuclear battlefield in the mid- and late 1950s marginalized special operations. The six-week course at the Special Warfare Training Center at Bragg did not appear that special. Attendees were not physically or mentally taxed. The attendees—two or three lieutenant colonels, a few majors, and the remainder captains—sat through not particularly well delivered daylong lectures explaining doctrine. The concept, derived from World War II experience—mostly operations staged by the Office of Strategic Services (the forerunner of the CIA) such as Jedburgh teams in Normandy and Brittany and Detachment 101 in the Pacific—called for special forces infiltrating by land, sea, or air behind enemy lines to organize, train, equip, and advise "stay behind" elements and friendly guerrillas. Cold War contingencies called for special operations, but the manuals produced in the 1950s lacked any agreed doctrinal statement other than defining the mission as conducting covert operations in enemy-controlled territory in conjunction with irregular partisan forces in support of a resistance movement, an insurgency, or in combination with conventional forces. The assignment centered on playing an unconventional role in the army's conventional concept of how to fight the Soviet Union and its Warsaw Pact allies in Europe. In the event of an all-out war in central Europe, conventional forces in Germany represented little more than a trip wire. Based on the theory of reliance on nuclear countermeasures, NATO would have to destroy West Germany from the inner border to the Rhine in order to save it. What role special operations might perform in an irradiated battle zone was anyone's guess. Special operations missions also entailed deep penetration into the "denied zone," behind the Iron Curtain. The Central Intelligence Agency theoretically would organize cells of anti-Communist operatives, and in the event of war, it fell to special operations teams to cooperate with these indigenous partisan bands. Given the highly publicized covert operations failures of the CIA in the Balkans and Eastern Europe, deep-penetration missions came with extremely high risks. Army doctrine continued to view special operations through the lens of World War II: as clandestine operations working with partisans in the enemy's rear. Nothing passed for instruction on counterinsurgency warfare because the partisans/guerrillas/insurgents were on our side. Obviously in six weeks we could receive no training on the languages, geography, or cultures of areas where we might operate or on dedicated communications; the course focused on doctrine. These specifics—nebulous though they were—would be the focus of unit training.

The last week featured a major tactical exercise. Field grade officers were excused from participating with the other trainees in the field. I thought exempting field grade officers was a mistake. They needed the training and experience; where else would they get it before assuming a command? Maj. Bob Rheault, a Leavenworth classmate also on his way to the Tenth Group, joined me in requesting that we participate since we believed that we would benefit from the training. After gaining permission, we took part in a compacted refresher jump course and requalified; the school staff wondered why we would go to the field when not required. The week in the field provided us with limited but valuable experience. We graduated 18 May 1960.

When we flew to Germany on a completely full civilian aircraft, our son, Tommy, then about eight months old, made the trip in a cardboard box on the floor. We landed in Gander, Newfoundland, for refueling before the flight over the North Atlantic. After a night in Frankfurt we flew to Munich, where we met our escort officer, Capt. Jim Jackson. As we continued our trip in a staff car south to Flint Kaserne in Bad Tölz, the home of the Tenth Special Forces Group (SFG), I "interrogated" Jim about life in the unit. What I heard pleased me very much. Bad Tölz, on the Isar River at the foot of the Bavarian Alps, has to be one of the most picturesque places on earth. The town boasted an interesting military history; it had served as the site of the SS officer candidate school, and Gen. George Patton selected it as Third Army headquarters during the occupation.

Team Leader

Initially the Tenth SFG was split in half, with one segment deployed to Bad Tölz and the other remaining in Fort Bragg. In 1960, the Fort Bragg element became the Seventh SFG. The Tenth SFG (A) consisted of the Headquarters and Headquarters Company and Company A. The company had eleven operational detachments (OD) "A." Rheault assumed command of OD B1 with six detachments; I took over B2 with five. My team sergeant was M.Sgt. Charles

Petry, a very experienced, knowledgeable, and personable noncommissioned officer, as were the other members of my "B" Team.

The Group participated in the annual theater-wide Unconventional Warfare Maneuver two weeks after we arrived. Upon alert, most of the teams moved to the Special Forces Operations Base (SFOB) in France. My "B" Team stayed at Tölz and immediately began a hurried preparation for a "new" method of infiltration officially referred to as "stay behind." We did not "stay" anywhere, but that night began a cross-country foot movement of about thirty miles to our contact point with the partisan guerrillas. We covered about fifteen miles the first night before holing up for the day. My feet were a mess. Blisters covered the scar tissue, skin graft, and "okay" portions of my feet. I bandaged them carefully and prepared for the second night movement. Except for my feet, I was in excellent physical condition and covered the thirty miles over rough terrain carrying about eighty pounds of equipment.

We went into a "hide" location a few hundred yards from our contact point to await the rendezvous time that night. Petry and I went to the main contact point, and Parker and our operations sergeant, 1st Sgt. Henry D. Goodwin, moved toward the alternate point. Unfortunately, they became disoriented and missed the contact. We had to hunker down another day and try again. This time we linked with our guerrilla chief, Capt. John Hayes.

During the next six weeks, "B" Team coordinated and planned numerous raids and ambushes with our "A" Teams. The exercise simulated attacks against the conventional enemy's vulnerable rear echelons and lines of communication. Experience and the high training status of the troops paid off. During the maneuver, I visited each of the "A" Teams, wanting to see them face to face and get acquainted with them. All our missions succeeded, and none of my men were "captured" by conventional force soldiers who played the part of the enemy. After the maneuver, we assembled for a major critique. While no particularly new lessons emerged, the field exercise demonstrated the validity of the "stay behind" concept. I thought the conclusions all too pro forma and resolved to do better next time.

One of the first challenges upon our return was the cross-training test that the group conducted each quarter. It consisted of a performance test on each of the four skills: demolitions, weapons, medical, and communications. A written test covered operations and intelligence. Rheault placed first on this portion, besting me by a half point. The weapons portion of the test concerned me. All special force personnel were supposed to know dozens of foreign weapons, but most of the soldiers, with the exception of the weapons specialists, consistently failed this portion of the test. We could not spend the time necessary to develop the knowledge required. I suggested to the group S3, Maj. Charles "Bill" Simpson, that each quarter we master three weapons for the next quarterly test. Our training would focus on what the S3, advised by his weapons experts, considered the most important. Always open to suggestions, Bill agreed. Thereafter, we spent our training time more productively and morale improved as a consequence.

Communications also presented problems. The cross-training benchmark demanded the ability to send and receive error-free seven words per minute for five minutes using Morse code in addition to other performance standards, including setting up a radio and passing a written test. Perhaps less than 10 percent of the noncommunications soldiers passed the Morse code portion. The reason was simple: nobody trained for the test. Deciding we needed focused training, I arranged for opening the code room one hour before reveille as well as during the day. I strongly urged my "B" Team members to practice and encouraged my "A" Team leaders to set the example for their teams and schedule code training during the day. Every morning I arrived when the code room opened, which made for a long day. Although I knew no code, my goal fixed on passing the code event in the next test. More of my soldiers began practicing before reveille (no other soldiers were present). I encouraged those who came and cajoled those who stayed in their bunks, dismissing as nonsense the claims of a few who said that they just could not learn code. The next test bore fruit: over 50 percent passed. This percentage rose in subsequent quarters until it exceeded 75 percent.

I paid close attention to the training schedules prepared by the "A" Team leaders, who had almost complete freedom to train as they saw fit. I scrutinized even more closely the conduct of the training. The group S3 set the goals, and our job centered on meeting them. Some resisted because for years they had done only what appealed to them. Slowly they came around, and in the next cross-training test, "B2" and three of its "A" Teams made up four of the top five teams. More individuals qualified overall and met the code standard. Officers who set examples and demand focused training produce results. Not exactly a formula out of rocket science but one often disregarded.

The physical demands of our mission were high because fitness should not be a worry during an operation. I instituted a physical fitness test each quarter. The first test was a "diagnostic," using the then current five-event Army Physical Fitness Test. Lt. Herman Day, one of the "A" Team leaders, conducted the test. My guidance to Day: "Maintain the standards prescribed in the Field Manual."

On test day, Herman explained each event as one of his soldiers demonstrated it. I went first on each event, followed by each of my troops. Each demonstration and the testing were done to standard "by the book." Herman and his team members exceeded my expectations. Quarterly physical tests became the norm. These tests focused on the strengths and physical capabilities required on our missions: climbing a rope to a second-story window; unloading a pallet of "C" Rations and running with them to a shelf set at the height of a hay wagon (often used by our teams working with guerrillas to move rations and other supplies air-dropped during maneuvers); each soldier, carrying a combat load, had to complete a march over a mountain and return within a specified time. All events were mission-oriented and battle-focused.

During the first winter, the operational teams moved to a "tent city" in the mountains. Snow depths sometimes reached three feet on open slopes. The wind and temperature combined to make the weather miserable. We began three weeks of winter training focused on skiing. For a Georgia boy with no experience, this training was difficult, but I soon grew to love the physical demands and being outdoors. I welcomed the challenge, and by the end, though I was far from proficient, I had gained some confidence on the slopes. We ended the winter training with a seventy-two-hour field training exercise (FTX). The exercise really pushed us physically as we labored up and down mountains through the deep snow under loads of eighty-five pounds or more. My operations officer, Lt. Jerry Scott, a particularly competent officer, helped in meeting the challenges of the new environment. He had replaced Captain Parker, who had moved to the brigade staff after we returned from the theater-wide FTX. The exercise brought home forcibly the realization, if we had not already reached that conclusion, that we were far from competent military skiers. Living at the foot of the Alps allowed for off-duty skiing, and our capabilities improved slowly.

The group commander, Col. Salve H. Matheson, selected the "B2" Team to become the water-training experts for the Tenth Group. We participated in an outstanding "Instructor Course in Underwater Diving and Demolitions" presented by a couple of our experienced sergeants who concentrated on developing our skills by repeated exercises until they became second nature. They stressed that safety was the overriding consideration. After completing the course on 23 June 1961, we developed two programs of instruction: one a qualification course with the goal of producing soldiers capable of performing the skills and emergency drills correctly and safely and the other on instructor training similar to what we had just completed. Soon "B2" trained other teams.

"B2" received the mission of developing surface and subsurface water-borne techniques and mounting training programs in those skills for the group. The specific mission included developing techniques for infiltrating from and exfiltrating to submarines, a competency that would significantly increase our operational capabilities. Special Forces included within its mission statement infiltrating into denied areas by air, sea, or land. Operating from submarines expanded our waterborne capability from surface to subsurface, a critical skill when attempting to enter denied areas behind the Iron Curtain.

My "B2" Team and 1st Lt. Ray Celeste and his "A" Team went to the Mediterranean to work with the navy. Lt. Cdr. Grant Apthorpe, the submarine skipper, and his crew were a perfect band to work with. Surprising for a submariner, "Baby Whale" Grant must have weighed three hundred pounds, but he could move remarkably fast. He told me at the outset, "Ralph, you just tell us what you want to do, and we'll figure out some way to do it." We spent two weeks making four one-boat infiltrations and exfiltrations each night. Several problems presented themselves. How do we surface, bring small boats topside, inflate them, load the soldiers, and cast off in the shortest possible time and avoid detection by the enemy? How do we find our way to a specific landing spot without being seen and without someone on shore to guide us? How do we exfiltrate and marry up with the submarine? The latter proved the most interesting and challenging.

One technique for connecting with a submarine at sea was for the ship to use radar to locate us as we held up a paddle blade covered with aluminum foil to make it more reflective. The sub would get between us and shore so the radar could be pointed outward, thereby lowering the possibility of revealing the sub's presence to the enemy onshore. However, the enemy, if scanning the ocean with radar, would pick up our paddle.

We tried every imaginable technique to make contact. The best was strictly low-tech. Somebody in the boat would strike two pipes together beneath the water surface. The sound could not be heard by anyone onshore or even a few yards away. The submerged sub's sonar picked up the sound and homed in on the small boat. When the sub closed on us, it proceeded at its slowest speed that permitted some directional control. While still underwater, the sub turned on its "red eye," a rotating red beacon. This red beacon helped the boat team locate the sub's periscope, but the underwater flashing light remained invisible to anyone on shore. The boat team paddled rapidly to catch the periscope as the sub passed by. The bow man threw a rope bight (a horseshoe bend in the rope) over the periscope and held on as the sub, still submerged, headed for open sea. If there was a miss, the sub required thirty minutes or more to turn around and make another pass. After going far enough (ostensibly over the horizon) for training purposes, the sub signaled the boat to cast off. As soon as the sub surfaced, there was another mad dash to it. The sailors hauled the team and its boat aboard. As soon as the boat could be deflated and taken below, the sub submerged. We held a quick but thorough "after-action review" of what had transpired after each infiltration/exfiltration while events remained fresh in the minds of the participants. Team members and navy crew exchanged ideas and suggestions as we worked to do better next time.

Working with the navy stands as one of the most enjoyable episodes of my career. Grant Apthorpe and his crew were true professionals. They made good on their skipper's promise to figure out a way to accomplish every task that we set before them. I never worked with a more cooperative group of men than those sailors. This cooperation on a junior, face-to-face level was the rule whenever I worked with the other services. The doers—those charged with accomplishing the mission—always rendered cooperative assistance to get the job done. It is at the very top levels where interservice rivalry causes real problems.

Upon returning to Bad Tölz, we prepared a complete after-action review and submitted it to group headquarters. The techniques were rudimentary but provided a basis for continuing development and enhancement. This material should have been forwarded to the Special Warfare Center at Fort Bragg for dissemination and retention in file. The army is often remiss in disseminating lessons-learned to other commands and even to subordinate units within a command. What one unit learns often disappears as members transfer to other assignments.

Bill Simpson was an energetic and far-sighted officer. He saw the opportunity for the Tenth Group to act as military ambassadors establishing working relationships with special units in other armies. Sending Mobile Training Teams (MTT) to work with NATO partners and participating in joint field training exercises would greatly benefit our training, boost morale, and build personal affiliations with officers and men we might operate with in the event of a war. B2's MTT to Greece was one of the first of many that Simpson arranged.

In Greece, we worked with the Raiding Force, an airborne unit similar to our Rangers composed of some of the best cadre in the Greek army. Our job involved qualifying a handpicked group of eight Raiders as scuba instructors, teaching them some small boat techniques. We also helped them develop an in-house capability to conduct their own scuba training. While in Greece, we executed a short tactical exercise that included raiding a target that required us to scale a cliff. After destroying the target, descending the cliff, and moving to a pickup zone, we were exfiltrated by air.

Part of our mission involved building rapport with a NATO partner. Our team—a composite of the core of "B2" plus 1st Sgt. Joe Lisi, an outstanding archer, and a couple of supplemental medics—prepared a special demonstration for the Raiders. The medics performed some surgery on a sedated dog, and Lisi demonstrated his prowess with the bow and arrow. We spent one day at the Greek army's parachute school. To qualify for Greek parachutist wings, we made three jumps from a C47. That day, 26 July 1961, was a high point in our MTT. We fostered a relationship that would benefit both the Greeks and the Americans in the event of war. As always, we submitted a carefully prepared after-action review, and Col. Lloyd Gomes, the chief of the Army Section, Joint United States Military Aid Group, Greece, sent a letter of commendation.

During my second year, B2 participated in another NATO special operations maneuver in Sardinia. We would take off from a carrier, jump into Sardinia, and work with a special operations clandestine group from the Italian army. The navy sent a small, wheeled aircraft and two pilots to Bad Tölz to work with us for several days. We made five or six jumps—because of the small doorway we exited in a crouched or sitting position—identifying any significant difficulties requiring adjustment. Since the navy pilots never had worked with paratroopers, we taught them to align themselves with the "T" on the drop zone that indicated the final approach and take corrections from the jumpmaster. After several days, we felt the pilots possessed enough orientation to put us over the DZ.

When the time arrived to conduct the maneuver, we went to Naples. Unfortunately, the pilots we trained with had been transferred. The assigned pilots had never worked with paratroopers. Having had some jumpmaster experience on USAF tactical troop carrier aircraft and guiding small aircraft on several free-fall jumps, I expected no difficulty. There was another change. We would not take off from a carrier. Disappointed, we made do.

The flight over the Tyrrhenian Sea was uneventful, and as we approached the DZ the illuminated *T* appeared. I began giving corrective hand signals to the inattentive pilot. The exit would be from a seated position because the mammoth rucksacks and other equipment precluded anything else. Seated right behind me was Sfc. Jim Beatty, my old friend who shared the foxhole with me on Hill 205 in Korea. Beatty was making his first jump in about ten years. My troopers, in the second aircraft, exited when they saw me leave the aircraft. Our landing and assembly left much to be desired. The DZ was small and very rugged. My landing was as soft as I ever experienced, but I found myself perilously near the edge of a cliff. My team sergeant, Command Sgt. Maj. William "Pappy" Greer, broke two ribs. The medic dislocated his shoulder. One of the communication sergeants slashed his knee, which required several stitches to close. Another team member twisted a knee. All four had to be evacuated, leaving us short-handed.

A steady downpour added to our misery as we struggled up the mountain that bordered the DZ. We passed back and forth the extra equipment taken from our injured troopers. The twenty-five-pound hand-cranked radio generator was a pain. We reached the ridge at about three in the morning. Our contact, who spoke limited English—none of us spoke Italian—took us to a hovel occupied by an old shepherd and his grandson. The old man wanted to know if we were Germans and broke into a big smile when he learned we were Americans. Exhausted after a very long and tiring day, we pulled off our soaked clothes and climbed into our bags for a few hours' sleep. As Ben Ivey observed, "There is nothing like a dry T-shirt when you are cold and wet." Little pleasures mean a lot to an Infantryman.

The next morning, we arose bright and early and made our way to the assigned position. We were attached to the Italian special forces, who bore responsibility for planning the next two weeks of the exercise. It became apparent that nothing had been accomplished. Unless significant changes happened, the maneuver would be a bust. I immediately radioed to the Special Forward Operations Base in France. Only a few hours elapsed before Capt. Dick Kim, an assistant group S3, arrived and set things straight. We moved to a secret training camp operated by the Italian equivalent of the CIA for training in preparing and retrieving cached equipment, weapons handling, and special operations. Over the next two weeks, we instructed our contacts on American procedures and equipment. At the end of the exercise, I concluded that the exercise amounted to another "win-win" situation. We expanded our capabilities, improved our performance, and established relationships with our Italian counterparts. Returning to Bad Tölz, we prepared a thorough after-action review and submitted a detailed written report. I had learned the value of both early in my service.

Caught a Lucky Break

After the most enjoyable eighteen months that I ever spent in the army, the group underwent reorganization into three operational companies. Because we lacked seniority, Rheault and I lost our "B" Team commands. The S2 and S3 assumed two of the three commands, and we took over their sections with me as the intelligence officer. I set about learning my new duties, and as was typical of the group, I was surrounded by people, both commissioned and noncommissioned, with better qualifications.

In a few months, our annual theater-wide maneuver would be conducted. Simpson, now a company commander, broke his leg on a jump as did his XO, Maj. Bill Hinton. I took over Simpson's "C" Team. Our designation was once again Greece. "C" Team would infiltrate from a sub, and two of the "A" Teams would jump in after we were in country. I focused the training program on honing the capabilities required for Greece with emphasis on physical fitness; we stressed preparing ourselves for the great physical demands that lay ahead. The exercise shaped up to be a very challenging one, and though I was sorry Simpson and Hinton could not lead their troops, I was happy for the opportunity.

We boarded a sub in Naples and prepared for the covert voyage and infiltration into Greece. The only Greeks aware of the operation were the king and select members of the Greek Raiding Force. On the day of our infiltration, the sub entered a bay where we would land and make our initial contact. We surveyed the shore and the landing zone through a periscope: the bay was completely empty. By nightfall, the same body of water was filled with dozens of small fishing boats. Not only a safety concern, the presence of the boats might compromise security and certainly complicate matters by slowing our movements. As I watched through the periscope a brief flash of light appeared, our signal to proceed. The sub surfaced, the boats were quickly inflated, and we made our way to shore. The delays convinced the Greek contact team that the operation was scrubbed, and they departed. We went into a hide site and spent a miserably cold day waiting for nightfall. We made contact with our guerrillas using an alternate contact plan.

Our contact, a Greek Raiding Force lieutenant, led us over the side of Mount Olympus, a hot, dry, dusty trek. The first night we slept on a steep incline. Each of us made a makeshift anchor for our sleeping pads by putting our packs on the downward side of the slope to keep from rolling downhill during the night—not very comfortable but amusing. The second day was more challenging than the first. We were out of water and never saw a stream or spring to slake our thirst and replenish our canteens. At a break in the early afternoon, all of us were parched and feeling somewhat dejected. At that moment, I remembered the two packages of gum in my pack. I pulled them out, broke each stick in half, and gave each trooper a piece. After the first couple of chews, each of us was rejuvenated and eager to continue.

In the end, the maneuver played out as fairly typical. Several nights later, our two "A" Teams jumped onto drop zones that the Raiders had selected. Some of the Raiders were those we had worked with previously. We staged a few operations and both the Special Forces and Raiders developed a better appreciation of how each operated. Then back to Germany and Bad Tölz. As always, we submitted an after-action review about our experiences cooperating with the Raiders and the U.S. Navy. We focused on both the tactical play and the relationships with members of a foreign army and a sister service.

The group grew rapidly. Almost none of the volunteers had any Special Forces experience and few held airborne qualifications. The group set up its own jump school and began a continuing cycle of training. I became the company commander of the to-be-formed Company D with the mission of training the intake of officers and enlisted men. We ran a three-week course in each of the four Special Forces skills together with a special operations and intelligence course for the officers and team sergeants. All participated in a week-long round-robin tactical exercise at the end of their skills course. This tactical exercise, planned and coordinated by M.Sgt. Bud Malone, my S3, and Jim Beatty, my S2, was one of the best I had ever seen thanks to the good work of my officers and NCOs.

The question of prioritizing between training and operations presents a perpetual challenge. The trainers produce the caliber of troops that operators demand yet starve the training establishment of the cadre they need. I encountered difficulty convincing the group XO, Lt. Col. Harrison J. Merritt, to place the staff I needed on temporary duty to establish and conduct the training company's programs. The caliber of the cadre would affect significantly how well the training was presented, and in large measure, how well the graduate performed. Trained cadre constitute the seed corn for future success. While the other company commanders recognized the necessity of the school, they proved reluctant to lose key personnel even for a short period. Merritt decided that my instructor staff, as opposed to my headquarters personnel, would be rotated through D Company for only three months and then return to their previous assignments. Disappointed that my staff would constantly rotate, I saw the benefit to the group as some of its senior NCOs would gain experience and higher levels of skill from a three-month tour in the training company. Our instructional standards were very high; they set the norm for the group.

The rotation system worked because of the extraordinary men who served in the group. My guidance for the XO and command sergeants major was simple: they would run the front office, and make the day-to-day decisions and take whatever actions deemed appropriate with the proviso they kept me informed. I spent my time in the field observing training, free from any administrative burdens. Naturally I bore responsibility if something went wrong, but it never did.

My principal instructors—the chief instructor for each program—received the same guidance and a free hand. After all, they were the subject-matter experts. I directed them to maximize practical exercise—learning by doing—rather than lecturing. Students learned the skill, and the instructors objectively evaluated their mastering of a clear set of training objectives. Although written tests were part of every evaluation, the emphasis remained fixed on performance in the field.

Not only did my duty with the Tenth SFG rank as the best in my career, the post in Bad Tölz topped the list for Jeannie and me. The children were too young to derive much benefit from living in Bavaria. We had fine quarters, and the kids went to good schools and made many friends. The area south of Munich is fairy-tale beautiful with its quaint towns, beautiful Alpine lakes, breathtaking mountainscapes, and Mad King Ludwig's fantasia castles. We never lacked for exciting things to do on my free weekends. The mountains afforded us the opportunity to learn to ski. Our family trips took us to a number of beautiful ski resorts. Some of our best times as a family took place on these outings. We all progressed in our skills, especially the children. Every year Jeannie and I took advantage of a program offered by the Swiss Ski School to stay in a resort with a package of all-day ski instruction, lifts, and room and board.

Another family activity was camping. Jeannie was not at all enthused, but she agreed to camp in a beautiful Alpine area featuring a waterfall. We did not exactly rough it since we hauled every conceivable convenience on top of the station wagon. Still not convinced, Jeannie was offered a deal she could not refuse: a ten-day trip to Lake Garda in northern Italy where I promised to do all the cooking. A day trip to Venice was thrown in as a sweetener. The kids loved it—swimming at the U.S. officers' beach, picnicking every day, meeting kids their age from different western European countries—and if Jeannie, always the good sport, did not, she hid it pretty well.

One thing that enhanced my time in Bad Tölz was my discovery of freefall parachuting. I joined an active group of skydivers that consisted mostly of Tenth Group men. The skydivers were not troublemakers but free spirits. Occasional violation of regulations pertaining to free-falling angered Colonel Matheson, who threatened to disband the club if it did not mend its ways. To ensure that it did, Matheson ordered me elected president of the club. Surprisingly, club members supported the "election" as they saw me as one who would ensure that they retained the support of the colonel. Another reason the group leadership were not thrilled with the club stemmed from the risk of serious injury. I broke my ankle on my third static line jump—two short of the five needed to qualify—and resumed training as soon as I recovered. Jeannie proved less sold on free-falling than Matheson. In all I made twenty-nine free falls; my longest was thirty-five seconds and a drop of 5,600 feet before the chute opened. Over time the club members modified their behaviors enough to avoid further censure.

Sadly, our three-year idyll in Bavaria came to an end. The Special Forces—as my first airborne assignment—provided the challenge, excitement, and satisfaction I sought in the army. Colonel Matheson, who commanded the group during my last two years, was the ideal boss. He gave me twenty-eight months of command time and the freedom to chart my own way. Far from causing a so-called detour on my career path, the tour with Tenth SFG boosted my prospects. No longer the pariah it had been in some quarters—although hard-core traditionalists, including those populating the senior ranks, remained unconvinced—Special Forces enjoyed a certain éclat, and as my experience amplified, a deserved reputation of an elite force.

9

Three More Way Stations Cleared

Armed Forces Staff College, the Pentagon, and U.S. Army War College

In June 1963, we left Germany and returned to the United States. Unbeknownst to me at the time, my promotion to lieutenant colonel came through a couple of days before relinquishing command of Training Company. Jeannie, the kids, and I were on the way to the Armed Forces Staff College (AFSC), a joint service school at Norfolk, Virginia. I had never heard of the school before and then was told the personnel managers sent officers there because they did not know what else to do with them. After discovering that Sid Berry had attended, I concluded that a five-month stint at the school certainly could not hurt my prospects.

Armed Forces Staff College

The Armed Forces Staff College occupied a nebulous position in the hierarchy of service schools. In the lead-up to the formation of the unified Department of Defense, the army—based upon the experience of joint and combined operations in World War II—pushed for the formation of an all-services national security university and an armed forces college. Neither emerged because the navy and newly independent air force were not about to surrender control over the development of their future senior leadership. Despite opposition from the other services to the scheme, the army suspended the reopening of the Army War College until 1950. The two joint educational institutions that emerged from this failed effort at amalgamating were the Industrial College, located in the former War College at what became Fort Leslie McNair in Washington, and the Armed Forces Staff College in Norfolk.

We moved into far from satisfactory quarters on what used to be a navy base. Not for the last time did I conclude the army had a long way to go before it could truthfully say that it was family friendly. Fortunately, a separate house on post came available, and we moved in. Family life immediately improved. Virginia Beach was nearby as well as ample camping opportunities. The family enjoyed our time in the Virginia Tidewater.

The course began in August and lasted into January 1964. It consisted of a series of guest lectures in the mornings, with afternoons given over to small group discussions. Usually around fifteen members were selected to bounce questions off the lecturer. The information presented in lecture—and the lineup of speakers was impressive—supplemented the theme of the current subcourse. Reading assignments meshed with the presentations. Classroom time usually ended at three in the afternoon. The remainder of the afternoon and evening was for study, physical fitness, and family. The diversified views of the consortium—consisting of soldiers, sailors, airmen, marines, and civilians from government agencies—provided for lively exchanges and insights to other points of view. The curriculum included staff planning exercises, usually with an army representative—all graduates of Leavenworth—holding the chair as the operations officer. The other services had no equivalent to the Command and Staff College. Rewarding both from a personal and professional point of view, the school exposed me to many other matters that impacted the United States and the world: health, education, the civil justice systems, and the lack of potable water in many countries; the world economy; population growth; and many others. The speakers, seminar sessions, parallel reading, and discussions opened my mind to aspects of the armed forces—not just the army—and the other governmental departments and the civilian world of which I possessed only a vague awareness. The school provided a stress-free learning environment where I gained an appreciation for joint and interagency attitudes and perspectives.

While at Norfolk, I joined the local Toastmasters Club to improve my speaking ability. The club consisted of perhaps fifteen officers on the AFSC staff. I benefited from these associations, and in my last evening, a formal dinner, I was selected as the emcee. It just so happened that emceeing a dinner was the next task in my training regimen. The president made a complimentary speech, thanking me for my participation during the year. Despite being under the gun, I enjoyed the evening and regretted that it would be my last with this group.

"The Building"

Completing the AFSC hurdle, the next step was a tour in "the Building," the Pentagon. I received assignment to the Office of Personnel Operations (OPO),

Infantry Branch. Since we would be staying in the Capitol District for at least two years, we decided to buy a house. While still in Norfolk I made several trips to the DC area before finding a house in Annandale, Virginia. Like so many of my contemporaries, I obtained first and second mortgages and a loan from my dad to buy the house in a brand-new development. We made a good choice. The children went to a particularly good school within walking distance.

For the next ten months I learned something about the personnel business. Lt. Col. J. J. Walsh, the current holder of the Regular Army (RA) Desk, taught me the ropes. He converted much of his official correspondence into standing operating procedure paragraphs that could be cut-and-pasted in response to inquiries from the field. Unlike in many previous assignments, I would not start from ground zero. The office handled assignments for all infantry officers of the ranks lieutenant colonel and below. The RA Desk reviewed applications from reserve officers applying for Regular Army commissions. I discharged additional functions. One involved reviewing records of officers who met the standards for Regular Army but had not applied. Discovering a prospect, I sent a letter to that officer's commander stating that a routine review of the subject officer's file indicated he possessed the desired qualities and stated, "If you agree, you may want to recommend to this officer that he submit an application for a Regular Army commission." In all cases a request was approved because I made the final cut and needed only my boss's concurrence. Naturally the applicant never knew what transpired. One officer could not be convinced to apply, although his commander made three attempts. I wrote letters with every sort of encouragement except saying "apply and you will be accepted." Finally the officer came by the Pentagon and explained that, despite his commander's endorsements, he still felt unqualified. "I'm the officer who has been reviewing your record and writing your commander," I said. "While I can't guarantee it, if you apply you are almost a cinch to be accepted." He did and received a Regular Army commission.

While serving in OPO I decided to review my file and make a disinterested appraisal of my record from the viewpoint of an action officer reviewing my record as if considering some personnel action such as an assignment, schooling, or promotion. I was amazed at what I saw ostensibly for the first time. While the file contained compliments about my demonstrated leadership capability both in combat and elsewhere, many entries pointed to my lack of tact. Enlightened by the exercise—and wondering how I had made lieutenant colonel—I vowed to overcome those faults.

Like hundreds of officers in the Pentagon, I started work on a graduate degree. I selected the personnel management program at George Washington University. The Kennedy administration shook up the defense establishment by placing a priority on improving the functioning and cost-effectiveness of the Pentagon and armed services through the application of scientific management and system analysis. To reinforce the point and drive reform, the administration added the office of systems analysis in the Department of Defense at the assistant secretary level. With me in OPO, personnel administration appeared the best choice, and the tick of a master of science degree in my 201 File certainly would not hurt. Two courses each semester required that I attend two-hour classes twice a week. Two additional nights and four to eight hours each weekend were set aside for studying. It was a heavy load, but the classes and readings opened new and intriguing horizons for me.

Expecting to write my thesis on the selection, education, and assignment of officers for duty with army missions in emerging countries, I tailored my term papers in each course around these themes. The subject was of major importance to the army at that time. Army Chief of Staff Harold K. Johnson had proclaimed stability operations—counterinsurgency and nation building—as the third principal mission of the army after fighting and winning a general or limited war. The Cold War and the avowed Soviet intention to support "wars of national liberation" translated into the containment policy. The army's job entailed stemming the spread of communism by aiding emerging countries to resist insurgencies by establishing a degree of stability and security to allow for the formation of democratic governments. The war in Vietnam certainly fit that profile and soon became the focus of much of the army's effort. I coordinated much of my writing efforts with members of the OPO staff.

The OPO assignment proved interesting. It provided insights into the workings of the Building and in particular the thinking behind the army's personnel management system. The office came in for more than its share of abuse. Each day the Infantry desk officers labored over their decisions, knowing the good of the branch and the service depended upon matching the right people with the appropriate job, and that the genuine strength of the army rested in the quality of its personnel.

After my short stint in OPO, I moved to the Office of the Deputy Chief of Staff for Military Operations (ODCSOPS) in the Special Operations Directorate. The Infantry Branch chief, Lt. Col. John Spears, wanted more OPO officers on the army staff. The director of special operations was Col. Hank Schweiter. The chief of plans, Lt. Col. Clarke Baldwin, was my immediate boss. Both eventually made flag (general officer) rank. My task focused on contingency planning for Latin America and Africa. Commanders in chief of the various commands submitted operations plans for various contingencies that might affect their area of responsibility. My job: prepare a written outline of each plan and, when appropriate, comment on the adequacy of the plan. I also evaluated other planning documents and advised Colonel Schweiter whether he should "chop" (approve) or disapprove them and what comments he should make.

One plan foresaw an American invasion of Colombia in reaction to a Communist takeover. The contingency plan called for the landing of a division on the Pacific coast followed by an advance over the rugged Andes to Bogotá. Only one narrow and winding route traversed the mountains. Having traveled that road I knew a well-led and supported company could delay a division for an extended time. My critique prompted a significant change in the original plan. Nothing substitutes for firsthand knowledge. Another contingency plan I reviewed and commented on involved an intervention in the Dominican Republic that went to, and was approved by, the operations division.

The job also included making trips. One lasted twenty-six days, beginning 7 September 1965, that took me to the U.S. Army missions in Panama, Guatemala, El Salvador, Colombia, Brazil, Peru, and Bolivia. Given my background in special operations, my assignment centered on assessing our counterinsurgency assistance programs in these unstable regions of Latin America. The short stay in Guatemala allowed me to get reacquainted with the Koontz family. In Bolivia I lodged with my classmate John Chandler and his wife. John accompanied me on a long jeep trip into the high Andes to visit a Special Forces Mobile Training Team (MTT) working with the Bolivian military. The adaptability of these soldiers and their ability to build working relationships with their hosts impressed me.

The Seventh SFG was going on a training exercise to Vieques Island, off Puerto Rico, opening with a night jump. I finagled my way into going along. The briefing, preflight rigging, safety instructions, and other planning and precautionary activities went like clockwork at Fort Bragg. It was late in the afternoon as we flew over the shimmering Caribbean. We rigged again in the aircraft and went through another safety check as we neared the drop zone. Then the prejump commands: "Get ready! Get Set! Stand up! Hook up! Check your equipment! Sound off for equipment check! Stand in the door! Go!" I felt that old surge of adrenaline.

Once more a leap into the darkness fueled by faith in the equipment, the rigger, the training, and the confidence (hope) that the air force had found the right drop zone. All of these things and more tumbled through my brain as I leaped into the darkness and hurtled through the air at perhaps a little more than 100 knots (about 110 miles) per hour. Then a shock and jerk as the canopy of the parachute blossomed open and the forward and downward fall came to a quick and bone-jerking stop as the chute filled with air. I watched for other chutes and steered clear of all while keeping an eye on the fast-approaching ground. DZ Vieques looked as bad as reported, with old pickets and other debris scattered everywhere among the cacti. Keeping clear of the obstacles as best I could, I slammed safely on the ground, which I followed, as always, with a silent "Thank you!" Aside from the usual cuts, scrapes, and bruises, nobody was injured. During the remainder of the week, I participated in as many different activities as possible, including time spent with the Air Commandos, the Air Force's Special Air Wing that worked closely with the Army's Special Forces. The training proved opportune. The Seventh SFG would soon deploy to the strife-torn Dominican Republic.

Pentagon duty made people claustrophobic. Not only were we were housed in a crowded, noisy, and windowless office, but I also had the sense of being a very small widget in a huge bureaucratic machine. Every day I struggled to transfer the mountain of paper from my "In" to my "Out" box, all the while juggling phone calls while simultaneously everyone else in the office did likewise. I sometimes wondered how we ever accomplished anything. Some officers spent nights on cots to meet deadlines on studies that would die a lonesome death somewhere in the maze. Everybody seemed to be in a rush: junior officers to win the favor—and the preferments that came with it—of their bosses; the services competing for influence and a bigger share of the budget. Careers were made or busted in the Building. There was also a sense of unease in the Pentagon. Many officers directed their suspicions, if not hostility, toward the secretariat of the Department of Defense, McNamara and his Ivy League advisers, and the bevy of "whiz kids" who exercised influence far outweighing their experience. Also many felt disquieted over the administration's policy in Vietnam—1965 saw the beginning of the bombing campaign against North Vietnam, the commitment of American ground combat units, and the Battle of Ia Drang—and the lack of input from the uniformed heads. I was glad when my name appeared on the list for the U.S. Army War College.

As usual, I sat for my annual physical. Completing his examination, the doctor, citing my damaged feet, said, "You should never be sent overseas again." I was stunned. Salve Matheson promised me a battalion command in Vietnam after I finished the War College. After I told the doctor about being slated for a tour in Vietnam, he said he would give me a profile that would ensure I stayed in Saigon in Military Assistance Command, Vietnam (MACV) headquarters. Not wanting any part of that, I told him about the battalion command. "Fine," he replied, "I'll give you a picket fence." Now all that stood in my way of that command was completing the War College.

U.S. Army War College

In the summer of 1966, we moved into a nice apartment at Carlisle Barracks, and I joined with 204 other officers in the War College Class of 1967. The atmosphere was relaxed. As constructed back in 1920 by Gen. Peyton March, then chief of staff, the War College occupied the apex of the army's education triangle and would prepare the elite of the officer corps for senior command slots and high-level staff functions in the War Department. From the beginning, Leavenworth usurped the War College's position as the premier army school. Careers were made at Leavenworth, not at the War College. From its origins in 1902 through the American entry into World War II, the War College acted as a planning adjunct to the War Department; student studies informed policy-making. The War College closed during the war and did not reopen until 1950, first at Leavenworth and then in historic Carlisle, Pennsylvania, not far from Gettysburg. The postwar school suffered from the lack of a clear mission and bore the reputation—which proved true—as the ultimate "gentleman's course."

Until the New Year, classes were held in Bliss Hall, a converted stable. In January, we moved into newly completed Root Hall. As at the AFSC, the Carlisle curriculum featured frequent guest speakers but mostly centered on cooperative work performed in student consortiums. The program of study consisted of eight courses; the core of the curriculum rotated around a small bloc on comparative military strategies from World War II through Flexible Response, a seminar called "Command and Management" that had no discernable command content but instead examined economic questions and system analysis approaches, and one that passed for stability operations. For the first time, the War College experimented with case studies, one looking at the recent operations in the Dominican Republic. It was interesting examining the intervention in the Dominican Republic given my prior work on contingency planning in DCSOPS. I was surprised that we would not be studying military operations as such.

Grades were not given, and the single academic demand involved a writing assignment. We had four options: a thesis, an individual research paper, a case study, or two essays. Still working to fulfill the master's requirements and the thesis—which meant a few trips back to Washington—I naturally selected stability operations. Our consortium made a trip to a think tank the army had contracted to conduct counterinsurgency studies. At the end of a conference, the action officer announced, "You have the expert on this subject in your class. He is Lt. Col. Ralph Puckett. He has written the only paper ever prepared on this subject." I had submitted the paper, a twenty-page essay, in one of my classes months before. If I was the leading expert on counterinsurgency at the War College, the army was in serious trouble.

The demands of the course were not taxing; we were done by three in the afternoon, which freed up time for me to work on my thesis. In the past, War College students had been allowed to opt for additional night classes. Unfortunately for my class, this option had been terminated. The college leadership decided that students should not concentrate their efforts on completing graduate credits at the cost of their War College work. My George Washington University thesis supervisor, Dr. William Torpey, a tough taskmaster, returned my submissions with a sea of red ink, but I doggedly persisted. The subject held a great amount of interest for me, and since stabilization operations and counterinsurgency were such hot-button issues, I considered my work of some potential value to the army.

The War College curriculum trained generalists for high command and staff positions and schooled us on management theory, but it was not very army-centered. Even though the cloud of Vietnam hung over the army and the nation, it made no imprint on the "business as usual" curriculum. Troubled by this shortsightedness—and still intent on going to Vietnam—I submitted a written recommendation that Carlisle develop a subcourse that examined our involvement in Southeast Asia. The paper recommended the seminar focus on decision making beginning with the French in Indochina through the steps leading to the expanding American involvement. At each major turning point, the decision would be analyzed based on what was known at the time, what conclusions emerged, and why. We would also discuss what might have been a better choice using the information available to the president, his advisors, and the joint chiefs at each juncture. There would be no Monday-morning quarterbacking. The goal was twofold: analyze and develop an understanding of the decisions with a view of critiquing the decision-making process. The college leadership never responded. Several other students made similar recommendations concerning Vietnam. The general verbal response from the faculty was that the War College did not exist to prepare officers for battalion command.

I entertained plenty of misgivings about our involvement in Vietnam. It seemed to me the wrong strategy against the wrong enemy in the wrong type of war. I had a gut feeling we already had made major mistakes and should not be there unless the president clearly stated our political objective and allowed the military leadership to fashion the appropriate strategy. By the end of 1966, we had more than 380,000 troops in Vietnam. The strategy of graduated pressure—bombing and covert operation against the North; the insertion of ground troops; the shift from "enclave pacification" to division-strength search-and-destroy operations. The problem with an attrition strategy is that it cuts both ways; and the United States had an enemy willing to pay the price. Gen. William Westmoreland talked about the "crossing point," yet troop ceilings continued to rise. So, too, did casualties and the spread of antiwar opposition. The aim of nation building became nation defending. South Vietnam appeared to be an army—and not a very good one—without a government. In 1966, a civil war broke out between rival factions. Nobody clearly understood our overarching objectives because the goalpost constantly shifted or could define the victory we sought. Plenty of platitudes were offered but nothing concrete.

Despite my unease with the war, I wanted to go to Vietnam and serve in the field for several reasons. First, as a professional soldier it was my duty. Second, all the conflicting accounts of how we were fighting the war made me want to experience it firsthand. Third, I wondered how I would perform. After my experiences in Korea, could I lead from the front and set the example for my soldiers? I did not want to miss out on this war and could not let others do all the fighting. My country and the army had invested time and money in my development. Now was payback time.

In a discussion with one of the chaplains in my class, Tom McMinn Jr., I expressed these concerns. Tom had been a first classman (senior) when I was a plebe at West Point in the same company during Beast Barracks. I knew him well and respected his views. When Tom heard me express my reservations about what we were doing, he asked incredulously, "Ralph, how are you going to Vietnam as a battalion commander feeling the way you do about the war?" "Easy," I said. "I am a professional soldier. I will do my best to be the best soldier that I can be."

Vietnam aside, the year at Carlisle broadened my perspectives. The academic work proved challenging and nicely dovetailed with the preparation of my thesis for George Washington University. The biggest rewards came from association with topnotch people. The prevailing assumption stood that one out of every three students would become a general officer. The attendees were dedicated, ambitious, and competent. Their comments either in class discussions or informal chats always proved insightful, well-informed, and thought-provoking.

Except for Bad Tölz, no post proved more enjoyable than those months in Carlisle. Marty and Jean wanted to ride, so we bought a half interest in two horses and joined the horsey set in the Hunt Club. Inevitably the question arose, Which half of the horse did we own? I joined the local Toastmasters in weekly meetings, improving my public speaking and making friends among the townsfolk. Although southeastern Pennsylvania is a far cry from Bavaria, we managed to continue our family skiing. Good quarters and schools for the kids, horseback riding, skiing, and sightseeing in the Pennsylvania Dutch Country, coupled with the wonderful people with whom we associated, combined to forge fond memories of our stay.

I wanted to complete as many of the requirements for my degree as I could before my deployment to Vietnam. With the thesis approved, all that remained was the two-day comprehensive examination and three electives. The three electives could wait, but I wanted to take the exam. The trouble was scheduling. Even though my requirements remained incomplete, I asked the dean for special permission to sit for the exam. When he discovered I was headed for Vietnam, he readily agreed. The university always treated us as mature professionals and made special allowances for officers who have to serve at the pleasure of their superiors and not themselves. The exams duly taken and passed, I would complete the electives when I returned home.

The motives for embarking on a graduate degree might have been professional, but the gains were mostly personal. The coursework, research, and writing all opened new vistas and different ways of looking at leadership, organization, and management and their underlying principles and philosophies. Research sharpened my analytical skills and provided insights that proved of lasting value. Previously disinterested in scholarly pursuits, the more I researched and thought, the greater my interest became. I never regretted the effort required for the degree.

We arranged for the packers to take our household goods to Columbus, where Jeannie and the children would stay during my tour in Vietnam. Collier Ross, a classmate at West Point and the War College, and I reported to the Infantry School for a three-week precommand course for soon-to-be battalion commanders. There were approximately thirty officers in the course; several had just completed the War College.

It was obvious from the first day of classes that the program of instruction was totally unsuitable. It focused entirely on a major land war in Europe against an invading Soviet Union army. We discussed maneuvering armored and mechanized divisions across vast expanses of the European continent. Here we were on our way to Vietnam, anticipating a combat battalion command, yet we were learning nothing about what to expect in Southeast Asia. Since I knew Maj. Gen. Sidney Berry, the commanding general—we had overlapped at West Point, and he was my student company commander at the advanced course—I volunteered to approach him and raise our objections.

Berry was very receptive and called in Lt. Col. Bill Lober, an old friend, who headed tactics instruction. The general asked, "What would you like for us to do?" "Sir," I responded, "we want instruction focused on Vietnam. We want to hear from Infantry battalion and company commanders, NCOs, chopper pilots, artillerymen, signals people who have experience in doing what we will soon be doing in Vietnam." A no-nonsense commander, Berry turned to Lober and said, "Bill, make it happen." How great it is to be around people who can make a decision and give an order without staff studying it to death. The program that Lober prepared was perfect. We had hands-on experience with equipment we had never seen before. Captains and sergeants told us how they had conducted air assaults and extractions. The artillery guys talked about fire support. The training was battle focused, the way it should be. Our total lack of experience in what we would soon be doing under fire may be surprising to some. For most of us, our first battalion command would be with a unit in combat. Lessons learned in training come cheap; those learned in combat are expensive.

As the time for my departure drew near, the specter of going off to Vietnam hung over the family. Every day the press provided more coverage of the conflict. I reminded Jeannie that the choice was mine and recalled that talk we had before we were engaged. Trained to lead men in combat, it was my duty to go where needed. She could have resisted and pointed to the family obligation of remaining with her and the children as they entered those difficult preteen years, but Jeannie, always the perfect army wife, was supportive.

It rained the entire day I was slated to leave. Whenever Jeannie looked at me she wanted to cry, but, for the kids, we acted as if nothing was out of the ordinary. As a family we played board games until it was time for me to go. Of course, our experience was no different from that of generations of families who have sent their husbands and sons off to the summons of the trumpet, but that knowledge did little to soften the hurt. Whatever fate held for me on the other side of the globe, I derived strength from the knowledge that Jeannie would be in charge. I knew that I could depend on her. I was reminded of the words of the poet John Milton: "They also serve who only stand and wait." Army wives do not stand and wait when their husbands go off to war. They continue doing all the things they always have done: see that the kids are properly dressed and fed; help with their lessons; nurse them when they are sick; and comfort them when they are sad. Then they shoulder the tasks that the daddies performed before they left. Army wives are combat force multipliers. Time management experts need to talk to army wives to learn about real efficiency. Jeannie was wonderful. I knew she and the kids would be okay. I wondered if she knew how much I loved her.

There is no doubt that Jeannie has had a tremendous impact on me. Her influence has been as strong as Daddy's. She held our family together. She has been the one whose wise counsel guided us through the normal travails of family life and those times when we experienced severe stress. I have often wondered what we would have done without her. We could have existed, but our life would have been empty. How fortunate I am to have found her and made her mine. She and I both know that we are blessed.

The day I left was the saddest day of my life to that time. I had never felt so alone as on the day of my departure. I had no premonition of any dire outcome. I just saw how lonely the coming year would be. I wondered if my family knew how much they meant to me. We said good-bye at the Martins' house. Frank, Jeannie's dad, drove me to the airport. I did not want the family sitting in the airport waiting for the loading call. As Frank drove, he said, "Ralph, if there were any way I could take your place, I would." I knew he meant it. I will always remember and appreciate that.

I met Maj. Don Bowman at the airport. He had married Cynthia Young, who grew up in the house across the street from Jeannie. Don and I would be leaving on the same plane. After a few moments we boarded the aircraft. We flew to Chicago's O'Hare Airport, where we met Ross. Thankfully, connections were tight, and after a short wait, we were on our way to Vietnam.

10

Strike Force

Battalion Command in Vietnam

The Pacific crossing proved mind-numbingly long. We arrived in Saigon on 10 July 1967. What impressed me was the heat, humidity, dust, smells, and the cacophony of strange tongues. Somebody more graphically remembered the mixed odors of sweat, excrement, jet fuel, and the fish sauce that the Vietnamese slather on all their food. Having served in similar situations, and despite the difference in language, I experienced a sense of déjà vu, although I realized that a distinctive environment would present novel challenges. I figured if I did my best I would be all right. We moved to our temporary quarters and spent three days awaiting our assignment orders.

Collier and Don left first, a day before me. They both received details to the First Air Cavalry; it was an infantry division with enough choppers to make it airmobile. Collier assumed command of the Second Battalion, Twelfth Cavalry, with Don as his operations officer. I reported to headquarters of the First Brigade (Separate) of the 101st Airborne Division (1/101st), Strike Force, at Base Carentan, near Duc Puo in southernmost Quảng Ngãi Province. Duc Pho was situated on the coast about 520 miles north of Saigon.

You always run the risk of getting selected out of the pipeline for another assignment, so I was relieved that Brigadier General Matheson's request for me went through. I would command the Second Battalion of the 502nd Infantry Regiment (Airborne). The brigade staff all appeared competent, dedicated, and professional, although many of them had held their assignments for only a few weeks. Matheson designated a moniker for all incoming commanders and staff for the purposes of radio communications; his was Iron Duke. He asked for my first choice, and without hesitation I replied, "Ranger." The name meant a lot to me, and each time I heard "Ranger" it reminded me that I had to live up to all that the name represented. It would identify me during my twelve months in Vietnam. My first order of business involved visiting each brigade staff officer and the artillery battalion commander and listening attentively to what they said. I also solicited the advice of the commanders of the other two battalions.

At lunch one day in the general's mess, the deputy commander, Col. Oscar Davis, mentioned that I had not been officially initiated into the brigade. Since World War II, downing a flaming drink constituted the rite of passage into an airborne unit. Matheson knew me as a teetotaler and wondered about my reaction. I thought, "What the heck!" I took the proffered "prompt blast" and killed it. With that, although most of it ran down my chest, Ranger became a full-fledged member of the 101st Airborne.

"Fire Brigade"

By the time I arrived in Vietnam, the army had worked out a sequential three-phase system designed to counter the enemy's political organization and military tactics and further the pacification process. All three levels were dedicated to fulfill the basic mission: "find, fix, fight, and finish" Viet Cong (VC) and North Vietnamese Army (NVA) resistance. The first type involved search-and-destroy operations. By 1967, this mission was performed by multibattalion elements; airmobile ground units moved into enemy base areas, seeking contact with concentrations of enemy forces in the hope of inflicting heavy casualties before they dispersed into the broken terrain and heavy forests. There was no single template. Most common was the hammer-and-anvil operation; a blocking battalion took up position, and one or more attacking battalions drove the enemy (the hammer) toward the anvil. A variation included posting small units in ambush positions along the most likely avenues of retreat. Once the main force VC and provincial battalions had been removed (by 1967, unless the operation took place in the border districts, NVA units were rarely encountered), the second operation "cleared" any stay-behind elements, allowing the South Vietnamese government to initiate pacification efforts. Clearing operations resembled search-and-destroy tactics: multibattalion forces established a cordon and then conducted sweeps with the intension of neutralizing provincial VC guerrillas and disabling the main force's support base. Clearing operations typically lasted longer. The final phase "secured" the area. Company-size elements conducted saturation patrolling and cordon-and-searches of hamlets, concentrating on uprooting the enemy's political infrastructure, eliminating the logistical support base, and suppressing VC guerrillas. Clearing operations often involved elements from the Army of the Republic of Vietnam (ARVN); Regional and Popular Forces and police participated in phase-three efforts.

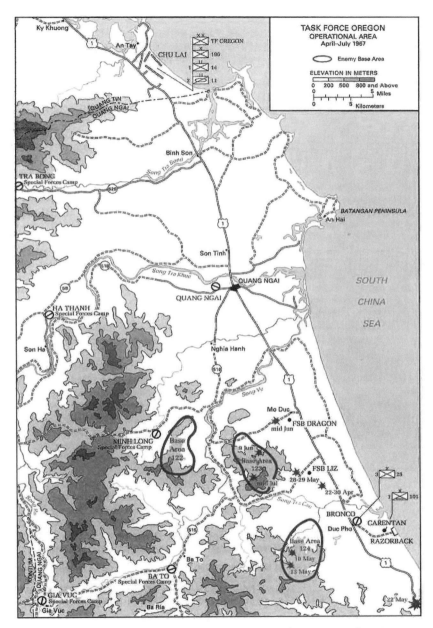

The operations of Task Force Oregon in the weeks preceding my arrival in Vietnam. From George MacGarrigle, *Taking the Offensive: October 1966–October 1967,* United States Army in Vietnam series (Washington: Center of Military History, United States Army, 1998), 234.

In each case, the ground forces found, fixed, and fought the enemy; artillery, gunships, and close air support finished them. Rare was the operation staged beyond the range of an artillery fire support base. Coordinating and employing supporting fires stood as a central feature of U.S. Army tactics.

The First Brigade belonged to a composite command, Task Force Oregon. Gen. William Westmoreland, commander of Military Assistance Command, Vietnam, created a provisional division, the first employment of large army forces in the I Corps Tactical Area, with a designated area of operation (AO) in Quảng Ngãi and Quảng Tín Provinces. Task Force Oregon's deployment in the corps area's southern provinces allowed the marines to consolidate their efforts, dealing with division-size North Vietnamese Army elements operating south of the demilitarized lines in Quang Trị and Thua Thien Provinces. The task force headquarters identified potential enemy concentrations, oversaw supply, and coordinated and established liaison with the III Marine Amphibious Force and other army commands but otherwise granted wide latitude to its brigades to conduct search-and-destroy missions against enemy base areas in the highlands. The brigade had been attached to Oregon for more than two months by the time I arrived and had suffered their highest rate of casualties since coming "in country" at the end of July 1965.

The Second Battalion, commanded by Lt. Col. Harry Buckley, an old friend, was in the jungles and highlands of Quảng Ngãi conducting combat sweeps as part of Operation Lake. Not wanting to sit around headquarters, I asked the general for permission to spend a few days with each of the companies before assuming command. He hesitated, then looked me in the eye and said, "Okay, but don't go get yourself killed!" I laughed and answered, "Sir, that's my number-one priority while I'm here."

I visited and spent one or two nights with both B and C Companies and the Recondo Platoon, a special, nonstandard organization composed of some of the battalion headquarters troopers. When I arrived at Bravo Company's location, its commander, Capt. Ron Odom, had his platoons and squads dispersed over a wide swath of jungle prepared to launch night ambushes. After dark, Odom received orders to move immediately through unfamiliar jungle and across streams to a new location about a mile away. I accompanied one of the platoons. The hike played havoc with my foot, which started to bleed, but I managed to keep pace. The next morning word got around how the colonel made the march on his chronically bad feet.

The last element visited was Company A, where I would spend a day. When I landed at Company A's location, Capt. Steve Arnold (a future lieutenant general) reported to me. Explaining I held no command authority, I promised to stay out of his way. When I asked what he was doing, he remarked that one of his platoons was about to depart on patrol. I told Steve that I would accompany the platoon if he had no objection. Of course he replied he had none and introduced me to Lt. James Peake, the platoon leader. I repeated the remarks I had made to his captain, and we departed. Task Force Oregon's primary mission involved keeping open the "Street Without Joy," the vital north-south artery of Highway 1 that ran along the narrow coastal plain. That meant mounting large-scale search-and-destroy operations to hit the enemy in their upland base area sanctuaries. To accomplish that, American forces forcibly ejected the civilian population deemed supportive of the insurgents—which meant much of the rural population had been removed. Both provinces, especially Quảng Ngãi, were enemy strongholds. The province had been a center of armed resistance against the Japanese and of the Viet Minh during the Indochina War against the French. Not long after leaving the base camp, the patrol came upon an extensive bunker complex but made no contact with the enemy.

The patrol pushed on, and after a while, Jim halted the platoon, pulled out his map, extracted his compass, and began to shoot azimuths. He then called his platoon sergeant up for a conference. I knew exactly what was happening, having seen the same actions so many times while instructing at the Ranger School. Peake came to me and stood at a rigid attention and asked, like a plebe at West Point, "Sir, may I make a statement?" Controlling a smile, I responded, "Certainly." "Sir," Jim reported, "I'm lost!" "Don't worry about it," I replied. "I don't take command of this battalion for another ten days. You have nine days to find where we are and get me back to the change of command." Jim broke into a big smile and called his company commander on the radio. Arnold flew circles until he was over the platoon's position. Peake popped a smoke grenade, and Arnold provided the coordinates. A great young officer, Peake was as handsome and personable as anyone I had ever met. After Vietnam, he transferred to the Medical Corps, completed medical school, and became a doctor, finishing his career as a lieutenant general and as surgeon general of the U.S. Army.

We never made contact with the enemy on any of my visits. By the time I arrived, the enemy had broken into small groups and withdrawn deeper into their base areas in the mountains to the northwest. Still, my little tour paid dividends. I met the company commanders, first sergeants, and platoon leaders and sergeants, and many of the men. By spending the night, making marches, and going on sweeps I gained firsthand knowledge of the personalities, strengths, and capabilities of my subordinate leaders and soldiers, at the same time providing the men of Strike Force with the impression that "Ranger" was a little different than the norm.

The brigade returned from deployment, and I took command on 31 July 1967. Immediately after the change of command, we conducted a memorial ceremony for the twelve troopers, including an attached Engineer, who had been killed during Operation Lake. These memorial ceremonies, the first I had ever seen, although short and simple, were very emotional. A rifle with bayonet was stuck in the ground for each man who had been killed. A pair of spit-shined boots stood in front with a helmet perched on the butt of the rifle. A set of dog tags hung from each rifle. I made a few remarks specifically mentioning by name our Engineer, who had died fighting as an Infantryman. The adjutant read the name of each trooper, and then a squad fired a three-round volley, and the bugler played Taps.

A number of troubling questions entered my mind as I stood there. Although antiwar dissent crested the following year, the wave of opposition to American involvement in Vietnam grew throughout 1967. I wondered what my soldiers were thinking. They were well aware of the discord in the States. How were these soldiers, paying homage to buddies who gave their lives in defense of their country and the freedoms we hold dear, impacted by the outpouring of resentment toward the military? At the same time those very liberties—the rights to gather, protest, and petition, and the freedoms of speech and the press—were constitutionally guaranteed. Disgust welled up inside me directed at those who condemned our soldiers, every one serving his country at the orders of the president.

Immediately after the change of command and memorial ceremonies, the adjutant, Lt. Tom Throckmorton, a son of a tactical officer at West Point when I was a cadet, approached me, smiled, and said, "Sir, give me twenty-five dollars." I asked, "What's that for?" "Sir, that's for your going-away present," he responded. We always contributed to the "Fund" used for the purchase of gifts for new babies and departing officers. It just struck me funny the way Tom expressed it.

As I walked toward my headquarters tent, my executive officer (XO), Maj. Herndon Godfrey, approached me, saying, "Sir, I have some bad news. Your driver was picked up in Saigon with some marijuana on him." Godfrey hesitated, and then said, "Sir, now you are a commander." Belying the popular image of the dope-smoking GI in Vietnam, this incident was the only one that required disciplinary action while I commanded the 2/502nd.

First I addressed my company commanders and staff. I spoke about how today was a proud day as I assumed command of a battalion boasting such a great World War II combat legacy and added that they and their predecessors had added to that reputation in Vietnam. The brigade had acted as a "fire brigade." Staging out of air bases at Biên Hòa near Saigon, Cam Ranh Bay, and Phan Rang, the brigade had fought in six coastal provinces and in the Central Highlands in II and III Corps Areas before redeployment to Task Force Oregon in May 1967. The army made it a practice never to acknowledge the existence of elite units, but we all knew *the* First Brigade, as it styled itself, represented the flower of the best division in the army. All the junior leaders—company commanders and lieutenants—were combat-tested, and unlike other brigades we did not face a famine of experienced noncommissioned officers; in fact, many NCOs had extended their service or returned from stateside assignments to serve with the unit. Morale was high. Since coming into the I Corps Area, the brigade conducted lengthy search-and-destroy operations in the Duc Pho District and Song Be Valley of Quảng Ngãi. These operations supported my contention that Vietnam was a company commander's war, and I explained it was my primary responsibility to establish an environment that permitted the company commanders to do their jobs without having to look over their shoulders for support. I assured them they would have that support—artillery, gunships, tactical air, medevac—whatever they needed to accomplish their missions. I concluded by telling them that they knew more about their soldiers, local conditions and the geography, and commanding their company than I did, then expressed my full confidence in them and my expectation that I would receive their 100 percent support. I finished with the exclamation, "Strike Force!"

As I was told and soon experienced, Matheson worked the same way. Since he possessed full confidence in his subordinates and troops, the brigadier allowed battalion commanders to conduct their own insertion operations: from selecting the landing zones and the sequence of assaults through conducting the sweeps. The only rule was that, although companies and their platoons must remain constantly on the move, they had to stay in proximity—for companies, that meant within a two-hour march—to allow for quick assembly in the event of running into trouble against sizeable enemy forces. The units also carried three to five days' supplies. The burden of carrying the extra weight—which slowed down movement—was balanced by the greater concern for preserving security; the enemy could not detect your location by observing the coming and going of resupply helicopters. Matheson and his staff provided the battalion commanders with a concise statement of the mission and intelligence, and identified our respective areas of operation. The battalion commanders did

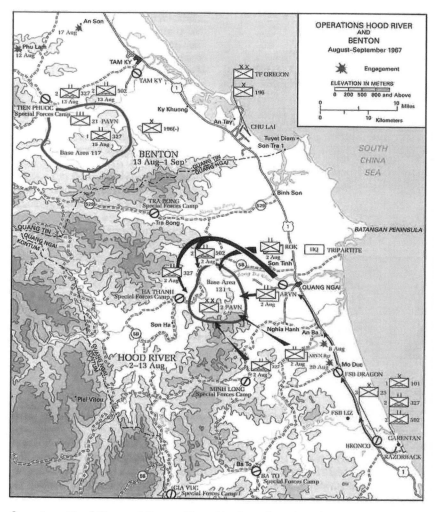

Operations Hood River and Benton. From MacGarrigle, *Taking the Offensive*, 247.

the same for their company leaders. The system proved simple but extremely effective.

Three days after I assumed command, we made our first combat air assault as part of Operation Hood River. Other than the precommand course at Benning and the orientation on commanding an air assault, I lacked any real experience. Turning to Maj. Skip Perrine, my operations officer (S3), I said, "Skip,

I have never done this before. I am responsible for all that happens and accept that responsibility. You tell me what orders to give while we insert those companies, and I'll give the order. I need your help." That's the way we made that first assault. It went smoothly, thanks to the outstanding people who served under me: Perrine, the Artillery liaison officer, Capt. Ben Melton, the company commanders and their troopers, and the air force pilots and Army gunship crews who prepped the landing zones before the troopers put down.

The fire coordination was particularly impressive. Melton flew in the command and control (Charlie Charlie) chopper and managed the fighter-bomber, artillery, and gunship support. The assault went like clockwork. The fighter-bombers arrived first, dropping five-hundred-pounders on all probable enemy locations. The jungle erupted with dirty orange-and-black explosions. Other aircraft then dropped daisy cutters (bombs with fuses on an extension to the nose of the bomb, causing the bomb to detonate above ground, spewing steel bomb fragments over the terrain) on the landing zone in the hope that the fragments would set off any land mines. When the air treatment finished, artillery blasted the entire perimeter and much of the landing zone. Immediately following the artillery, the gunships zoomed in, blasting away with machine guns and rockets. Within seconds the first slicks (choppers carrying troopers) set down. The troopers leaped out, ran across the landing zone, regrouped, and moved into the jungle. All in all, it was a beautiful, deadly symphony choreographed to split-second perfection. The operation went smoothly: the intelligence proved good, and the companies made contact with the enemy soon after landing.

I had been forewarned that Matheson always pulled a little joke on commanders conducting their first air assaults. No matter what time the commander would report, Matheson would tell the commander that his watch was incorrect. As I reported the insertion of the first company, he asked what time the landing had been made. I asked him for the time, and when he told me, I reported that the assault had been made at that time. Col. John Collins (code name "Cottonmouth"), the deputy brigade commander, told me Matheson got quite a kick out of having the tables turned on him. That was the only time that I would put something over on Iron Duke.

Hood River was a big operation involving two battalions from Task Force Oregon and Army of the Republic of Vietnam (ARVN) troops as well as South Korean marines. An ARVN regiment acted as the blocking force while we and our sister battalion, the 2/327th, were inserted on the northern and western perimeters of Base Area 121 that intelligence reported was held by two regular regiments of the Second Division, North Vietnamese Army (NVA), and a VC regiment. In combination with the Republic of Korea marines, the three battalions advanced south, inflicting damage in sharp small-unit actions against local guerrillas, while pushing the elusive enemy toward the ARVN forces. Base Area 121 lay about a dozen miles west of Quảng Ngãi City, south of the Trà Khúc River, in heavily forested mountainous terrain. Temperatures exceeded 100°F. For the next ten days the allied forces tightened the cordon but never brought any main-force VC or NVA to battle. As with so many operations, both past and future, the intelligence proved faulty. We uncovered no evidence that the identified enemy units had ever occupied the area.

After being pulled out of Hood River, we drew a couple days of downtime before being committed to the next operation, Benton. On 13 August the battalion conducted another airmobile assault in conjunction again with the 2/327, west of Chu Lai just across the border in neighboring Quảng Tín Province. The mission centered on finding, fixing, and destroying VC/NVA forces and neutralizing enemy base camps north of the Trà Khúc River. Intelligence indicated enemy forces were consolidating in Base Area 117 for an attack on the provincial capital, Tam Ky, in an effort to disrupt upcoming elections. Following the air insertions, our instructions called for saturation day patrolling and night ambushes working eastward, where elements of the 196th Infantry Brigade would be positioned.

All the insertions were complete, and around 1730 I flew over the area of operations, checking on how things had progressed. Odom's Company B put down in a "hot" landing zone. Immediately upon landing, the company came under fire from enemy mortar, automatic weapons, small arms, rifle grenades, and rocket-propelled grenades. Attempting to maneuver, the company met with intense enemy fire. Odom consolidated his position and reported he had several wounded, one of them his First Platoon leader, Lt. Thomas Petromalo, hit by a rocket-propelled grenade and in serious condition. He added ominously, "The LZ is mined!"

What to do? Should I land and take the chance of getting a chopper shot up? That was uppermost in my mind. The mines also concerned me. Mines make such messy wounds, and I had always dreaded going through a minefield. The thought occurred that Iron Duke might think I was playing the hero. Suppose I got involved in an action with Bravo Company and could not get out? If other elements of the battalion became heavily engaged, I would be needed elsewhere. All this ran through my mind, but it took me only a few seconds to decide. The action was here, and my presence was needed. I decided to land and assess the situation for myself. That was my job. I asked my pilot to take us down.

Once on the ground. my radio operator, Pfc. James Spears, and I jumped off the chopper. The chopper hurriedly lifted off and began circling overhead, expecting to pick me up in a few minutes. Another chopper landed and evacuated Petromalo. Odom ran to meet me and repeated what he had told me over the radio. The company's situation was dire. Watching my chopper leave foreshadowed what lay in store; we had a fight on our hands with an enemy as resourceful, tough, and more experienced than we and just as determined to win. It appeared a zero-sum game. There would be a winner and a loser, with no prize for second place.

Odom explained that First Platoon had stopped on the ridge running to the northwest from the landing zone. Lt. Donald A. Nemetz, the forward artillery observer (FO), was going to call in artillery to cover the withdrawal. "Sir, I'm nervous as a cat," Odom confided. "Ever since I heard I was going home, I've had short-timers' fever." "Don't worry," I assured him, "you'll make it." I knew Ron would do his usual good job; he was solid. I never mentioned to him that I was nervous, too.

Dreading the walk across the landing zone, I knew I had to get the company moving. I started toward the First Platoon, trying to step lightly (I smiled at myself as I unsuccessfully tried to make my 175 pounds weigh less than 4 ounces, the pressure required to set off the anti-personnel mines). The First Platoon soldiers sat in single file along a trail. Two troopers pointed to mines marked with toilet paper. All that could be seen were three small prongs sticking above the ground. I had been told a good point man could spot these types of mines. As I moved along the trail I cracked jokes that drew a few chuckles. Adrenaline was pumping inside me, but I struggled to appear calm.

Since no other option existed, I suggested to Ron that he return to the landing zone, form a perimeter, dig in, and hunker down for the night. Nemetz readied to call in artillery as the platoon started moving slowly to the landing zone. One element spotted some enemy in the draw and opened fire that slowed the movement. When we reached the landing zone, the requested artillery began to explode on the suspected enemy positions. "Ron, I'm going to spend the night here," I declared. "This is your company. You command it. Don't worry about me. If I can help, let me know." As Odom later related, his confidence shot sky-high.

I radioed my chopper circling overhead and told the pilot to return to base. Then I contacted my Tactical Operations Center (TOC). They informed me that a chopper would be dispatched to extract me. "This is Ranger. That's not necessary. Some of my men are in a fight here. I think I'll just stay with them till it's over." Then I directed that artillery, Dustoff choppers (for casualty evacuation), flare ships, and Puff, the Magic Dragon (C130 with Gatling gun) be alerted. I expected all would be needed before the night ended. While I could have marshaled the support just as well, if not better, from my TOC, I felt that my presence on the ground would be helpful.

Spears began digging us a foxhole about ten yards from where Odom located his. I would be close but not in his way. While Ron busied himself with the preparation of the defensive position, I checked with my TOC. As the company dug in, the enemy continued to fire rocket-propelled grenades, mortars, and automatic weapons onto our position that sat astride a flat plateau-like feature.

As darkness fell, enemy fire intensified. I thought that Odom might need buoying up. Early on I ran to his command post during each lull and checked in and complimented him on his leadership. He did a great job throughout and got better as the night wore on. It was obvious to me that he did not need me. Every now and then a tremendous burst of fire lasting a minute or so came from Company B or the enemy, clearly main-force VC of undetermined strength. Whenever it appeared the enemy was preparing to launch an assault, Odom and Nemetz called in defensive concentrations that appeared effective, causing the enemy to regroup. The first few times Odom called for support, I followed on my command net with a "Do it!" It really was not necessary, but it demonstrated that Ranger was monitoring the situation, which exerted the desired steadying influence on Ron and his men. Odom had matters under control. Despite the sometimes withering fire, I ran from foxhole to foxhole, giving "attaboys." The moon was up. I called Capt. Dennis Anderson, my S2, to see when the moon would set. He replied, "0001." I figured we would really get it then, so I encouraged everyone to dig.

Around eleven, my regular Charlie Charlie pilot radioed, "Ranger, this is Bronco, I can come in and get you if you want me to." He had been forced to take downtime for pilot rest. I thanked him and said, "Bravo has fixed me a nice comfortable bed. Think I'll spend the night here." I had to stay, but it gave me a good feeling to know that Bronco wanted to come for me. Warrant Officer Marti (Bronco) was courageous, totally unflappable, and a first-rate pilot; I always felt better when he was on duty because I had complete confidence that he would do whatever it took, no matter the difficulty or danger.

As predicted, after midnight the fire falling on our position increased significantly. In return, we used everything we could get—flare ships, Spooky (Puff, the Magic Dragon), artillery, and, of course, our machine guns, M79 grenade launchers, rifles, and hand grenades. Things often appeared critical. Whenever the gunships and Spooky departed and the artillery stopped, we received a pounding from mortars. When that occurred, I busied myself trying to get fire support: Nemetz brought in artillery on his fire direction net while I got on my command net and informed my command post how badly we needed it. The Viet Cong employed 60mm mortars, 40mm rocket-launcher fire and rifle grenades; the mortars were the worst. Lying in my foxhole with Spears and another trooper, I could hear mortars firing in the distance and then the explosions that came closer and closer, some shaking the ground. Naturally I thought about Hill 205 in Korea. I knew I was safe unless one landed in the hole, but, then again, that had happened before. I was scared and tried to say the Lord's Prayer about six times but never got through it. Then I tried the Twenty-Third Psalm but finally gave up and said, "Lord, I'm in your hands." I also remembered what Colonel Mendez had told me: if I thought about myself, I was not doing my job. So I got up and checked on some of the troopers. About this time a particularly intense mortar barrage fell on one of the advance positions. Hearing cries for help, I instinctively ran forward, grabbed a wounded GI, and carried him back to our improvised aid station. Then I repeated the process with a second soldier. Returning to where they lay, I administered what aid and comfort I could.

A little bit of levity helped the situation. Although not good radio procedure, I made glib remarks on the radio: "I told you I'm a lover not a soldier. I need all the help I can get." Or "Webster 2 [Captain Anderson], are you sure you signed that certificate?" I always told Andy that I wanted him to sign a certificate each night guaranteeing that I would be safe. Or in a singsong voice, "We could really use some artillery." Once my XO, Webster 5 (Godfrey), got on the radio and told me Bravo 6 (Odom) should give me the certificate; it was his responsibility to look after me. I ran over and told Odom that during a lull. He got a kick out of it. I kidded the men, "I'm never going to spend the night with you guys again. The first night I did, you tried to walk my legs off. Now you're trying to get me killed. You're the most inhospitable bunch I've ever seen." They ate it up. Several times during the night, different men would say, "Sir, we appreciate you staying with us. You're good for morale. We never had a colonel spend the night with us before." How can you leave when your men talk like that?

Three times during the night choppers arrived, delivering ammo and evacuating the wounded. Each time I helped remove supplies and load wounded. I ran to one of the pilots and said, "Hi, I'm Ranger. Thanks for coming." I wanted them to know we appreciated the risks they took. The chopper pilots, from the

"Minutemen," the 176th Aviation Company, logged more than six hundred sorties in twenty-four hours in support of the brigade's operation. Warrant Officer Dennis D. Bostad flew nearly nineteen consecutive hours during the first day of Operation Benton on four types of missions: combat assaults, command and control for me, and later air resupply and air evacuation of wounded. As Capt. Matthew M. McGuire flew his gunship in support, a caliber .30 bullet smashed his windshield and hit him in his chest. He was saved by his armored vest. He logged fourteen hours. We brought the choppers in during lulls after our counterfire suppressed the enemy mortars, and amazingly, none of the resupply/evacuation missions received fire. The terrain—the steep-sided plateau—also factored in the enemy's inability to sight his weapons.

At around 0200 the firefight slackened, and the enemy broke contact and withdrew. Sporadic sniper fire continued throughout the night. I checked my watch every few minutes and finally spotted the first hints of daylight. I ran over to Odom and suggested a "mad minute" at dawn—Ron convinced me that about five seconds would do the job—every soldier would fire his weapon at any and every potential target area in the event that some of the enemy had remained to surprise us if we became careless. We received a few sniper rounds in return, but that was all.

Before leaving, I walked the perimeter and spoke with the men, congratulating them on the great job they had performed. They were proud of themselves and chattered about their victory and how close the enemy had come. Some enemy dead sprawled grotesquely less than twenty yards in front of Bravo Company's foxholes. The troopers thanked me for being with them, and I replied, "I enjoyed it. [I imagine they knew that was a huge fabrication.] See you later." Odom came up and said, "Sir, I never would have made it if it hadn't been for you. I was scared to death." "Ron," I replied. "You did great. I'm proud of you." Ron's calm, professional leadership made the difference between success and failure. He and his company had beaten a ferocious, disciplined enemy; all I did was provide a little steadying influence.

I flew back to my command post, and within a few minutes Iron Duke came in. I briefed him and suggested he visit Bravo, which he did. The general never said anything, but I sensed he now believed I was "Airborne all the way." Since Odom was due for rotation in two days, I asked Matheson to expedite a Silver Star award for Ron so I could present it at the change of command ceremony. The general responded, "How can I get that processed that soon?" "Sir! You're a general," I reminded him. "You can get anything you want." In this instance my brashness paid dividends. Matheson went to bat for Ron, and the next day I pinned the medal on a very surprised Ron Odom. I made a few remarks congratulating a representative from each platoon—the rest of the men occupied the perimeter—and said there would be a "helmet full" of medals for the company as soon as we could process the recommendations. Capt. Dick Boyd, a highly respected and well-liked young officer, replaced Odom.

The day after Ron left, Colonel Collins came by and said that Odom had spoken very highly of me. He described an incident when he had come by my foxhole during a lull and found me asleep. Odom said, "I figured if Ranger wasn't worried and could go to sleep, I shouldn't worry either." Collins thought that was funny. I was not asleep but pretended to be, expecting that Ron would conclude that I had total confidence in him. That was what I wanted, and it happened. The firefight received plenty of press attention. Steve Rowan of CBS News and Henri Hurst, an Associated Press photographer, both told me that all the men lavished praise on me. Bravo's XO, 1st Lt. Tom Courtney, thought, "Having the Ranger on the hill that night was the same as having another rifle company with us in the fight." I told the press the same thing I expressed to anyone who asked: Ron Odom and his troopers deserved all the credit for an outstanding job. His actions and demeanor reassured me that, although in for a rough time, we would prevail. The night with Bravo Company, other than Hill 205, had been the toughest night I had ever spent; thankfully the action in Vietnam ended a lot more happily than the one in Korea.

Operation Benton continued through the rest of August but with diminishing results. On 15 August, the general committed his reserve, the 1/327, but the enemy avoided major confrontations with our forces; the infrequent contacts involved squad-size but usually smaller elements. Matheson was constantly in the air, kept plugged into our communication nets, and visited the battalion command posts every day, but he never micromanaged. The battalion commanders got together. Lt. Col. Bob Yerks—who was in my company a year behind me at West Point—Lt. Col. Gerald Morse, and I took turns hosting. We never had any real agenda other than to pick each other's brains, trying to improve on what we were doing. My battalion's saturation patrolling did uncover two extensive bunker systems and a hospital; ample rice stocks were torched. Company A discovered a bunker complex on 25 August. A medevac chopper approached the area and took a round in the transmission and came down. The company would spend the night guarding the downed aircraft.

I took Command Sgt. Maj. Walter Sabalauski, an airborne legend, and my radio operator with me to the company's location. The landing zone was minuscule, and Arnold, the company commander, reported to me as soon as I landed. I told him the same thing I had said to Odom: "You are in command. I will spend the night and see to it you have all the support you need." As Steve returned to his business, I walked the perimeter. I encountered four soldiers standing in a cleared area smoking and laughing. I pointed out if the "bad guys" dropped in a few mortar rounds or rocket-propelled grenades they would be out of luck and directed them to get into a protected position. After completing my rounds, I returned to Arnold's position and, anticipating the men had ignored my directions, asked the captain to check. As soon as Steve reached their area, eight to ten 82mm mortar rounds landed on the position, killing three men and wounding several others, some seriously. The damaged chopper received a direct hit. Steve received slight fragment wounds and experienced difficulty seeing as his eyes were filled with debris from the explosion. It was now dark, and I climbed into the foxhole dug by Sabalauski and radioman Bill Hill, a son of a grade-school classmate of mine, fully expecting further enemy attacks, but none came. The next morning a maintenance crew arrived, checked the chopper, and concluded that it could not be repaired in the field or lifted from its present location, so Steve ordered it destroyed.

Although a small action—like innumerable others just like it fought every day in Vietnam—it produced twenty-eight casualties, including six killed. I always made a point to visit my wounded men. The aid stations and hospitals were filled with the worst casualties—men without limbs and some of the most horrible wounds imaginable—but I never heard a whimper or complaint. Somehow my troopers always managed a weak smile as they gave the "thumbs-up" sign and said, "Hello, Ranger." Returning that smile was a hard task. I kept close tabs on my troopers and how they were progressing; then I passed that information to the companies. The soldiers always appeared most appreciative; they wanted to know how their buddies were faring.

The next day, Company B found itself involved in a similar situation. A trooper was critically hurt, and for whatever reason the medical choppers refused to land. I ordered my chopper pilot to land at the insecure landing zone. Not only was there intense enemy ground fire in the area, but a severe thunderstorm threatened. During the fight, Dick called for tactical air support. The air force, in addition to strafing the bunkers, dropped some five-hundred-pound bombs only one hundred yards from Dick's position. I was surprised at the way the ground shook at that distance from the explosions. As I felt the reverberations from the five-hundred-pounders, I wondered what it must be like to be caught in an "Arc Light" strike, the name for B-52s dropping two-thousand-pound bombs. The "bad guys" had to be emotionally tough and motivated to continue fighting. Lieutenant Courtney informed me the company stood low on ammunition and was vulnerable to being overrun. As soon as we evacuated the wounded soldier to the hospital, we loaded up the copter with a resupply of ammo and delivered it to the landing zone. Casualties increased, and medevac was still unavailable. Again we went in with the battalion command and control chopper and evacuated the dead and wounded. The company succeeded in repelling the attacking enemy. Although using Charlie Charlie for medical evacuation was unorthodox, on this occasion no other option presented itself. In addition, I gained firsthand information about my company.

Company B had the bad luck of often running into harm's way. The unit suffered something approaching 50 percent losses, forty-five to fifty in combat, with the rest from disease and exhaustion. Daytime temperatures reached triple figures, with humidity nearly 100 percent. I marveled at my men's tenacity and resilience, but the time arrived to pull them out, knowing they would be ready to do it all over again after a few beers, a shower, some sleep, and plenty of hot chow.

Matheson selected the 2/502nd for a special mission, dubbed Operation Strike Force, set for 1 September. An escaped Vietnamese POW provided information about the existence of two prisoner of war camps. He had escaped around 1 August but had not approached American authorities for another three weeks. Subsequently, the ex-POW (the "Source") was flown over the identified area in a normal daily courier run so as not to alert the enemy by increased overflights. The Source isolated two locations, about fifteen miles apart, something that was extremely difficult to do while looking at the jungle canopy from an aircraft. The air force took photos of the areas, and the Task Force Oregon G2 briefed me on the mission on August 28. The G2 estimated the camps contained as many as one hundred prisoners, with many Americans among them.

The battalion came in from Benton the next day. My staff formulated plans and briefed the company commanders, who had been alerted and had executed some concurrent planning with their key subordinates. I directed the commanders to return with a detailed plan of how they would conduct their part of the battalion raid. One asked a logical question, "Why should we make a detailed plan when things never go according to plan?" "You are right," I responded. "Nothing goes according to plan. However, if we have a plan known to all, we can more easily adjust and coordinate than if we are winging it."

We then moved the battalion to a staging area the next day far enough away from the designated area so as to preserve security. The target areas were out of range of any supporting artillery, so we planned on relying on air force tactical aircraft if we ran into trouble. In addition to coordinating tactical aircraft, we planned on the use of gunships, psychological operations aircraft, medevac—everything we might need.

On 1 September, Arnold lifted off from his pickup zone at 0840 and assaulted into two landing zones, one on each side of the suspected POW camp location. After being on the ground about ten minutes, he radioed me that Company A had landed in the wrong area. Just as my officer had suggested during the briefing, our well-laid plans had gone awry. We now had to make adjustments.

The Source told Steve they had passed over the correct area on the way into the landing zones. I told Arnold to sit tight: we would pick up his company and move to the correct area. Steve loaded his troopers onto the choppers, reversed their route, selected landing zones for his platoon leaders, briefed them, and landed. He found the POW camp with seven prisoners, none Americans.

While extracting Steve, I briefed Dick Boyd, who decided to precede his Company B assault elements by five minutes so he could fly over his target area with the Source to ensure that he was going to the correct location. Over his intended target, Boyd radioed that the Source did not recognize the area. Dick said that he wanted to fly around to see if the Source could orient himself. In about ten minutes, Dick reported they had discovered the proper site about one mile north of the planned target. Boyd picked his landing zones and briefed his platoon leaders as they flew to the location. When they arrived, they landed on the selected landing zones and found two POW camps that contained thirteen prisoners, no Americans and two Viet Cong. We had them all out and on the way to base camp by about 1530.

The troopers were really let down because they had expected a bigger prize. The VC said that the captors and prisoners had moved. We were two weeks late at one camp and a month late at the other. The escape of our Source may have triggered the move. Because of the delay between his escape and when he turned himself into authorities, we had missed a great opportunity for rescuing some Americans POWs. Although disappointed by the results, I was very pleased with the outstanding level of professionalism displayed by Captains Arnold and Boyd and their companies.

Following better than two weeks in the field, the troopers deserved some rest. They returned to Chu Lai filthy, unshaven, and tired, but happy. They looked forward to a shower each day, steak every night, plenty of beer, and spacious hex tents in which to bunk. On the night following Strike Force, par-

ties broke out all over the compound, including one for the battalion officers. Within thirty minutes, my Companies A and B were having a shaving
cream war. Pretty soon all of the junior officers were engaged. Colonel Collins
"retired" safely.

After the colonel made his retreat, Lt. Bob Berry, Bravo Company's forward artillery observer, launched a surprise attack on me. I grabbed Berry as
another lieutenant, Ted Orvald, jumped on me and we tumbled to the ground.
My face got scratched in the scuffle, and I wondered if a Purple Heart could be
authorized for being "wounded" in a shaving cream fight. Finally I wrestled the
can from Berry, but it was empty. Without ammunition, I surrendered. I made
a couple of comments about how they had destroyed my "image" and how I
had told Collins what a mature bunch of officers I commanded. They thought
that was hilarious and roared with laughter. I made Arnold the "investigating
officer" to determine who started the fight, promising to "hang" the responsible company commander along with my attacker, Bob Berry. Later it turned
out that the investigating officer was the instigator of the insurrection. Secretly
I was pleased at being included in the battle. Before it started, I had heard some
of them whispering about "getting the Ranger" and wondered if they had the
nerve to jump me. I was not disappointed. Climbing into my cot, I thought
whimsically that we had better get into the field soon. It was too dangerous during stand-downs.

For me, stand-downs proved far busier than when the battalion was in the
bush because so many tedious odds and ends demanded attention. But something that never became routine was the after-action ceremony for the fallen.
Benton cost the battalion the deaths of eighteen troopers. I expressed sadness at
our loss, recognizing each of those no longer with us, and stressed the importance of their sacrifice. Those left behind were reminded they could number
among those honored at the next memorial service. I had tears in my eyes when
the bugler played Taps. Although I did not know all the men lost, they were
still mine.

In sharp contrast to my earlier doubts, I no longer entertained any misgivings about the commitment of these young soldiers—boys most of them, just
out of high school—to the struggle. Regardless of their background (or their
views on the war), they always acquitted themselves as men. They drove themselves day and night for sometimes as many as two months in the field without
respite. While in the bush, they received a hot meal every four or five days. The
physical environment—jungle, heat, monsoon rain, insects, deadly poisonous
snakes, and mountainous terrain—was enough to whip most men. They spent

days scouring the jungle, never knowing exactly the location or strength of the enemy. They might spend several futile days "ghost chasing"—trying to bring the enemy to battle—in what they called a "dry hole"—making no contact—when suddenly all hell would break out and an intense firefight would erupt. The blinding flash of light from a deafening explosion, pain shooting through the body like an electric charge, the numbness as you watch your life blood oozing from your body, and the resulting fear and confusion as you try to regain mental control were all too real.

Add an ever-present yet elusive enemy—highly skilled, well led and armed, and dedicated to their cause—and an inert if not hostile population, and one can imagine the tremendous emotional strain these men endured. Yet, their sole objective was to close with and destroy the enemy; their only complaint was the inability to find him. These airborne troopers represented the finest fighting men I ever had the privilege to serve with, and although I was in command of them for only a short period, an amazingly strong bond welded us together.

After the mostly barren results of Hood River, Benton, and Strike Force, I began to question the efficacy of what we were doing. On paper, the sequenced search-and-destroy, clear-and-secure operations made perfect sense, but there is always a huge gap been theoretical and real war. For one, since Westmoreland's attrition strategy placed almost exclusive priority on destroying the enemy's forces in the field, airmobile battalions continually executed search-and-destroy missions; pacification efforts would be sidelined until the main mission was achieved. That never occurred.

The troops were doing their job, and we suffered casualties, but it seemed like we just nibbled away at the enemy. A sniper would fire a round, a soldier would fall, and the enemy slipped away. Other men fell victim to booby traps or mines, all without the ability to retaliate. Mobility and firepower became the hallmarks of American operations. Air mobility sought to locate and bring enemy forces to battle. American units were exceptionally mobile as long as they remained in their helicopters. Once on the ground, the lightly equipped infantry of the adversary enjoyed a marked advantage. That meant they possessed—in most circumstances—the option of accepting combat or evading it. The greatest frustration was pinning down an elusive enemy that always enjoyed the imitative and, unless surprised, fought on his own terms. By any metric, enemy forces absorbed tremendous punishment. Knowledge of local terrain, long experience in their craft, and intense devotion to the cause made the VC formidable adversaries. As long as the will of the NVA and VC remained unbroken and they stood ready to pay the blood price, they were prepared to play the attrition game. Fortunately I did not have too much time to ponder such questions. Ten days after coming in from Benton, the brigade commenced another set of airmobile insertions and search-and-destroy operations in the highlands west of Tam Ky, just north of where Benton was conducted.

"Sir, God Was Really Looking after You"

Operation Wheeler was a complicated multibattalion attempt to clear the enemy from Base Area 116, a potential staging area for attacks against Da Nang to the north or Chu Lai to the south. On 11 September, the 1/327 landed in the southern sector of the base area. The next day we and the 2/327 did the same, with my battalion in the western sector and Yerks's battalion in the north. For two weeks the saturation patrols and multiple squad-sized ambushes produced few serious contacts. Concluding that the enemy had dispersed and pulled back about twelve miles into the mountains around the abandoned district capital of Hiep Duc, Matheson instructed the two 327th battalions to remount and insert themselves north and south of the town as blocking forces. My battalion would advance in columns of companies overland and attack the suspected enemy concentration. To enhance our battalion firepower, Matheson attached two artillery batteries. The second phase of the operation was set to begin on 26 September.

That night I took to my tent in the tactical command post compound for some much-needed rest. For some reason it occurred to me that big events in my life occurred on the 26th of a month. I was wounded and my Ranger company destroyed on 26 November 1950, and our wedding anniversary also fell on a 26th. But I had no premonition of anything happening. I sat secure inside a heavily defended command post and artillery firebase. For the first time since Wheeler began, I took off my boots before crawling into the sack.

Around midnight there was a blinding flash of light and simultaneously a deafening explosion. It felt as if some giant had slammed both of his hands over my ears. Sitting up, I screamed an epithet. The explosion blew out my eardrums. The concussion produced searing pain, then numbness, followed by fear and confusion as I struggled to recover my mental control.

As I scrambled to put on my boots, another explosion rocked the tent, shattering my eardrums again and lodging a small fragment in my left arm. Immediately adrenaline coursed through me, and I burst out of my lacerated pup tent and raced toward the Tactical Operations Center (TOC). Incoming ordnance exploded everywhere. It occurred to me how my feet had plagued me since being wounded in Korea, yet here I was sprinting in my socks over pierced-steel planking. All of a sudden, my right little toe caught in one of the holes in the planking and I toppled head-over heels to the ground. Despite the precarious situation, I could not help thinking how funny it must have looked as I tumbled down. I picked myself up and made for the hooch of the headquarters commandant, Capt. Stan Gorski, which was sandbagged and had overhead cover. His hooch was connected to the TOC. Not wanting to be shot as an infiltrator in all the confusion, I let Gorski know I was coming. As I entered the hooch, Stan asked if I was all right. Stan then called through the opening to the TOC, "The colonel's been hit!" Despite being dazed and bleeding and having my hearing impaired by two punctured eardrums, I assured everyone I was okay.

My first thought centered on organizing our defense, but Gorski and my S2, Capt. "Andy" Anderson, were already on top of the situation. Our close-in supporting fires began exploding. Reports had been received from my troops, and the artillery battery and brigade headquarters had been notified. My staff had already done everything they needed to do. Gunships were already making runs, firing in support of our perimeter defense.

The enemy continued to mortar the TOC and artillery battery. I moved from position to position, encouraging the men and directing their fire. One of the first officers encountered was Melton, my artillery fire support officer. When I asked him how he was doing, he had difficulty understanding me and appeared dazed. I had Specialist Poinsetta, my ranking medic, check on Ben. Poinsetta reported Melton seemed okay. After completing my inspection I saw Ben again, and he still appeared muddled. I remarked to Anderson that Melton did not seem in control of his faculties. Later, I learned that Ben had reported that I also gave the impression of being dazed. We had both had our eardrums punctured. The troops remarked how funny it was watching Ben and me standing in the open yelling, "What?" back and forth.

Soon, Dustoff choppers flew in to evacuate our wounded. Gorski insisted that Ben be on one of the first ships. After checking with Poinsetta, I had Ben stay. He was in no danger and could still fight. I remained at the TOC until well after daylight, when I was sure that all damage had been or was being repaired

I returned to my tent to take a look. The grenades that shattered my eardrums had exploded eighteen inches from my head, ripping the tent to shreds. My air mattress was riddled. The grenade could have blown my head off. Around my tent, there were several holes left by exploding mortar rounds, and my soldiers found six dud hand grenades. When my radio operator, Private First Class Hill, saw my tent, he said, "Sir, God was really looking after you."

Gorski showed me the fence around our position. A "killer team" had crept up using grass as cover, cut through more than forty strands of protective wire, coming within a yard of a bunker, and infiltrated the firebase. A tuft of grass tied to the wire marked the gap. Gorski had made a communications check with that bunker about twenty minutes before the attack, but the soldier on "alert" told me he had not heard or seen anything. Once inside the perimeter, the VC threw grenades with the intention of sowing as much death and mayhem as possible before a mortar barrage provided cover for their retreat. Lucky for us, the VC mortars fired the barrage prematurely; otherwise the damage would have been much greater. Five days later, a *Hoi Chanh,* a surrendering enemy, walked into the Tactical Operations Center and said that the attacking force had consisted of eighteen Viet Cong and eight had succeeded in infiltrating our position. Obviously, I had failed to ensure the safety of my command post. More personal checks may have prevented what could have been a major tragedy.

I flew to the aid station, where the doctors examined my ears and the superficial wound in my upper arm. Matheson expressed concern over the doctor's warning that if I got water in my ears from rain or even a shower, an infection would probably develop and result in permanent hearing loss. He called me to his tent and, with Colonel Collins present, told me Lt. Col. Howard "Dan" Danford would assume my command. I would take over Danford's job as brigade executive officer, but the general assured me I would return to the 2/502 as soon as the doctor gave his okay. Although I was perhaps as disappointed as I had ever been, I recognized Matheson was only thinking of my future. I knew he was right; with my hearing seriously impaired, I could not communicate effectively on the radio. I called my company commanders and very tersely informed them that Danford would replace me and enjoined them to give him the same devotion and support that they had rendered me. I signed off without waiting for comment. The command shift occurred on 28 September.

The army gave those soldiers whose wounds were not serious the right to determine whether his family would be officially notified. I decided against informing Jeannie. Father Murphy strongly counseled me to change my mind. "She needs to know," he said. "Suppose she hears from someone else?" As it turned out, she did. A reporter from the Columbus newspaper called to ask Jeannie how she felt about me being wounded. Fortunately, I followed the padre's advice and patched through a call via a ham radio. The connection was so poor and my hearing so bad that Murphy had to act as interpreter. The conversation lasted all of two minutes, but Jeannie at least knew I was not badly hurt.

On 7 October, Tom Courtney brought me a most appreciated surprise. He handed me a handful of torn pieces of cardboard—parts of C-Ration cartons; there was no stationery in the jungle. The soldiers in Company B had scribbled many heartfelt messages expressing support, disappointment, and best wishes for a speedy recovery and return to the field. Their demonstration of concern meant everything to me.

When it became obvious my ears would require several months to heal, I thought it unfair to keep Dan Danford and the 2/502 troopers in limbo. First I went to the brigade commander and proposed he make the change permanent, and then I urged Colonel Collins to back up my suggestion. Matheson finally agreed, and on 26 October we held an informal change of command ceremony at the 2/502 TOC. Although I was deflated by knowing I would not return to Strike Force, the decision was best for all concerned.

Ranger-ready at four years old.

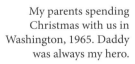

My parents spending Christmas with us in Washington, 1965. Daddy was always my hero.

Flyboy mounting a Stearman biplane trainer, airfield near Gainesville, Florida, 1943.

Captain of the West Point boxing squad, 1948.

Maj. Gen. Bryant E. Moore, the superintendent, presenting me with an award for being an outstanding boxer.

Bill Walls, who, along with David Pollock, dragged me off of Hill 205 under fire.

Eighth Ranger Company. Taken after I had been evacuated to the States, the picture names, except for our KATUSA Kim, the survivors of the original sixty-six who marched off Ranger Hill.

Convalescing at Martin Army Hospital, Fort Benning, Georgia, 1950. This photo appeared in the Columbus newspaper and prompted Jeannie and another girl to visit me.

Distinguished Service Cross. Maj. Gen. John Church, commanding general, Fort Benning, presented the award. The other officer is Lt. Richard Sanders, a classmate at USMA, who received the Silver Star.

Wedding bells, St. Paul Methodist Church, Columbus, Georgia, 26 November 1952.

Cadre and first graduating class, Escuela de Lanceros. Maj. Hernando Bernal Duran, the commandant, is pictured front and center. Lieutenant Moros is to his right, and Lieutenant Negret is to his left. I am looking over Lieutenant Moros's shoulder.

My Special Forces team, Germany, 1961. Preparing to stage scuba training for members of the Greek Raiding Force.

An astonished Ron Odom being awarded an expedited Silver Star after a hot action near Duc Pho, Vietnam, 13 August 1967. Ron displayed great courage and coolness under fire.

Operation Strike Force, 1 September 1967, succeeded in liberating some South Vietnamese POWs, but occurred too late to rescue any Americans, who had been moved a few days earlier.

To the family of Col. Ralph Puckett Jr —
who distinguished himself in very exceptional service to his country —
a proud son of Georgia — a great national patriot.
Lyndon Johnson

Second Distinguished Service Cross. President Johnson pins on the medal awarded for the same fight near Duc Pho on the first day of Operation Benton.

Taken later at Phan Rang. I received a Silver Star at the same ceremony for landing my command and control helicopter twice under intense fire while ferrying ammunition to and evacuating wounded from a hot landing zone. The action occurred on 26 August 1967.

Reunited after Vietnam. Newly promoted Colonel Puckett with Jeannie and the kids. Martha Lane, age twelve, and nine-year-old Thomas are in front; eighth-grader Jeannie stands beside her father. West Point, 1968.

Civilian life brought our family together but challenges lay ahead.

Distinguished Graduate, West Point, June Week, 2004.

Hard Rocket Café, somewhere in Afghanistan. Lt. Col. Jeff Bannister, deputy commander and a fellow Georgian, and a local Afghan pose with me on one of my visits to the Seventy-Fifth Rangers.

Celebrating my eightieth birthday in Afghanistan, November 2006.

Honorary colonel, Seventy-Fifth Ranger Regiment, January 1996–January 2008.

11

Tet

The Unexpected Crossover

The night following the command shift, just after midnight, Lts. Tom Courtney and Jack Keane (a future general and vice chief of staff of the army) came to my tent. After Tom reported and he and Keane took a seat, Tom blurted, "Sir, Bravo 6 is dead!" Tom had tears in his eyes. Bravo 6 was Dick Boyd, a favorite of mine. Tom knew that and wanted me to hear about it firsthand. Boyd—always smiling and so full of life—was always cool under the greatest pressure. Although the details remained unclear, Boyd fell about an hour before, the victim of a single round. Even though in stand-down, the brigade still conducted security sweeps and still took casualties. Dick had spent about an hour and a half in my tent during the last stand-down discussing his future in the army, which I thought was bright. I inquired how they and the men of Company B took the loss of their well-liked and respected commanding officer. As expected, the troopers were stunned. I considered it fortunate they had a mature person like Courtney as the XO. It fell to him to assist the men in accepting one of the ugly realities of war. After bidding them good night, I climbed back into my cot. My mind raced from one memory to another about Dick and our many shared experiences.

I wrote an expressive letter to Dick's parents. Later Dick's father replied. Shortly after returning to the States, I called Mr. Boyd and asked to pay him a visit. He thanked me but said that he was not up to it. Several months later, I called again, and Mr. Boyd asked that I not come; he was heartbroken. All these many years later I cannot think of Dick without recalling the sorrow in his father's voice.

Capt. Tom Mercer took command of the company the next day. He had big shoes to fill, but I had pegged him for company command from our first meeting and entertained no doubt he would measure up. I took advantage of a resupply flight to visit Bravo Company, still in the field but after Wheeler closed down. The men were shaken, but platoon leaders Lts. Ted Orvald and Bob Berry spoke very highly of Mercer. The company had gotten into a firefight immediately after Tom took command. Ted remarked that Mercer established a base of fire and maneuvered just like in a Fort Benning field problem.

I visited with as many troopers as possible during my one-hour stay. They were chastened by Boyd's death but glad to see me. Bravo was not the same. It had only been a month, but the unit already had many new faces. The old hands wanted to know when I would come back to the battalion. I told them Danford was their commander and urged that they continue giving him their complete support. He was their commander and a good leader.

A couple of nights later, I decided to "eat out." I called Bud Connett, the 2/502nd chaplain, and then went to Bravo Company to get Tom Courtney. As XO, Tom commanded the company rear. I knew Tom was in the dumps and needed a change. Two soldiers in his company had been killed that day, and Tom was on the way to identify the bodies in the morgue. Wanting to get Tom's mind off his troubles, I insisted he join us. A leader can be emotionally involved with his soldiers but must not become so embroiled that it affects his performance. We stayed at the Navy Officers' Club in Tam Ky for about an hour and a half before returning to our headquarters. We dropped Tom off in his area and then went to my tent. Bud stopped in to shoot the breeze. After about thirty minutes, I had a call from Tom. He said that Jim Smith (not his name), a young lieutenant, had a problem that Tom wanted me to discuss with Jim. I told Tom to come by and bring Smith with him.

Smith was in the rear area because he had a significant reaction from a bee sting. When Jim and Tom arrived, Bud left. Smith confessed he could not bring himself to kill and cited a couple of times when he had an enemy in his sights but shifted his aim on purpose. After expressing his feelings at some length, he said that he had considered suicide. A son of a Methodist preacher, he had not discussed his feelings prior to deployment. Before arriving "in country," Smith had convinced himself that he could overcome his conscience and had been very proud when he earned the right to wear the crossed muskets insignia of the Infantryman. He said that he wanted to stay with the brigade even though he knew that he might be subjected to some verbal abuse.

Sympathizing with his feelings and believing it took real moral courage to say what he had just told me, I wanted him to discuss his problem with his battalion commander and see if Danforth could use him in his battalion. Jim said he knew that he had to discuss his problem with Danforth but wanted to talk to me first—I was still "the Ranger" to the battalion. We talked for more than an hour, during which time Tom and I convinced him that he should talk with Father Murphy or Father Connett, both outstanding chaplains. Murph might be the better choice since he was older and had been in Vietnam longer. I called Murph and then accompanied Jim to Murph's tent. Then I went to see Dick Kupau, the S1. Dick knew of four jobs in the brigade that Jim could fill. We agreed that Jim could earn his pay, although we had some concern that a real "reluctance to kill" might become contagious. Next morning I discussed the problem with Collins, who commanded the brigade in Matheson's absence (he was on R&R before moving to a job at division). He believed the danger too great and that Smith had to go. I then asked Kupau to contact Lt. Col. Bill Walby, G1 of our parent command, the American Division, if a slot existed for Smith. The brigade had been placed under the operational control of the Twenty-Third Infantry Division when Wheeler morphed into Wallowa back in October. Walby provided a solution. Smith had never shirked his duties or misbehaved before the enemy, but he needed to be taken off the line. Serendipitously, Jeannie sent me a clipping of one of Billy Graham's columns discussing the mental and emotional conflict that people wrestle with when confronted with tough moral choices. I forwarded it to Smith, thinking the clipping would not resolve all the questions but might prove helpful. It would also let him know that he was not forgotten. Jim contacted me and expressed his appreciation and told me that he was contributing in his new job. We had removed Smith from a situation where his presence might have had a detrimental effect on his company and at the same time found a position in which he could still contribute to the brigade's success.

Although I had not much pondered the morality of killing an enemy soldier, the thought had crossed my mind several times, particularly in Korea. Whenever the thought occurred, it was easily dismissed as just part of the soldier's trade. Killing, never personal, was the necessary by-product of seeing the mission through to its successful completion. No matter the carnage wrought on the enemy, I never grew accustomed to seeing the enemy casualties strewn grotesquely about the battlefield.

Death haunts the soldier in many guises. Too often we lost people through avoidable mishaps. Fratricides occurred; one example was a returning patrol that failed to follow the normal challenge-and-password procedure and lost people to friendly fire. These types of casualties were products of stress and forgetting elementary training. You take young American boys and equip them with weapons and vehicles, and the result is casualties from accidents. But older men, including officers, were not exempt. One of our captains accidentally shot and killed a fellow officer in his bachelor officer quarters, another case of carelessness and failure to follow proper procedures. The grief-stricken young officer visited me several times. I consoled him in the hope of snapping him out of his depressed state. He became withdrawn and stopped attending the informal officer parties. He became a liability to himself and those serving under his command. I cautioned him about taking any unnecessary risks. I told him that if he got himself killed, I would feel responsible. Colonel Collins asked me about him. A few days later he died in combat, although without any indication that he took an unusual risk.

Unhappy Reunion with the Rest of the Screaming Eagles

As XO the biggest task involved trying to find something useful to do. The staff—Maj. Richard Kupau (S1), Maj. Ted Geesey (S2), Lt. Col. Bud Sydnor (S3), Maj. Jerry Scott (S4), and Maj. Wayne Prokup (S5–Civil Affairs)—worked together like a finely tuned engine. The special staff—the commander of headquarters and headquarters company, public information officer, provost marshal, the surgeon, and the chaplains—likewise required almost no supervision. I accompanied Iron Duke or Cottonmouth on a few visits to the field, but since I made no contribution, I stopped going, instead spending most of my time at brigade headquarters and with the supporting units.

One advantage of being on the brigade staff was the ability to see friends who visited our brigade. My old friend from Korea and Benning, John Vann, came by on three occasions. John had come up in the world. A disgruntled Vann had retired from the army after his celebrated tour as an advisor for a Vietnamese division—celebrated because his scathing criticism of the inadequacies of the Saigon government and ARVN received wide press reportage. Equally unhappy out of the army, he accepted a position that allowed him to return to Vietnam as pacification representative in the Agency for International Development. Before long, Vann took over direction of civilian pacification programs in all the provinces around Saigon. In May 1967, the Office of Civilian Operations that exercised jurisdiction over all American civilian agencies underwent reorganization, received a military chain of command, and a new impetus, as suggested by its new name, Civilian Operations and Revolutionary Development Support (CORDS). Pacification no longer would be reactive, and the head of CORDS, Robert Komer, pushed for and, against army opposition, got Vann as his deputy in charge of the pacification campaign in III

Corps Zone. John now held the equivalent rank of a major general. Although Vann remained acerbic as always, he never launched into any assault on West-moreland's attrition strategy and multibattalion search-and-destroy operations. Mostly we talked about the old days. He looked very tired and worn. He urged me to extend and promised that I would get a brigade. I thanked him but said, "Nothing doing. I'm ready to go home."

Wheeler, the largest operation of its type in 1967, began winding down in the middle of November. The brigade would redeploy to Phan Rang, its "home" in Vietnam. The 3/506th Parachute Infantry Regiment (PIR), our fourth battalion, preceded us, arriving "in country" as an intact unit—a real rarity in Vietnam. The 196th Infantry Brigade was moving into our area, and their support battalion was occupying our headquarters area. The commander of that battalion was Lt. Col. Frank Clarke, a West Point classmate of mine whom I had not seen since 1950, when we graduated from the Infantry School. The handover of responsibility for the area went smoothly.

Frank's mess hall assumed responsibility for feeding my troops. One morning, Frank's mess sergeant came to me apologizing because breakfast had been late. I assured him that it was of no consequence and that I appreciated what he was doing for us. He then told me that some of my troopers had launched a night raid and cut down the cooks' tent on top of them as they slept. The cooks were so frightened they ran away and had not been seen since because they had heard so much about airborne soldiers. After issuing blanket apologies including to Clarke, I wanted to place the culprits on "C" Rations and put them to work for Frank's first sergeant until we left the area. At the same time, I understood their prank—and that nobody gave up the names of the perpetrators—reflected the esprit de corps of airborne troopers and their contempt for "legs" (troopers wore their khakis and green trousers tucked in and bloused as opposed to "straight-legs," or nonjumpers).

We completed the move to Phan Rang in time for a four-day Thanksgiving stand-down. Around the same time, word arrived of my selection for promotion to colonel (number 761 on the list). The papers probably would not come through until July or August. Although I was pleased at being selected, it did not seem particularly important at the time.

The brigade did not have much time to adjust to its new surroundings. We drew responsibility for performing another search-and-destroy operation about sixty miles west of Phan Rang, in the highlands around Bảo Lộc. Intelligence indicated the area served as an enemy staging zone. Operation Klamath Falls, the last staged by the brigade as a separate command, was set to open on

27 November. Just as the jumping-off date arrived, Lt. Col. Bob Yerks, the commander of the 2/327th, and his XO, Maj. Jim Waldeck, ended up in the hospital with food poisoning. Collins placed me in temporary command of the battalion. With no time to spare, I explained to each company commander the reason for the hasty change, stressing that Yerks would return as soon as he recovered.

We moved to Bảo Lộc on 30 November. The flight proved interesting. The highlands appeared much different from the coastal area I just left: a famous tea-growing region, it was more prosperous and less densely populated, the fields were well kept, and the houses larger and supplied with power lines. The pilot lost his bearings and started flying in circles. When he flew over the town, I borrowed his chart and had him oriented in about fifteen minutes and we landed safely. At three thousand feet, Bảo Lộc at least provided a break from the heat of the coast.

The battalion bivouacked in Bảo Lộc with the 2/502 immediately adjacent. I threw some of its troopers for a loop when I responded to their "Strike Force" greeting with "No Slack," the slogan of the 2/327. They did not know about the temporary command shift. Lt. Col. Paul Mueller, the senior provincial advisor, put on a briefing for us. A member of the same cadet company at West Point, Mueller had been a classmate at Carlisle.

The two battalions staged out of Bảo Lộc with the 2/327 area of operations halfway between Phan Thist, on the coast south of Phan Rang, and Bảo Lộc. The assault did not proceed according to script. Although in Vietnam for months, because of rotations, the Tenth Aviation Battalion had very few personnel experienced in conducting an operation of this size. The flight schedule went through a series of alterations that created confusion that caused slippages in the scheduled lifts. Consequently, the air support hit the area two hours before the insertion, and we had no artillery prep. Fortunately, the assaulting troops met no resistance.

Little else went right with Klamath Falls. Once again the intelligence proved flawed, out-of-date, or had been compromised. Our sweeps uncovered little evidence of an enemy buildup and made only sporadic contacts with local force units. After about ten days in a "black hole," we were extracted. Yerks resumed command as soon as the battalion returned from the field, and I went back to brigade headquarters. I welcomed the opportunity to work with the 2/327th, and during the stand-down the battalion officers invited me to a small gathering and presented me with a plaque commemorating my brief command of the battalion

When the rest of the 101st completed its movement to Vietnam, the "Always

First" Brigade would revert to division control. None of us were happy losing our "separate" status and the freedom it afforded while under what amounted to the titular command of Task Force Oregon and the Americal Division. Jealous of their deserved reputation as members of the finest brigade in the army, many of the brigade staff made no secret of their feelings. I decided to reel them in before the situation got out of hand. At the next day's afternoon briefings, I heard the usual snide remarks. As Matheson and Collins left the briefing tent, I told the staff to remain behind.

Mounting the podium, I told the staff that I understood that we would rather maintain our separate brigade status, together with our own combat team composed of all the support that we needed. The brigade had established an unparalleled working relationship among the staff and commanders. We not only functioned well together but liked and respected each other. But I reminded them we belonged to the 101st Airborne Division. Not only was it unprofessional to criticize division, its commander and staff, but it demoralized our subordinates and set a bad example for our troopers. In a stern voice I told them criticisms of higher headquarters would terminate as of that moment and dismissed them. My admonition must have worked because carping and fault-finding ended.

Some things did change under division control. For starters, Matheson left us, replaced by Collins. The staff respected Collins but missed the Iron Duke. Coordination with supporting units never ran as smoothly. In future, brigade operations would be supported by whatever assets division assigned. Naturally plenty of areas of friction developed, and morale suffered. My self-esteem took a dip because the command shift had no bearing on my position.

Maj. Gen. Olinto Mark Barsanti commanded the division. Barsanti, the son of immigrants and a mustang (worked his way up the ranks), might have been the most decorated officer in the army. He now held the plumiest appointment as commander of the 101st. An original Ranger and the youngest battalion commander in World War II, he assembled an outstanding record in Korea and in all the right staff assignments. Barsanti was a force of nature who possessed a mercurial temper. He probably bore no love for West Pointers and definitely had a chip on his shoulder against the First Brigade.

While the First Brigade won laurels in Vietnam, the rest of the division had been constantly bled of its best airborne personnel. Because of the rotation rules, officers and men with combat experience in Vietnam bore no obligation to return. The division also provided replacements for the heavy casualties suffered by the First Brigade and the 173rd Airborne Brigade. In particular, the division lacked its quota of officers and especially experienced NCOs. Most of the replacements funneling into Fort Campbell were the products of recent training cycles, not airborne-qualified men. Virtually every member of the First Brigade wore the Combat Infantryman Badge, in sharp contrast to men in the Second and Third Brigades.

My first contact with the general proved memorable. As XO, it fell to me to escort Barsanti on his first visit to the brigade. We proceeded to the center of the area where some Vietnamese were filling sandbags to revet the Tactical Operations Center. He asked where we had obtained the civilians. I began, "Sir, we usually. . . ." With that he exploded and berated me for all he was worth. Barsanti informed me in no uncertain terms that the First Brigade was not the only unit that had any combat experience. The eruption went on for what seemed forever; when he finally finished, he immediately became placid and we continued on our walk through the brigade area as if nothing had happened. Obviously, my "we usually" hit a raw nerve. His tirade took place in full view of enlisted men; Barsanti got his message across loud and clear.

December meant my time for R&R (rest and relaxation) had arrived. I needed a break. The rotation system deservedly drew much criticism, but after six months in Vietnam, the time and the rapid tempo of operations all seemed to meld. Emotionally, I needed some downtime and the opportunity to see Jeannie. We met in Hawaii. Aside from doing the normal tourist things—like taking sightseeing drives on Oahu—we chiefly sat on the beach and relaxed. Because of my ears, I could not even get into the water. One day we sat beside a lady from the mainland. When Jeannie mentioned my pending return to Vietnam, the lady asked in all seriousness, "My dear, are you going with him?" That told me all I needed to know about how much the public knew about conditions in Vietnam. Jeannie was concerned about my safety, but our time together seemed to allay many of her fears.

Returning to Vietnam required some mental gymnastics. Not long after, just before Christmas, I received instructions to report to Cam Ranh Bay for a special decoration ceremony. President Johnson, making his second and last tour of Vietnam, wanted to meet with the troops and pin on some medals. About two dozen of us stood there in ascending rank of award—DSCs and Silver Stars. Johnson, accompanied by Westmoreland, talked about his Silver Star in World War II. What pleased me most was that I saw Maj. Gen. Hank Schweiter, who had been a colonel in special operations in the Pentagon, my boss, in the stands. I had always admired him and the way he conducted himself, and I was pleased he witnessed the ceremony.

In most respects, matters continued as before under the new command structure. As the only operational reserve, the division reverted to "fire brigade" status. In our first operation under Barsanti's command, the First Brigade acted independently, with two ARVN battalions and Special Forces attached, in far-distant Phuoc Long and Quang Duc Provinces, on the Cambodian border astride the II and III Corps Zone boundaries.

Operation San Angelo, conducted much of the time in abandoned rubber plantations, was intended to prevent infiltration of manpower and materiel across the border during the Tet truce. By the middle of January, the San Angelo task force was in place and began conducting sweeps. Even though an ARVN battalion had been roughly handled by a NVA regiment at Son Be in Phoug Long as recently as October, our units again made only rare contacts. Given that not much was going on in our sector and with the beginning of the holiday truce, Collins decided the time was right to take some R&R. He flew off for Hawaii and left me in command of the brigade. The date was 29 January 1968, two days before the NVA/VC launched their Tet Offensive.

Light at the End of the Tunnel

As 1967 drew to a close, all indications pointed to headway being made. Westmoreland told the president the end was in sight; the crossover had been accomplished, and the NVA remained under control and the VC were on the run. The bombing campaign of the North began to bite. The revolving door government in Saigon appeared stable; voting was held under a new constitution for the National Assembly and Gen. Nguyễn Văn Thiệu's election as president. The Phoenix Program, dedicated to eliminating the enemy's leadership, gained momentum; CORDS reported 68 percent of the population under Saigon's control. The leadership in Hanoi came to a similar conclusion; they could not win a war of attrition. Just before New Year, the North signaled their willingness to open diplomatic negotiations. It was a diversion, as was the request for the cease-fire during the Tet celebration of the lunar new year. Hanoi was not looking for a settlement; rather, it had decided to go for broke, launching a massive offensive on South Vietnamese cities designed to hammer ARVN, inflict casualties on American forces, spur the peasants into open rebellion, and topple the Saigon government.

The Tet Offensive represented a colossal American intelligence failure. Since major American forces had deployed in Vietnam, U.S. Military Assistance Command, Vietnam (MACV) had tried to force the enemy to fight our kind of war and persisted in conducting more than one thousand battalion-level search-and-destroy operations. Despite the general's rosy claims, with a half million troops "in country," we achieved a stalemate. The frontier battles—Dak To, Con Thien, and the massive buildup around Khe Sanh—convinced Westmoreland the enemy was prepared to go to Phase III, conventional warfare; and he decided it would center in the northern two provinces. Half the American maneuver battalions were deployed there (including the Second Brigade, moved to the vicinity of Hue, in I Corps Area). MACV was not entirely wrong; the NVA/VC were poised to come out and fight, but nobody knew in what strength and that their center of gravity lay in the heavily populated coastal areas, not the borders and at Khe Sanh. Just after midnight on 30 January 1968 they hit Saigon, thirty-six provincial capitals, and sixty-four of the 242 district towns in addition to multiple fixed positions and airfields.

Barsanti wanted San Angelo closed down, and the brigade moved with dispatch to Biên Hòa, which housed division headquarters, in the northern environs of Saigon. Already on 1 February, elements of my old battalion had been rushed by air and engaged in heavy fighting for Ton Son Nhut airport and around MACV headquarters. Our headquarters was tasked to begin the movement of the rest of the brigade no later than 3 February. Barsanti and several of his staff arrived at headquarters in Song Be. I escorted him and his entourage to the tent, where the brigade operations officer, Maj. Othar Shalikashvili (brother of the future chairman of the Joint Chiefs of Staff), stood by to deliver the briefing. Shali, one of the sharpest officers I have ever known, enjoyed that same reputation with both commanders and staff. We expected everything to go smoothly.

Shali began, and after completing a two-minute introduction said, "Sir, we recommend. . . ." Barsanti exploded and launched into one of his patented harangues, while Shali stood stiffly at attention on the stage. I sat uneasily beside the general. When the tempest subsided, Shali proceeded. Almost immediately, Barsanti went off again. The depth of Barsanti's belligerence was more than an old "brown shoe" general tearing into a junior staff officer. When the storm did not abate, I mounted the stage, took the pointer from Shali, and stood at attention by him. When Barsanti's wrath subsided, I told Shali to take a seat. Given my track record, the chances of me pouring oil on the flames stood pretty high: "Sir, what Major Shalikashvili was presenting were my recommendations to you for your employment of this brigade." Without pause, I continued, "If you will listen to me, I will go over those recommendations. You will see that they support your concept for the division." I proceeded, and the general remained silent. When I finished, he said very calmly, "Come down and take a seat," indicating the one I had vacated.

In the next ten minutes—it seemed much longer—he told me how he operated. He said that he listened to his commanders and staff and took care of them. He mentioned that Col. Larry Mowery had recently been awarded the Silver Star. The general was completely at ease and spoke calmly and softly. I could not fathom his intent any more than I could his command style, unless this was Barsanti taking a page out of Patton's playbook. The general and his staff departed, evidently agreeing with my proposals. The artillery commander called me aside and complimented me on my defense of Shali and for defusing an explosive situation.

Sydnor, who left the brigade staff to command a battalion in the 327th, confronted a real problem. Because of poor flying weather, the uncertain security situation around Biên Hòa airbase, and the lack of availability of overstretched transport aviation, Sydnor could not complete his move before the day ended. After careful consideration, I instructed him to reverse his movement and return his deployed elements to their original position. I was not going to be caught with a battalion Tactical Operations Center split into two locations. It was my call, and Bud happily concurred.

I immediately radioed division, and Barsanti got on the radio. In his usual manner, he began to raise hell and ordered me to "Relieve Sydnor." I told the general several times I had given the order to Sydnor to reverse his movement. Barsanti would have none of that; I am not sure he ever heard what I told him. Finally, I said, "Yes, Sir!" That ended the conversation. I flew to Sydnor's location and pulled him aside. Bud was obviously distressed when I related what had transpired. With a smile on my face, I relieved and immediately reinstated him. We shook hands, and I promised him all the support that I could muster and departed. I guessed correctly that the general would let the episode pass. Sydnor continued as battalion commander, and nothing was ever mentioned about the incident. Needless to say, I was immensely relieved when Collins returned.

By the time the brigade arrived and deployed, the intensity of the fighting around Biên Hòa had slackened. Now the job centered on sealing the approaches to the capital district and destroying Communist forces attempting to withdraw from the built-up areas. Although we received alerts of impending enemy actions and nerves remained raw as terrorist incidents in the city continued, basically we settled into the familiar pattern of setting up cordons and conducting security sweeps. With the threat to Saigon removed, the brigade returned to Phan Rang for some rest and relaxation.

The respite proved short-lived. On 14 February, we loaded on air transport for a flight to the new division headquarters, Camp Eagle, a few miles south of Hue, and then an overnight shift into the A Shau Valley, located in Thua Thien Province, I Corps Area. The battle to regain Hue, under way since the NVA raised their flag over the citadel on 31 January, had approached its climax as the battalions moved into their areas of operation. The brigade's mission involved sealing the A Shau Valley, the chief infiltration route adjacent to the Ho Chi Minh Trail and the Laotian border, along Highway 547, denying the enemy the ability to move reinforcements and supplies into the fight for Hue. Conducting sweeps on either side of the highway, the brigade made contact with stay-behind-parties but no large enemy units. Once Hue was secured, the forces in I Corps Zone concentrated on writing off as many of the exposed enemy as possible as they pulled back into their mountain sanctuaries (Operation Carentan I). The First Brigade remained in place blocking the escape routes until 31 March, when Carentan moved into its second phase. Higher command ordered two brigades of the First Cavalry Division to launch air assaults into the heart of the A Shau (Operation Delaware). The brigade, pulled from Carentan II, now became the blocking force for the First Cavalry Division but shifted its front, now moving west down Highways 547 and 547A into the mouth of the valley.

Other than overseeing administration and logistics and backstopping the commanding officer, I almost felt left out as XO. Whenever a general or brigade commander visited our headquarters, I stole a couple minutes and asked him for another command. Several responded, "You have already had your battalion. I need to look after my own men." The army's personnel policy—making sure battalion commands were widely distributed—took precedence over placing officers with experience in combat units. To keep myself busy and improve the unit's readiness when the next command shift transpired, I enlisted the aid of Kupau and began recording best practices and putting together a manual on administrative, supply, and tactical procedures. When commanders and staff rotate at any level, the incoming team usually starts cold. Practical experience may be the best teacher, but it is often very expensive in lives and combat efficiency. We gathered input from others and completed the document, but whether it served any purpose remained a question. I would not be around to see.

In spring 1968, vacancies opened in two battalions: one in the Third Brigade commanded by Colonel Mowery and another in Col. John Cushman's First Brigade. Collins gave me the choice, and I picked Mowery's without giving it much thought. Cushman had a reputation of being hard to get along with.

I knew and liked Mowery from serving together in the Infantry Branch in the Pentagon and considered him a highly competent officer.

At my request, Collins held a small ceremony in a jungle clearing attended only by a color guard. Collins also arranged a small send-off in his mess. "The Ranger wants another command," he remarked, "although he doesn't need one." As far as having my battalion commander chit, he was right, but from my perspective, for my professional development, there remained much to learn. After enduring all that time feeling worthless as XO, I needed that command for my peace of mind. Although unjustified, my sentiments were real.

The "Bastard Battalion"

On 9 April 1968, I traded assignments with Lt. Col. Enzo Klinner and assumed command of the 1/506 "Currahees." The Third Brigade resembled the old First Brigade in that it was designated as the "fire brigade" under II Field Forces command—at least in theory. As a result of Tet, II Field Force oversaw all the combined assets of American elements—including three divisions—deployed in and around Saigon. My arrival coincided with the opening of Operation Toan Thang, which translated as Complete Victory. The mission: drive all remaining NVA/VC troops from the III Corps Area and the capital district and complete the destruction of company-and battalion-sized enemy units before they withdrew into their safe havens. Since Tet, Third Brigade had moved from one OPCON (operational control) assignment to another, eventually in four corps zones. When I caught up with them, the brigade held a static defensive position in coastal Gia Dinh Province, south and east of Saigon, in IV Corps Area under operational control of the Ninth Infantry Division.

The First Battalion held a ring of sandbagged bunkers surrounding a village. Gia Dinh is in the Saigon River delta. Flat as a pool table, the heavily populated and intensely cultivated area was segmented by tidal estuaries, rivers, and innumerable canals. The brigade's role centered on guarding the southern approaches to Saigon, but it struck me as odd that an airborne battalion's combat power was expended providing security for a village having no discernible military value. I soon discovered the Third Brigade did a lot differently.

After the change of command ceremony, I walked the perimeter by myself. In the first dugout, I happened upon a trooper sitting on top of the bunker in his skivvies reading a magazine. As I stood in front of him, he passed a glance my way and resumed his reading. I introduced myself as his battalion commander and required him to come to attention. In response to my questions, he replied he was manning the bunker. When asked about the whereabouts of his weapon, he replied he kept his rifle in the barracks because it saved him from cleaning it. When I pointed out the village had recently come under rocket and small-arms fire, he assured me that if that happened he would return to the barracks to retrieve his rifle. Here stood a soldier in my battalion who saw nothing unusual about being on perimeter security without his rifle. I instructed that he return to the barracks, get into uniform, and return with his weapon. Proceeding to the next bunker, the same sight greeted me. I never chewed out either of these soldiers because they bore no blame if their superiors shirked their leadership responsibilities. Officers set the benchmarks; junior officers and NCOs rise to or fall below basic requirements based on the standards set by their commanding officer.

Returning to the barracks area, I called the company commanders together. I clearly, specifically, calmly recounted what had transpired and then made clear my expectations. End of meeting. I made no threats; that was not my style. The next day's inspection of the defenses revealed the same story. I reassembled the company commanders, pointed out the lack of improvement, and explained I would not tolerate any more slackness. Several of them were thinking about applying for Regular Army status so I told them about my experience in the Pentagon selecting reserve officers for commissioning. "I do not like making threats," I said, "but if you do not correct immediately the shortcomings I have enumerated, I will relieve you from command." I assured them they could forget about getting a regular commission or making major. Things did improve but grudgingly and not quickly enough.

I found it hard to believe the difference between my old unit and this battalion. The 1/506 also had a number of instances of soldiers sleeping on guard, an unpardonable, and potentially deadly, breach. I appointed my executive officer as trial council, and he won every case, which was not difficult since an official record, signed by a duty officer, existed describing each violation. The number of cases provided yet further proof that the battalion suffered from a very real discipline problem. The officers and NCOs in the 502nd knew their business and performed. But they were all volunteers, many of them had returned to Vietnam from prior tours, and they were proud bearers of the airborne tradition. The officers, NCOs, and enlisted men of the Currahees, despite the unit's proud history, exhibited no esprit de corps. Most were the scraping of training facilities in the States. The replacements that filtered in came from the same category. The Third Brigade had never completed its in-country training before being loaded on copters and receiving their baptism of fire during Tet in the fighting around the Biên Hòa air base. Their second deployment, thirty-six hours later, took them to Phuoc Long Province in the Central Highlands, where they saw bitter street-to-street fighting at Song Be. Toward the end of March they returned to performing security operations for the air base before shifting south of Saigon into their static role in the Delta. Whereas Strike Force relished their "fire brigade" role, the Currahees called themselves the "bastard battalion"; they were nomads who moved from pillar to post without much rhyme or reason. Determined to change this state of affairs, I put the men to work improving the defenses, strengthening some of the bunkers and building others that covered routes of approach. Mowery, on one visit, told me that we would soon assume a more active role. I hoped morale and discipline would improve once these men ended their static role.

Intelligence indicated the enemy was engaged in a buildup in preparation for a second offensive against Saigon-Cholon. The brigade's mission shifted to interdicting and blocking the flow of enemy supplies by cutting infiltration routes that converged in neighboring Long An Province. The brigade operations officer briefed the assembled brigade staff, my staff, and me on the new mission. I requested the normal tactical air, artillery, gunship support that preceded every First Brigade assault. The S3 said that the prep would be planned but not fired unless we faced opposition. I was incredulous and expressed my disapproval. "Why not fire the prep just in case?" I asked. "It's only ammunition. Why not do everything reasonable to protect the troops as they make the landing?" The S3 said that Third Brigade policy called for fire preps only if needed. I responded quietly and firmly, "My battalion won't go unless we have the prep." Taken aback, the S3 said he needed to check with Mowery. The expected confrontation never happened. Mowery said, "Give Ranger what he wants." We got the prep, and firing preparations became part of the standing operating procedures for the brigade, at least for the 1/506. The change was well received in the battalion.

The Third Brigade routinely extracted the patrolling troops every day. Companies, inserted at dawn and extracted early in the afternoon, had less opportunity to find and eliminate the enemy and were more exposed to attacks while being pulled out, always a potentially dangerous operation. I briefed the brigade S3, informing him my battalion would employ the First Brigade method and remain in the bush for several days with resupply every five days. The surprised S3 again went to Mowery, who again approved. Mowery knew I was not trying to upstage him, and he merely wanted to tap into the First Brigade's experience.

For once, intelligence proved correct. During the early-morning hours of May Day, the Communists opened the second phase of the Tet Offensive. The brigade conducted a series of reconnaissances-in-force, Eagle Flights to fix enemy positions, sweeps seeking enemy camps and supply caches, night ambush patrols, and airmobile assaults against targets of opportunity—all designed to intercept and destroy the enemy units before they reached Saigon. We began experiencing heavy contacts. Mowery gave me a free hand to fight my battalion. Instead of crashing through the bush in company-size formations, making enough noise to alert any enemy within miles, the units operated in small groups. Instead of always fighting the enemy on his terms, we began to locate him and initiate actions. The only time the elements united was for resupply. Another ambush trick I picked up involved prepositioning a platoon along trails leading to the extraction landing zone. The company, minus the platoon, would pull out as normal. The enemy, attracted by the incoming helicopters, typically sent in troops—our men always left behind what they considered excess baggage—to forage. The concealed platoon then tripped the ambush.

At that time I had a rifle company from another battalion under my operational control. The company was commanded by an exceptionally sharp first lieutenant. I selected him for the ambush mission and gave him a day to plan it. He came back with a well-conceived design. When he finished his briefing, I congratulated him and wished him good luck. He stood on the platform for a moment and then blurted, "Sir, aren't you going to tell me how to do it?" "No." I responded. "You're the company commander. You know your company and more about commanding it than I will ever know. You have an excellent plan. I will ensure that you have all the support you could possibly need. I have complete confidence in you."

It worked like a charm. Shortly after dark, the enemy in platoon strength approached the landing zone, and the unseen operational control platoon opened fire and killed approximately eight enemy. When Mowery received the report, he immediately ordered his Charlie Charlie fired up and invited me to accompany him. We flew over the platoon and radioed congratulations to the company commander, who had stayed with his platoon. Mowery called this technique "bushmaster." The company walked back to base the next morning. During the debriefing, the young officer did not attempt to cover his elation. He and his company had performed perfectly. As the young lieutenant said goodbye, he remarked, "Sir, I hope you'll ask for me again. I like working in your battalion. You don't tell me what to do." I thanked him again and wished him well.

Not long after I had taken command, my outstanding battalion communications officer, Capt. John "Jay" Hendrix, told me that he had applied for a transfer from the Signal Corps to Infantry and wanted command of a rifle company. I promised him he would have the next company that came open. Mowery, demonstrating the typical operator's dismissal of the support branches, took a dim view of the suggestion. "Ralph," he asked, "have you lost your mind? Hendrix is Signal Corps!" True, Hendrix lacked any of the Infantry background required of a rifle company commander. Not deflected, I expressed my complete confidence in Hendrix—which had nothing to do with him being a Georgian who had gone to Georgia Tech—and the conviction he could more than handle the assignment. Mowery, as always, supported my decision. When a vacancy appeared, Hendrix got his company. My instincts proved on the mark; Jay earned two Silver Stars in Vietnam and ended his career as a four-star general and commander of U.S. Army Forces Command (FORSCOM).

After heavy contact one night, Hendrix returned with his company from one of his early forays into the jungle. As the company entered our battalion area, I told Jay that General Westmoreland was visiting and that I had invited him to speak to the company. Flabbergasted and visibly upset, Jay blurted, "Sir, we're filthy. We can't let the general see us looking like this!" I dismissed his concerns, telling him the general wanted to meet troops fresh from an action and that it would provide a big morale boost for the troops to speak to and shake the hand of the commanding general, himself a former commander of the Screaming Eagles. Assuring Hendrix I would take any flak—and expecting none—I told him to assemble about twenty of his soldiers.

The meeting was memorable; the troops were grubby after five days in the bush. I was proud of Jay and his troopers. When Westmoreland approached, in his starched and creased fatigues, I reported and explained that these troopers had just come in from a sweep and the night before had engaged the enemy in a hot firefight. Westmoreland went from trooper to trooper asking questions and commenting briefly. In one exchange, a soldier said that he had been wounded by a punji stake. The general turned to Mowery and said, "We don't give Purple Hearts for punji stake wounds, do we?" I never knew the policy but as Westmoreland continued down the line, I remarked quietly, "Don't worry, son. If there is any problem with your Purple Heart, you can have one of mine." A seemingly pleased General Westmoreland bid us good-bye and left.

My XO informed me that Hendrix had recommended that I be awarded a medal for some recent action. The event had something to do with directing my helicopter into a hot area; I felt that no medal was deserved. If anybody merited a medal, it was the pilot. While appreciative of Hendrix's sentiment, I worried the citation might cause Jeannie undue concern about my taking unnecessary risks. No recommendation was submitted.

Toward the end of May, MACV selected the brigade to take part in a major operation in the Central Highlands. Intelligence indicated large concentrations of NVA in the triborder region in Kontum Province. To preserve security, we received no briefing, and all division patches were removed from the uniforms and unit markings from the helicopters. On 24 May, the brigade completed its movement in C-130 transports to Dak Tek Special Forces Camp in western Kontum Province, where we passed under the operational control of the Fourth Division. The landings took place on a cold landing zone because our twin unit, the First Brigade of the Fourth ID, had been inserted the day before against no opposition. Over the next three days the brigade conducted a reconnaissance-in-force and detected nothing. The enemy had evidently withdrawn into Laos and Cambodia. The next day, 28 May, the brigade airlifted to Dak To.

The enemy used the same "rope-a-dope" technique they had employed in Phase I of Tet. The NVA units that moved into Kontum Province prompted the movement of American strength from populated centers—their objectives—into a black hole in the border regions. The day after we arrived, the NVA/VC unleashed Mini Tet against Saigon. For the next two weeks, the brigade conducted a series of fruitless operations to locate the enemy. It rained the entire time, with drizzle and low fog in the mornings giving way to heavy downpours in the afternoon. We humped up steeply sloped and rugged mountains and through double- and triple-canopied rainforests and never saw an enemy soldier. The entire brigade captured a grand total of four small-arms weapons; my battalion captured none. We had a single casualty and that was obviously noncombat. Operation Mathews was scrubbed on 8 June, and the other two battalions began their redeployment.

The airborne troops were leaving the area, but the NVA stayed. Although organized in conventional battalions, regiments, and divisions, the NVA could readily break down into squads and platoons and operate as guerrillas, avoid detection, and withdraw under pressure into their sanctuaries and with amazing speed reconstitute themselves, fully capable of executing relatively large-scale missions. This is what happened here. On 10 June, they launched a battalion-size assault against the Dak Pek camp. For the next forty-eight hours the area was pounded by artillery and the largest concentration of Arclight attacks to date. After the B-52s finished, my battalion mounted a reconnaissance and pursuit operation. Again the enemy had melted away. The survey of bomb damage revealed destroyed bunkers but no bodies or weapons; there was no demon-

CONFIDENTIAL

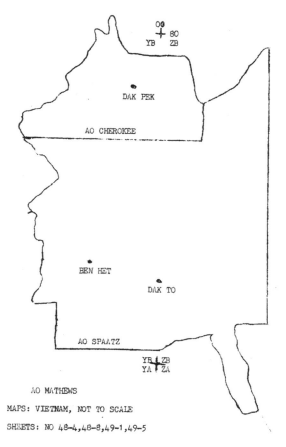

AO MATHEWS

MAPS: VIETNAM, NOT TO SCALE

SHEETS: NO 48-4,48-8,49-1,49-5

Inclosure 1

CONFIDENTIAL

Task Force Mathews, 24 May–12 June 1968, Kontum Province. Cambodia is west; Laos is north. From Headquarters Fourth Infantry Division, *Combat After-Action Report,* 13 June 1968, Vietnam Center and Archive, Texas Tech University.

strable return for the massive investment of firepower. The next day Task Force Mathews was deactivated, and the battalion boarded C-130s for Biên Hòa.

Even before the other two battalions could unpack their gear, orders came instructing them to move about thirty miles from the Phouc Vinh base camp to Cu Chi. The brigade now fell under the operational control of the Twenty-Fifth Infantry Division. When I went to the headquarters of the Twenty-Fifth ID brigade we were replacing, the commander barely acknowledged my presence. Looking around, I saw Lt. Col. Gordon Sumner, the artillery liaison officer whom I had first met in Task Force Dolvin in Korea. Later I attended a staff meeting of the battalion holding the area we were assigned. The battalion S3 issued instructions to each company. He went into minute detail specifying what trails to follow, almost yard by yard. Accustomed to our battalion's procedures that delegated responsibility, I was confounded. Obviously line Infantry did things differently.

Be that as it may, once our battalion moved into our designated area of operations, I never had any face-to-face contact with any member of the Twenty-Fifth Division. About a third of the division held security positions. Initially placed in this role, we went immediately into the bush. The enemy had been launching nightly rocket attacks; our mission centered on suppressing the fire coming from a ridge overlooking a village. We believed that aggressive patrolling might keep the enemy off balance and prevent or inhibit their rocket attacks. The S3 developed a plan that gave each of our companies an area of operation and a general direction of movement. How each unit accomplished its mission was left to its immediate commander. That had always been my policy. Almost at once, one company surprised and eliminated a small enemy detachment as it prepared to fire some five-inch rockets. The enemy rocketing ceased.

After Mini Tet, the new Toan Thang directive called for active search-and-destroy missions to upset the enemy's plans for a third stage of their offensive expected in late July. At first operations centered on the sparsely populated Tay Nihn Province and War Zone C, often searching what had been the vast Michelin rubber plantations. When that proved unavailing—producing only infrequent skirmishes with scattered platoon-sized elements of local forces—operations moved into the western part of Nau Ngnia Province, hard on the Cambodian border. The hunting was better in the heavy undergrowth and dense bamboo thickets along the Oriental River. On 21 June, Company A ran into a VC base camp. The brigade conducted the standard "pile on" operation. Mowery inserted two companies from our sister battalion, the 3/187th, as a

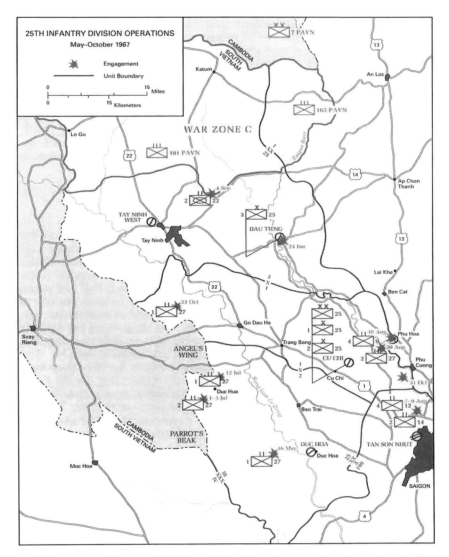

Twenty-Fifth Infantry Division area of operations. From MacGarrigle, *Taking the Offensive*, 366.

blocking force. Then the combat area received heavy doses of artillery fire and air support. The heavy firefight continued into the night before the remnant of the VC company infiltrated through the cordon.

Two days later the recon platoon discovered and seized a lightly defended guerrilla complex. Exploring the underground labyrinth, they found an ammu-nition cache and vast stores of rice. Destruction or extraction of the rice would be a significant blow to the effectiveness of the NVA or main force VC operat-ing in that area. We received orders to destroy it and were given Engineer sup-port. During the day, orders arrived to expedite the process and withdraw. I objected, saying that the Engineers had not completed their preparations. The order stood: "Move out." The rice remained where we found it.

Thinking this offered the perfect scenario for a bushmaster ambush, I asked for and received the green light. I briefed the company commander, stressing the importance of the stay-behind platoon getting into the defensive position before the rest of the company was extracted. The platoon members must remain totally silent, not smoke, and remain hidden before the company left the landing zone and until any enemy appeared. Without total secrecy, the ambush would fail. I talked to the platoon leader, stressing this vital element. Preparation for the demolition was a lengthy process. The extraction went off without any difficulties. Within a few minutes, I heard the platoon leader's pan-icky voice, reporting that he was under fire. I immediately called for artillery to seal off the area, thinking that the platoon had come under heavy attack. After much back and forth, I learned that the enemy consisted of a single rifleman. He had not fallen for bushmaster and had already inflicted several casualties, more when the platoon tried to recover its wounded without first suppressing the enemy's fire. Finally, the lone Vietnamese withdrew, and we pulled out our beaten platoon.

After interviewing the platoon leader, the company commander, and first sergeant, it became obvious the platoon leader had violated my specific instruc-tions concerning concealment. Instead of getting into his hole and hunkering down, he had sat on the lip smoking a cigarette and talking to his troops. That lone enemy, having spotted the platoon leader, waited until the last chopper departed and took the exposed men under fire, inflicting his first casualties. As other troopers tried to rescue their downed comrades, they, in turn, became casualties. The platoon leader had failed miserably, causing the needless death of some of his men. The platoon had been beaten by a single enemy soldier who deserved the enemy's equivalent of a Silver Star.

Saddened and bitterly disappointed, I believed the platoon leader should be relieved and reassigned but did not communicate that to his company com-mander. I again questioned the company commander and first sergeant, focus-ing on determining if they thought that members of the platoon trusted their leader. Without hesitation, they assured me the men still respected and had confidence in the platoon leader. Although finding it hard to believe, I concurred with the company commander's recommendation not to relieve the platoon leader.

The Big R

Happily my tour was coming to a close. Mowery informed me that I would receive a Silver Star as part of the package each battalion commander received when he left Vietnam. I balked, telling him I had done nothing to deserve it. He tried convincing me the award was merited, but I refused, saying a Bronze Star would be more appropriate. Mowery never gave up insisting, and I always demurred. I ended up with the Bronze Star.

Obviously I would have been honored receiving the award, but my whole experience with the Third Brigade left me feeling empty. Leaving one unit and joining another is always difficult. The army manpower system viewed American soldiers as interchangeable parts. Moving from one brigade to another in the same division should not have presented a problem. In my case, it did. I never established any connection with the Currahees; at least from my perspective, there was no sense of being a member of any "band of brothers." In Strike Force, the troops returning to base were greeted with barbeques and beer parties that rebuilt unit cohesion and morale after the rigors of being in the bush. Nothing like that happened with the Currahees. The frenetic pace of the operations and bouncing from the delta to the highlands to the rice paddies and thick hedgerows around Cu Chi and finally the jungles of the Oriental River—always under the operational control of a different division—left the battalion fighting its own little war. Moving from one area of operation to another for short periods of time for specific operations—almost always black holes—undermined our combat effectiveness and morale. Unfamiliarity with the terrain and the enemy—even our own parent organization—multiplied the problem. The sad Operation Mathews affair seriously eroded faith in the senior leadership. I never knew what the other battalions were doing. Much of my personal sense of alienation derived from not having shared in the heat of battle with any company in the 1/506. My efforts never slackened; my companies always had all the support they needed, but I never felt that unique bond that comes from the shared exhilaration and mortal fear of being together in a life-or-death firefight.

An old friend, Lt. Col. Dan Sharp, replaced me. Dan had just come from an Office of Personnel Operations desk in the Pentagon. He arrived a week or so before the change of command date and accompanied me on a few air assaults.

I remember one well. The 1/506 T/O&E (table of organization and equipment) called for four rifle companies—one more than in the 2/502. For this operation, I had a company under my operational control from another battalion. In the midst of a battalion insertion, with portions of companies on the landing zones, at the departure airstrip, or in the air, I received a call from Mowery ordering me to move my assaults to a new area. Amazed, I responded, "We're in the midst of an insertion!" Mowery knew that and, ignoring the frustrated tone of my voice, repeated his instructions. I gave him a WILCO (understand and will comply) and proceeded with the change.

Word went down to the aviation support commander and my company commanders, and the operations officer coordinated the fire support. When the new mission came off without a hitch, Dan appeared nonplussed. After all the companies had been inserted and we had landed, Dan remarked, shaking his head, "Ralph, I'll never be able to do all of that." I reassured him that he could and like me in my first air assault, he needed to rely on his operations chief: "Dan, we could do what we just did because we have been doing it over and over again. We have SOPs [standing operating procedures] that we follow. All the supporting arms—particularly the aviation and fire support—are real pros. All they need is to be told what you want them to do, and they will do it." I also stressed that we had good troops who could and always did perform.

As time for my Big R (rotation out of Vietnam) neared, I felt no particular apprehension; I had no short-timer's concern about not making it to the end of my tour. Physically tired and emotionally drained, I speculated on how our soldiers in World War II served "for the duration and six months." Some were separated from family and home for two or three years. I wondered about the Vietnamese we were fighting, away from home for years and years with no contact—mail, telephone calls, or whatever—with family. I marveled at their perseverance.

Although all departures are filled with mixed emotions, I was glad to be leaving. I missed my family so much. The pangs of separation—missing what my children were doing—troubled me more than any concerns about not going home. I labored under no doubt that Jeannie would do a wonderful job seeing to it that life remained as normal as it could be for children whose father was away in a combat zone. Her letters and tapes arrived every few days, filling me in on the happy times; whatever problems she confronted, she kept to herself.

Once the paperwork was cleared at Third Brigade, I made a courtesy call on General Barsanti. Although I was uneasy about it, the meeting went off without mishap. Lt. Col. Jerry Morse commanded the processing station. After

six months in battalion command in the First Brigade, Jerry had been transferred to this job. We knew each other from Leavenworth, where we had played
basketball during the lunch hour. Jerry met me with a warm bear hug, spoke
glowingly of our time together, and escorted me to my billet. I remained there
a couple days before catching that "7-O-Quick" (Boeing 707) back to what was
termed "the World."

Sitting alone on that dark plane during the interminable Pacific crossing
gave me plenty of time for reflection. As time passed, I became more dejected.
Leaving Vietnam left me with a hollow feeling. I had a job to do and did it.
Service in Vietnam profited me enormously from a professional standpoint.
Except for a brief time on staff, I was lucky to have been afforded the opportunity to command two battalions and, briefly, a third. Aside from personal
sentiments, the experience left me dubious about the prospects of winning in
Vietnam. Westmoreland's unfortunate forecast about the light at the end of the
tunnel inflated the impact of Tet. The North Vietnamese and especially the Viet
Cong took a pasting, and their hoped-for "general uprising" never materialized,
but though nobody saw it at the time, Tet proved to be the enemy's Saratoga, the
tipping point in the war. Operation Mathews demonstrated the bankruptcy of
the "killing flies with a sledgehammer" faith that ever-more firepower, bombs,
napalm, and Agent Orange would win the day. The army had lost its way and
needed to return its focus to old-fashioned soldiering. To make matters worse,
I was headed for a job I did not want. That aside, the best thing was that I was
returning to Jeannie and the kids.

12

West Point

Changing Times at the Academy

Only a soldier and his family can know the stress of combat separation and the emotions of "coming home." The two girls greeted me, a little shy around this strange man who, for the last year, had been someone they knew only through letters. Jean, almost fourteen, had blossomed into a beautiful young lady, and Marty remained just as pretty and vivacious as I remembered. Tommy, now eight, was away at camp. When Tommy arrived from camp, he jumped into my arms and hugged my neck for a long time without saying a word. His actions, more than anything else, showed the void my absence had created in all our lives. I had been away before—in Colombia when we had only Jean and in Germany on numerous occasions for four to eight weeks at a time—but none of those remotely compared to my being on combat duty in Vietnam.

Daddy was ill and had been for some time. While nothing had been said in any of the letters, I sensed he was not well. The day after arriving in Columbus, I drove to Tifton and visited him in the hospital. Mother was there by his side as she always had been. Daddy was so glad to see me. The feeling was mutual. After a big hug, he asked in a disappointed tone, "Why didn't you wear your uniform?" He wanted to see my ribbons. I returned to Tifton in about a week, and Daddy's condition had worsened. Early one morning shortly thereafter, brother Tommy called and said Daddy had died. During the funeral service I felt devastated and sobbed uncontrollably. Remorse swept over me, guilt for not having spent more time with him, even for not taking the time to purchase my ribbons so he could see them. I miss him still and feel his presence.

Several months before my DEROS (Date of Expected Return from Overseas), I had written Maj. Gen. Sidney Berry, the commanding general of the Infantry Center and commandant of the U.S. Army Infantry School. Our careers had often intersected, and he was clearly tabbed for greater things. I requested assignment as the director of the Ranger Department, citing my long list of credentials stretching from Korea through various Ranger postings stateside, including command time, to my experiences in Puerto Rico, Colombia, and Germany. I felt optimistic, knowing no other officer could match my Ranger qualifications. Soon Berry replied with the deflating news that he already filled the slot. Lt. Col. Y. Y. Phillips had been selected. No doubt Phillips possessed all the right chits in his 201, but he had skillfully dodged any "dirty sox" assignments, lacked my Ranger résumé, and left the army six months into his tour. By way of consolation, Berry mentioned that Benning offered a number of other good jobs. Disappointment mounted when around the same time word came through that I was under consideration for an assignment to West Point. I just wanted to stay with troops and thought the assignment to the Ranger Department perfectly matched my experience. Finally orders arrived for West Point.

Return to the Monastery on the Hudson

I was disheartened, but Jeannie was thrilled. West Point offered the best possible posting for the family to rebind. The Pucketts definitely needed some family time. The post was safe, and the kids could roam at will with plenty of activities and friends to share them. We drew quarters on Lusk Reservoir, the choice residential area. Jeannie's intuition proved on the mark.

I tried to look on the bright side. As regimental commander, a position of considerable prestige, I would serve as the senior tactical officer overseeing the tactical officers in the eight cadet companies of the First Regiment. Two of my classmates, Collier Ross and Dick Tallman, commanded regiments. My friend from Germany, Bill Simpson, commanded another regiment. Other old acquaintances and classmates held positions in the Academic Department. Most important, I would play an important role in molding some of the finest young men the country produced. Once I put aside my personal feelings, I decided a two-year stint at West Point presented plenty of positives.

Not long after arriving, Collier and I received promotion to colonel. The commandant, Brig. Gen. Bernard Rogers, presided over a simple ceremony. It proved especially gratifying to be promoted with my buddy Ross and with our families in attendance. A future four-star general, army chief of staff, and supreme allied commander in Europe, Rogers possessed all the urbane polish and intelligence you would expect from a first captain (Class of 1943) and Rhodes Scholar. Rogers had served as assistant division commander of the First Infantry Division in Vietnam before coming to West Point. As I gleaned from the beginning, Rogers would be a great boss.

Rogers was broad-minded, which proved a definite asset as commandant in a period of social disorder. The 1960s might be called the burnt-over decade: strife over civil rights set American cities alight; women demanding greater rights torched their bras; and the draft cards of many antiwar protesters went up in flames. The youth revolt assaulted all the bastions of tradition; the sense of innocence that pervaded American culture gave way to a cynicism that polarized—and still does—American society. While West Point appeared as an oasis of order and discipline, it could not entirely escape the turmoil and demands for change. The cadets, after all, were the products of that same overindulged baby boomer generation.

While a conservative, I was no troglodyte—a claim some of my charges might contest. West Point is a kind of monastery tucked away on a bluff overlooking the Hudson, far removed from the hustle and tussles of modern life (ironically within an hour's drive of Manhattan). Tradition was its bedrock. Cadets still wore the gray uniforms of the Battle of Chippewa in the War of 1812, and many of the practices dated back at least that far. For decades, adherence to hoary teaching practices—rote memorization, daily recitations, arcane grading methods—left the Military Academy trailing the best civilian universities. West Point was in the midst of changing its pedagogic methods and modernizing the curriculum, but that, too, widened old fault lines. I agreed with those who wanted to make tempered adjustments when called for but also believed in preserving the best of the old system and enforcing the rules as written, which applied equally to officers and cadets. The tactical officers bore responsibility for the discipline and military training of cadets; the former demanded most of our energies.

I arrived during the summer lull, when the cadets, except those at Beast Barracks, were at various installations participating in a variety of training activities. In typical Puckett fashion, I wanted to get my feet on the ground and learn the ropes of being the First Regiment commander before they returned. Fortunately, my adjutant, Maj. Bill Mullen, an exceptionally conscientious and loyal subordinate, served as the perfect sounding board. As time would tell, Mullen possessed an unerring sense of the subterranean folkways of cadet life at West Point.

When the cadets returned from their summer schedule, I had the cadet regimental commander, my student counterpart, report to my office. Mullen described Cadet Nardotti as probably the most respected cadet in the corps and recounted how he had quelled a student ruckus—just cadets letting off steam—simply by showing up and waving his arms. I came to West Point determined the cadet leadership would exert the same influence as their counterparts in the active army. Granted, that ideal of leadership was seldom achieved in the "real army," but it set a standard. The tactical officers always talked about how the cadets ran the corps. The cadets rated members of their company, their classmates, and all members of the underclass according to desired military traits. The cadets also regulated the holiest of holies—the cadet honor code. Virtually upon arrival at West Point, a cadet is counted upon to know and live by the oath, "A cadet will not lie, cheat or steal, nor tolerate those who do." Anyone charged with a violation sits before a committee of twelve cadets and if found guilty is separated from the United States Military Academy. The 1951 cheating scandal involving eighty-three cadets—many of them football players—still hung over the institution. Nardotti lived up to his billing; he exuded poise and strength of character that demanded respect.

I wanted to place more responsibility on the cadets by granting them more freedoms providing they bore greater responsibilities for their actions. The tactical officers, or tacs, resorted to the gig (demerits) for every infraction. Cadet leaders, on the other hand, used the demerit system sparingly if at all. As I told my tacs and the cadet chain of command, I wished we never had to gig anyone; it was an impossibility but something to shoot for. Instead of demerits, the tacs and cadets leaders should identify shortcomings and counsel offenders. To me, the gig was an admission of failure. Not many—if any—cadets ever gained any true enlightenment tramping back and forth across Central Area.

Nardotti called upon other top-drawer support—Claude Alexander, his XO, and particularly Jon Shine, one of the cadet battalion commanders who came as close as possible to being the ideal cadet. There were many others. On one occasion, Mullen and Nardotti confronted a problem. Bill explained what he considered the best plan of action. Nardotti expressed a contrary view. Mullen turned to me and asked for a ruling. "Go with Mr. Nardotti," I responded. Disappointed, Mullen persisted until I said, "I think my idea is better than both of yours. However, Mr. Nardotti's is certainly workable. He is the commander. I go with him."

The attempt at social engineering, empowering the cadet leadership, achieved very limited success. The cadet leaders were not exempt, as members of the corps, from peer pressure. One of the great strengths of West Point resides in building tensile-strong personal bonds between classmates. Officer corps ring pounding and membership in the careerist "West Point self-promotion society" are by-products of the "band of brothers" sentiment felt by classmates and associates. The same applied to cadets. Naturally, the standards of cadet leaders' discipline enforcement proved far too lax for the tacs. My effort to combat the decline in standards and defusing the popular attitude of "getting over" on the army by empowering the cadets never gained any traction. Attitudes were far too entrenched. A few years later, General Berry saw his career sidetracked by a massive cheating scandal that rocked West Point while he served as commandant. Honor code violations became just one more method of "beating the system."

Not long after assuming command, I invited Maj. Gen. Sam Koster, the newly appointed superintendent, to visit my regiment. The superintendent had commanded the Americal Division in Vietnam. Toward the end of the First Brigade's run as a separate unit, it served under the operational control of General Koster, whom I considered a genuinely outstanding commander. While I was XO of the First Brigade 101st, he asked me to take over as the division operations officer. Thanking him, I begged off in the hope of getting another battalion command. Koster wanted to visit his old company. I had not alerted the Company tac, wanting the general to see the normal day-to-day standard. The company's appearance fell far short of expectations. Koster appeared both dismayed and disappointed. (I wondered if he knew how I felt.) He asked me if the company had been alerted before his visit. When I said no and explained why, he queried me on my assessment of the company. When I stated the obvious, he asked what I intended to do. I told him that the company would meet the standard before the day was over, and he left.

I knew the general had to feel let down and probably thought that I should have informed the company before the visit. If the tac had been notified, the company would have been in inspection order and the visit would have made everybody happy, but the superintendent's visit offered me a great training opportunity. I took the risk to impress upon the tac that he should be prepared at all times. The tac was chagrined and apologetic, but I left wondering if he had learned from the experience.

General Koster would later be held responsible for the cover-up of the My Lai incident that occurred while he commanded the Americal Division. Although he may be criticized for not going to the site and investigating himself, I am convinced that he was an honorable man, told the truth, and had been lied to by members of his staff.

Of all army schools, West Point is the most resistant to change. On the surface, everything appeared pretty much identical to the Military Academy I had left in 1949. For nine months, the cadets were subjected to the same rigid academic regime—in both scheduling and content—with the six-week selection process and cadets segregated by class standing. Cadets attended mandatory physical education sessions and participated in intramural and intercollegiate sports. Cadets who lagged behind in their studies or fitness sat for remedial work and extra PT. But some things had changed, particularly the shift toward greater emphasis on academics at the cost, in my opinion, of the traditional mission of West Point to develop officers with the moral fiber to serve as junior officers and with the potential of becoming the senior leaders in the army.

In the contest between the Academic and Tactical Departments over cadets' time—another age-old point of friction—the cards were stacked against the tacs. The conventional wisdom held the tacs were the "brawn" (soldiers), and the Ps (instructors) were the "brains." That characterization, unfair to both sides, expressed long-held perceptions and offered partial explanations for the differences that divided the departments. The tacs were chosen primarily on their military records, and at this juncture, almost all were combat veterans. Except for permanent associate professors who remained at the Academy until they retired, most of the officers in the Academic Department, many also boasting impeccable combat records, were serving their three-year "utilization" tour as payback for the army's funding their graduate educations. As recent products of master's programs in leading universities, the Ps could not escape the ferment on American campuses. Many of them relaxed the admittedly archaic classroom pedagogic practices in the interest of producing an environment more conducive to learning. As a result, they paid less attention to regulations than many in the Tactical Department believed appropriate. Haircuts, uniforms, and the shine on shoes acceptable to the Ps fell far short of what the tacs expected. Often at cross-purposes and never reconciled, the tactical officers and instructors—often the best of friends—never appeared to be on the same wavelength.

The Tactical Department faced severe restrictions on the times we could assemble the cadets. The inviolable schedule defined every minute of a very busy day that began with reveille at 0600 and ended with "lights out" at 2000 hours. The Academic Department jealously appropriated the study time that the tacs would have used for "military" purposes. Often it was necessary to infringe on free time just to speak to cadets. At the regular meetings with the commandant, the regimental commanders expressed their concerns. Rogers explained he occupied an impossible position. In the Academy's senior leadership, his was but a single voice contending against those of the dean, also a brigadier general, and all the department heads, all senior colonels. The Academic Department held all the trumps.

Ironically, the tacs carried responsibility for maintaining discipline during the evening study period. Despite warnings, upperclassmen pestered plebes. Some of this went way beyond simple harassment. A cabal preyed upon those they considered weak and took it upon themselves to "get" the plebe, "run him out of the corps." The sons of Ps and tacs were often the targets. Granted, in some cases these cadets proved ill-suited to cadet life and had applied for admission only to please their fathers. To combat this, I often spoke of the leader's responsibility to develop his junior's potential. Every cadet had something to offer or he could not have met the admission requirements. I urged upperclassmen to help plebes meet the standards. Unfortunately, I never convinced enough of them that their approach not only defied command guidance but violated basic leadership principles. Frequent visits to the barracks during study periods did little to curb the practice.

Each semester, particularly in the fall, cadets—mostly plebes—were "found" academically deficient and either turned back to repeat the year or turned out (dismissed). In common with the rest of the army, West Point suffered owing to the public disquiet over Vietnam. Applications were down, vacancies existed, and admission standards eased. The curriculum remained biased toward engineering. Six days a week cadets sat through eighty minutes of math classes and recitations. After talking to each of these young men, it became clear to me that the problem derived from their insufficient academic preparation at the secondary-school level for the focused science and math courses. Many of them played football in high school and at the urging of their coaches avoided math and science classes to preserve their academic eligibility. They became academic cripples, and there was not much West Point could do to remedy the situation. What I saw angered me.

Demographers and the press made a great deal of the "generation gap" that existed between parents, products of the Depression and World War II, and their baby-boomer children. The cadets, while not exactly manning the barricades of the "youth revolution," nonetheless could not entirely escape it. One tac saw a cadet put on a wig as he left post for the weekend so he could pass as a "normal" member of society. Cadets clamored for more "privileges"—relaxation of the Spartan restrictions of cadet life. Nothing subversive about that.

One set of regulations that particularly rankled cadets involved "escorting" a family member or guest, but particularly a girlfriend, while on post. The regulation proscribed escorting in a certain area that might prove conducive to behavior deemed inappropriate. Rogers noted the convoluted regulation was inaccurate in that the area in question was not "below the level of the Plain" and therefore outside the forbidden boundaries. By the letter of the then regulation, cadets could escort in that area. The question arose: Should we eliminate the written ban since it contradicted our own delineation of appropriate physical locations? "Yes," I offered. "We either eliminate the prohibition from the Blue Book or we enforce it. We should not make rules and then not apply them." My view was rejected. The tacs did not want cadets escorting in that area, but if we removed the ban from the Blue Book, the sharp-eyed cadets would notice the change even though we would make no announcement to that effect. By leaving the prohibition and not enforcing it, so the wishful thinking went, cadets might not recognize that the rule was not being enforced and would stay out of the area after retreat.

"Public Display of Affection" (PDA) was taboo; even holding your girl's hand in public was verboten. Rogers broached the subject, remarking how he enjoyed walking hand in hand with his wife. He felt that the rule was too stringent. Several regimental commanders agreed and decided on the same solution as with the escorting ban. Again I objected—stating the same complaint. Rules should be enforced as long as they remained on the books. If inappropriate, they should be eliminated. Otherwise, we would be failing to do our duty and that dereliction would be perceived and exploited by the cadets. Once again I was a minority of one.

Tacs acted as chaperones—as Officers in Charge (OC)—at social functions. Jeannie and I drew duty as chaperones for a yearlings (sophomores) dance at Camp Buckner. Mullen, who knew about such things, warned that PDA would be widespread and glaring, adding that tac chaperones usually took no action. Before the hop, I instructed the cadet coordinators and conduct supervisors to announce I would act as the officer in charge. I had been at the Academy long enough that they all knew where I stood. So much for my fearsome reputation. The flouting of the rules on PDA were flagrant, particularly after the dance. Furious and embarrassed at the same time, I confronted a cadet with a girl in his arms and asked for his name and company. Obviously the cadets had been conditioned to expect that the regulation prohibiting PDA would not be enforced.

Another thing that disturbed me about West Point was the contradiction between what officers professed and what we did. The cadets read us like a book. Gambling—pools and wagering—was strictly forbidden, yet officers openly participated in football pools and other betting; there was a football pool in the tacs' barbershop. Well aware of this pool, cadets sometimes mentioned it to their tacs, and some even questioned why this discrepancy existed

between what the tacs did and the rules for cadets. The gambling never bothered me, but the double standard did.

The Times, They Are a-Changing

An innovative thinker, General Rogers wrestled with preserving West Point traditions while dealing with the demands of a new generation of cadets. He was
the perfect fit for that thankless task. Cadets lodged complaints about having to
stand reveille, return to their rooms for thirty minutes, then reform to march
to breakfast. For some obscure reason in the distant past, this probably served
a function. Rogers agreed the two-formation drill wasted time. In anticipation
of the inevitable fallout, Rogers solicited input from "old grads" before he ruled
cadets would form for reveille and then march directly to breakfast. To an "old
grad," the corps appeared to be "going soft" with increased speed with each
succeeding class since the year he graduated. To them, it seemed as if Rogers
had eliminated reveille. Far more sweeping was the overhaul of the plebe system, which Rogers viewed as wholly counterproductive in instilling in cadets
the proper leadership techniques. Any thinking soldier knew no officer could
treat his men the way upperclassmen abused plebes without being severely rep-
rimanded. Rogers wanted to eliminate the worst vestiges of these anachronis-
tic practices such as screaming at and berating plebes; the "brace" (holding at
severe attention) was replaced with a more realistic posture and discontinued
in the mess hall. Wisely these changes were introduced during Beast Barracks.
Responsibility for beast training fell to Ross, who modernized the plebe system
by thoroughly orienting the Beast Detail who trained the new Fourth Class.

My frustrations deepened toward the end of the academic year. On Sunday
afternoon, a few minutes before the First Year cadets returned to their barracks
after the weekend, I assembled them. The time arrived when they needed to
complete their "wish list," their branch preference form. Remembering the difficulties I had faced before deciding to go Infantry, what tipped the balance was
my desire to confront the biggest challenge—to be in direct contact with the
men who make up our army and lead them. Based on the cadets' comments,
their priorities looked to lie elsewhere. The army had undergone remarkable
change since 1949. The bureaucratized corporate army offered a broad range
of career choices outside the combat arms. Most of those required advanced
education. Some cadets stated their branch choices were based on purely social
factors such as their likely initial posting being located close to their families
or girlfriends. Most reckoned on the branch or service that held out the best

prospects for early entry into a master's program. What they were really stating was their intention to get the advanced degree best calculated for success in a civilian profession. They knew the army used the inducement of graduate school as a lever in recruitment and retention. In other words, they planned on "getting over" on the army, using the cache of West Point, a stint as an officer, and a graduate degree from a name university to parlay themselves into a high-paying civilian job. After serving their five-year commitment, many of them clearly intended on leaving the army. Also unstated, going to West Point, then getting their airborne patch, then attending their branch advanced course greatly increased their chances of not getting sent to Vietnam. Disgusted, I told them their "primary objective should be to get your master's degree in soldiering—in leading troops." Sadly, my premonitions proved correct: more than half of the Class of 1969 had left the service by 1975, a record.

In another of our Sunday-afternoon assemblies I cautioned the First Classmen on the dangers of drinking and driving. Denied alcohol on post, cadets drank heavily beyond the gates. A big day in a cadet's life is when he can have a car. In the 1960s a red Corvette was every cadet's dream. Drinking and driving made a deadly cocktail. Three cadets died driving back from a New Year's Eve party that year. Two more died that spring when the driver, drunk, drove his car into the Hudson. My admonition fell on deaf ears.

Aside from the head-butting over rule enforcement, I got through my first year without major clashes with superiors. That happy situation soon changed. One of the first things Mullen did after I first arrived was ask, "Sir, when do you want to see the General's List?" I was unsure what that meant, but I had a pretty good idea. "It's the list of First Regiment cadets who are sons of generals," Mullen informed me. I thanked Bill and told him that I never wanted to hear of it again. Mullen was taken aback and warned me to expect hearing from some of those fathers if something unpleasant in the way of discipline befell their sons. I stated emphatically that we would treat each cadet the same and hold them to identical standards regardless of who his father might be. Bill shook his head in a "you'll be sorry" manner as he left the room.

That summer I ran the new yearlings' training at Camp Buckner. A group had grabbed one of the interior guards (another cadet) and dragged him off his post. There was no malicious intent; it was a prank pulled just about every summer. One of my tacs offered up the names of the culprits and set up a meeting with me. When the crestfallen cadets reported and took their seats, I picked up my copy of the Manual for Courts-Martial, the Unified Code of Military Justice (UCMJ), and read them the charge concerning interfering with a guard in the performance of his duty. After finishing, I told them that I had no intention of preferring charges under the UCMJ but only wanted to impress upon them the seriousness of the offense. "Interior guard is important; I take it seriously," I said. I then asked for their justification. They explained that seizing the guard and dragging him off his post was just a practical joke. I dismissed them and turned the matter over to the regular disciplinary process. They were "awarded" some demerits and punishment tours. As far as I was concerned, that concluded the matter. I was mistaken.

I received a call one night shortly thereafter from an irate father, a brigadier general, who made it abundantly clear that I had overreacted to what was nothing more than a prank by exuberant boys that happened most summers. He remembered his summer at Camp Buckner when a similar incident occurred. He excoriated me for threatening to court-martial the cadets. I explained to him what I had stated clearly to the cadets, that I had no intention of resorting to a court-martial and that I used the UCMJ to underline the seriousness of what they had done. The general raged on. I mentally pictured him frothing at the mouth. After several more minutes of venting his spleen, he hung up. He treated me just like an upperclassman might a callow plebe (a strong argument in support for Rogers's revamp of the plebe system). I immediately called General Rogers and informed him of the conversation, fully expecting the fuming father would call him. I did not want Rogers caught off guard. The next day, Rogers told me that he received the complaint and dismissed it. I had figured he would.

June 1969 produced the routine change in command. During his two-year tenure, Rogers faced plenty of controversy and made important changes, stripping away some of the more arcane cadet rituals. Although not in total accord with some of his decisions, I admired him and the way he performed his difficult duties. Brig. Gen. Sam Walker took over. The son of Gen. Walton Walker, he had been a firstie in my plebe year.

That summer I served as officer in charge for the second class trip, which toured various army installations. Everything was routine: I briefed Walker on the plan put together by the Office of Military Instruction, and we headed out. So the cadets could enjoy themselves and get the most benefit from the trip, we suspended serving "confinements" (restrictions for disciplinary infractions) until the return to West Point. The trip went off without any major incidents.

Almost immediately upon our return, Mullen came to me: "Sir, today is the birthday of Cadet Walker, the commandant's son. He is under restriction. His mother has planned a party for him and expects him to be allowed to go

to the party." He wondered what we should do. "Bill, we do what we are supposed to do," I said. "I make no exceptions for Cadet Walker just because he is
the commandant's son. He knew and so did the commandant that the requirement to serve restrictions was reinstated when we returned from the trip."
Mullen warned, "Sir, you're going to catch hell!" I knew he was right and never
felt particularly courageous taking a stand that would almost certainly rever-
berate back on me. Mullen relayed my decision to Cadet Walker, but before
the day ended Bill informed me that Walker would be attending his birthday
party. I was not surprised. The next day General Walker summoned me to his
office and asked, "Didn't you tell me that confinements were suspended during the trip?" In my sometimes abrupt manner, I replied in the affirmative and
reminded him the trip ended three days before. I was curtly dismissed. The
only conclusion to be drawn from this sad affair is that I never learned how to
play the game.

The climax of the football season—one of the highlights of the entire
year—was the annual grudge match against Navy. I drew the assignment as
officer in charge. Army had not fared well in the 1969 season, limping into the
big game in Philadelphia with a 3–5 record. Fortunately, the Midshipmen had
only one win. The Cadets crushed Navy 27–0. Despite the losing season, any
win over Navy gave soldiers everywhere a reason for celebration; the cadets in
my charge proved no exception.

That evening I went to the Ben Franklin, then the premier hotel in down-
town Philadelphia, where many of the students on weekend pass congregated.
Entering the ornate colonnaded lobby, I was greeted by the sight of two cadets
with blouses completely unzipped and obviously inebriated. I took their names
and directed them to return to their rooms and get themselves straight. On
the second floor what confronted me was not exactly something out of *Animal House* but close enough. Cadets, clearly drunk and in all sorts of disar-
ray, ran amok. Spotting me, they scurried to their rooms. That was the first of
many forays back to the Ben Franklin that night. I called out the first captain
and instructed him to "get control." He accomplished nothing, and in fairness
to him, there was little he could do. For me, this was a harrowing and unsettling experience. Here we were representing the United States Military Academy, and the cadets could not care less.

The following Monday, I submitted numerous reports of violations. I again
approached the first captain and solicited his views. He informed me that in the
past the tacs never ventured beyond the lobby. The conduct I witnessed was the
norm. What made it worse, the first captain was very impressive—intelligent

and polished—with all the makings of an excellent officer. I could not get my head around his seeming indifference.

When I went to see the superintendent he was unavailable, so I unburdened myself to his aide. He informed me that what I had witnessed was no aberration; it had been going on for years. Hotels suffered thousands of dollars in damages yet made no formal complaint since they expected their rooms would get torn up and made up the loss and more on the steep prices charged for the rooms and services. I remained in disbelief until my faithful and knowledgeable adjutant clued me in. Even more troubling, in a meeting with the first class, Commandant Walker made light of the entire episode.

One of the anthems of the youth revolution held that "the times, they are a-changing." The author was right, but I did not have to change with them. The way Vietnam was being fought more than indicated the army had serious systemic problems, but at the time it proved beyond my understanding as to why. After a year and a half at West Point, it became clearer. The army held up the Academy as the font of the values and virtues that sustain the vision and ideal of American officership, yet the institution condoned a whole litany of breaches of regulations, some even court-martial offenses. The leadership, tacs, and instructors all bent the honor code in ways never intended. Cadets knew this and abused the code and spent their time dreaming up novel ways to beat the system. This game had been going on since at least the days of Sylvanus Thayer, but it appeared to me more pernicious than before, with destructive and long-term implications. Cadets who played the game well at West Point learned how to use the system to their own advantage—whether for promotions or laying the foundation for success out of the army—as officers. And that system was failing in Vietnam. In times of distress and self-doubt I thought back to what Daddy always said, "Son, you do what's right no matter what." So I continued rigorously enforcing the letter of the rules. The cadets hated me as a regular Simon Legree. They would cross the street to avoid me when they saw me walking toward them. They thought the scar on my head was the product of a war wound, that a metal plate in my head made me so ornery. The cadre probably thought I was some unregenerate old brown shoe—which I was—and it certainly did not make life easy, but I remained true to my core beliefs.

In professional and personal terms, the time put in at West Point probably constituted my worst years in the army. For the family, it was probably the best, especially coming as it did after our separation during my year in Vietnam. The kids loved West Point. Our oldest, Jean, attended school in Highland Falls, made loads of friends, and earned a spot on the ski team. She became quite the accomplished skier. Because of my rank and position, Jeannie and I had a very active social life. The social demands were eased by having Collier and Ann Ross there. West Point was close enough that we decided to indulge ourselves with a ski trip to Vermont together with Bill and Mary Simpson. It turned into a disaster. First the high-price condo was a construction site, then we managed to lock the only set of keys in the car, and finally I blew a ligament in my knee and returned to West Point before our week was up.

The head surgeon, Lt. Col. John Feagin, decided the knee did not require an operation, immobilized the knee with a cast, and after six weeks put me in physiotherapy. For weeks on end I put in the work but never made the hoped-for progress. A number of cadets joined me, injured in the very tough physical regimen they followed. One, a football player, received clearance to play after having had knee surgery only six or eight weeks before. After all my months of physio, working harder than anyone else, I could not believe he could play football. The PE instructor looked at me, hesitated, and then said, "Sir, you are forty-three years old—twenty-two years older than that cadet."

As could be expected, I had one further tussle with Walker before my tour ended. At one of our regular meetings with the commandant, he briefed us on officer assignments for the coming summer. Walker instructed me to write an officer slated for duty at West Point to cut short his leave by one month and report for duty. I thought the incoming officer deserved his leave, but that was not up to me. Disinclined to write the letter, I went to the person who handled personnel matters, the commandant's adjutant. The letter never went out, the officer took his leave, and a glaring vacancy appeared in the summer roster. Walker called me in. I related what happened, and he made no effort to disguise his intense displeasure. He later expressed that irritation in my efficiency report.

Before General Rogers left West Point to take command of the Fifth Infantry Division (Mechanized) at Fort Carson, I petitioned for an assignment under him. He seemed surprised by my wanting a reassignment from West Point but assured me if that was what I wanted he would do what he could. In spring 1970 both Collier Ross and I received notification of our assignment to Carson as brigade commanders. We would be cutting our programmed three-year tour at West Point short by one year; Rogers had come through. I was very pleased to have this opportunity to work for him again and return to troop duty.

13

The Fort Carson Blues

Troubled Birth of the New Army

Shortly before we left West Point, Jeannie and I bought a twenty-four-foot motor home. We planned a major cross-country trip, taking in all the tourist attractions along the way. We planned a leisurely sojourn with plenty of flex time built in for side trips and unexpected stops. The Winnebago was crowded with five of us and our dog, Pretzel. The children realized they faced several weeks of close confinement with each other and made accommodations. The most trying part of the trip was listening again and again to a seemingly indestructible 8-track Carole King–James Taylor tape. White Sands, Carlsbad Caverns, the Grand Canyon, Walnut Canyon, the Petrified Forest, the Painted Desert, the Mojave Desert, Muir Redwood Forest, Disneyland, the Great Salt Lake, and a host of other attractions filled the days. I am an early riser, so we hit the road by six in the morning. After driving for a couple of hours, we stopped at some wayside park, where all of us would enjoy the great breakfasts that Jeannie prepared. Then we would be on our way again. I did most of the driving, but Jeannie took her turn and proved adept at handling what we considered a very big rig. When we arrived in Colorado Springs, we had covered 6,600 miles in five weeks. "The trip" entered into family lore.

After getting us partially settled in quarters, I went to the required maintenance management course at Fort Knox, Kentucky, and sat through well-presented classes along with the other newly assigned commanders of mechanized and armor units. As always, too little time was devoted to practical, hands-on work. I needed the training since my previous assignments had always been in "light" units with relatively few wheeled vehicles and no "tracks." "Heavy" was totally new. I vowed to apply myself to my responsibility as a commander to see that our unit equipment was well-maintained.

The Sorry State of the Army

Fort Carson was very much in the news. During the Truman administration, the army petitioned hard for universal military training; the draft would "save" the army. With the rampant antimilitary sentiments engendered by Vietnam, the army looked back to the future; it viewed conscripted manpower as a huge political liability. The Pentagon began selling Congress on returning to an all-volunteer force. Carson was selected as the petri dish for the "New Army" that would emerge out of Vietnam. Rogers, with his deserved reputation as an enlightened innovator, was tabbed as the man to lead this transformation. Because the future of the army hung in the balance, senior leadership cut Rogers plenty of slack to execute some bold social experimentation. Because of his personality, high-order intelligence, and his track record at West Point, Rogers was probably the general officer best equipped to deal with 1960s soldiers on their own terms.

The baby boomers were different than their parents' generation. The World War II citizen-soldiers were products of the Depression; Korea was fought by young soldiers matured during the world war. The Vietnam generation—more affluent and better educated—knew only the Fat Fifties. Vietnam was not World War II or Korea—wars with clear distinctions between good and evil. The brutal insurgency that the United States clearly was not defeating in Vietnam bred a widespread rejection among the nation's youth of arbitrary authority and traditional roles and rules. The ambiguous war aims in Southeast Asia—never clear even in the minds of policymakers—blurred the values taught at home and reinforced in school about liberty, justice, fair play, and honesty. The gaps—generational and in credibility—were countered by a culture of drugs, promiscuity, and rock music, all expressions of the frustration and confusion arising from the clash between the values of the turbulent 1960s and the rigid mores of the staid 1950s. Nixon's "silent majority" probably existed, but powerful factions—not limited to opinion makers in the press—grew vocal in their opposition to the war, especially when manpower requirements might mean the curtailment of college deferments and the commitment of national guard units that would send the sons of the white middle classes and elites—men like Bill Clinton and George W. Bush—off to Vietnam. Vietnam was a catalyst, but tensions mounted across the social spectrum—conflicts flared over class, gender, sexual preference, and especially race.

Attempting to understand the 1960s soldiers, Rogers opened up the lines of communication. He chartered an Enlisted Men's Council; every soldier below sergeant elected a representative to air the complaints of the lower ranks in weekly meetings. Because issues of race featured so prominently, he formed a Racial Harmony Council. A guerrilla theater opened that provided a creative outlet for soldiers to express their gripes about the army; many of the productions dealt with racial problems. Greenwich Village–style coffee houses sprang up on post as a counter to those outside the gates that enticed soldiers into acts of civil and military disobedience. Rogers ended formations for reveille and retreat, close order drill, and bed checks. He put in place a liberal policy on passes, placed soft drink machines and allowed beer in the barracks, and even brought a fast-food chain on post, another army first. Carson also housed a volunteer-manned drug information and treatment center. All of these radical departures were designed to build a sense of community and tap into the energy of young soldiers. As word spread that Rogers cared about enlisted men and was serious about making changes prompted by their complaints about their lives and duties, more and more soldiers got involved. All of these innovations were central in restoring some measure of good order and discipline to Fort Carson and provided a template for recruiting and retention for the new volunteer army to come. All of this now appears clear in hindsight. The all-volunteer army that grew out this turmoil has been an enormous success. But for those of us who experienced the bedlam—that was how most of the senior line officers saw it—these times proved immensely troubling.

The army's manpower policies multiplied the morale problem. The personnel management brain trust in the Pentagon could not have dreamt up a worse policy than the one the army adopted. The vast majority of the men at Carson were draftees, and most served in combat ground units in Vietnam. Instead of basic and advanced individual training for six months followed by another half year of specialized training for the combat challenges they would face in Southeast Asia attached to a unit that would go intact to Vietnam, they received basic and Advanced Individual Training (AIT) and proceeded immediately to the war zone as individual replacements. After a one-year tour "in country," they returned stateside to finish their two-year commitment before discharge. Even without the detrimental impacts of Vietnam—drug problems permeated the ranks—morale would have soured. To make matters worse, infantrymen in combat units in Vietnam never worked with tracked vehicles. Now at Carson they would convert to mechanized infantry for six months before mustering out. Small wonder most of these men entertained one thought: F**k the army.

Clearly a brigade command at Carson required a great deal more than old-style soldiering. In the week before my assumption of command, I had visited each of the garrison special staff officers for a briefing. The provost marshal proved most enlightening. Visiting him on a Monday, he pulled the military police blotter for the weekend with pages upon pages of incident reports on personnel from what would soon be my brigade. With a disturbing nonchalance, he assured me the past weekend was typical. Many incidents occurred on post, including assaults and theft. He explained that a group of three or four white soldiers often would jump some African American in the barracks and beat him with fists and ax handles. Conversely, a group of African Americans would return the treatment on some white soldier elsewhere in the barracks complex. Hispanics had it worst because they suffered attacks from whites and blacks. Commanders seldom identified the perpetrators and rarely filed charges. Thefts were common. On average, one civilian vehicle went missing from the parking lot by my brigade headquarters each week. The off-post crime wave paralleled or exceeded the one on-post. My brigade was no better or worse than any other unit. Unclear how to tackle the problem, I solicited advice and cooperation from the provost marshal. I requested he book—fingerprint, photograph, and enter into the record—each soldier from my brigade brought to him. I vowed "normal" would be drastically improved.

The staff judge advocate (SJA) was next on my list. He described a system in chaos. The army wisely had established and published a timeline for investigating alleged crimes, preferring charges, and trying offenses. He told me most of the suspected offenders never faced charges or, if arraigned, never went to trial once the prescribed deadline passed. This situation was totally unacceptable. Every division roster had officers with law school degrees but who had not yet passed the bar exam. If the judge advocate's office would assign one of these officers to my brigade, I would have him tackle the problem. The SJA agreed, and in a few days an Infantry officer with a law degree, Lt. Bruce Reed, was assigned to my brigade. He was one of the most efficient and helpful officers I ever met.

Next came the visit to the public information officer (PIO). I had seen too many photographs highlighting a senior officer pinning a medal on a soldier. The limelight should be directed on the men. I would be pleased if my picture appeared in the post newspaper twice—when I assumed and relinquished command. The brigade would benefit from more motivated soldiers encouraged to try harder. I wanted as much favorable publicity for my soldiers as they deserved. My sergeant major would inform the PIO's office of anything considered noteworthy. His staff could decide whether the news merited publication. He assured me that he would cooperate fully. Command Sgt. Maj. Thomas E.

Fagan took on the task with relish. On occasion, more Second Brigade stories appeared than for the other two brigades and the support command combined. The articles focused on and named the soldier(s) who received recognition for the good jobs they performed. All units offered many publicity opportunities that could be exploited, rewarding the soldier and concomitantly benefiting the unit.

Assuming command of a brigade marked one of the proudest days in my life. General Rogers had demonstrated his confidence in me by selecting me to command a regiment at West Point and a brigade at Fort Carson. I steeled myself to live up to his expectations. At the same time, given the deplorable condition of the brigade—on par with our sister brigades—I knew what a tall order confronted me. Any notions that things could not be as bad as the many horror stories reported were immediately dispelled. The general and his wife invited the new brigade commanders—Collier and me—together with Jeannie and Ann, to his quarters for dinner. The assistant division commander, Brig. Gen. DeWitt Smith, and his wife also attended. No sooner had we been seated when I was called to the phone. As I left the table, knowing glances and comments were exchanged by the other officers. My Officer of the Day (OD) informed me of a budding riot in my brigade area. He explained that approximately thirty African Americans, most seemingly under the influence of alcohol and carrying pickax handles, had assembled at the service club and threatened violence because the facility was closed. He urged me to come immediately and, in response to my question, said the situation appeared too explosive for me to take the time to return to my quarters and change into uniform.

I spoke briefly to the general and his guests and left hurriedly. When I arrived at the service club, the situation was just as described. The soldiers, all African Americans, were in an angry mood. After quickly explaining my intentions to the OD, I approached the mob, held up my ID card, and in a nonconfrontational tone said to the first two soldiers I encountered, "I'm Colonel Puckett, the brigade commander. What is the problem?" The situation was volatile; all I wanted to do was disarm it. They told me they considered the club closure an act of racial discrimination. I explained that the service club was following its long-published schedule and urged them to return to the barracks. If they did, no punitive action would follow. They ignored my entreaty, and I directed the OD to take those who refused to disband to the provost marshal's office and have them booked. As he could only take two soldiers each trip in the jeep, I was left alone with the fuming throng. Some of the soldiers circled around me and whispered into my ear, "I'm going to kill me a white rabbit" or

"I'm going to get me a honky." There was no question that I was in a tough spot. If any of them perceived me as frightened or nervous, the situation might spin out of control. Despite a wave of anxiety, I preserved my outward calm and forceful resolve. As the minutes ticked by, some returned to their barracks. In about an hour, the OD finished ferrying the rest to the stockade, where they were placed in custody. All those who had not returned voluntarily to the barracks eventually were tried and found guilty. When it was over, I returned to the dinner party.

As their reactions when I left and returned indicated, Rogers and Smith were not surprised by what had occurred. Shortly before I arrived, a far more dangerous incident had nearly erupted. A carload of Black Panthers evaded the guard at the south gate and entered the fort, the truck full of loaded rifles. They tried to provoke a small contingent of military police under an inexperienced lieutenant to fire the first shot, which would have prompted an open gun battle. Smith, together with the division chief of staff, Lt. Col. Dave Hughes and a "brotherhood soldier" from the Racial Harmony Council, defused without incident what could have been an explosive encounter with far-reaching consequences. Resolving racial disturbances was part and parcel of the job.

In the aftermath of the service club episode, Dave Hughes admonished me for appearing out of uniform but particularly for resorting to punishment. A lieutenant colonel holding a full colonel's slot as chief of staff, Hughes had been Rogers's choice to implement the ongoing social engineering experiment. A very bright, articulate, and opinionated officer, Hughes had served with me in the Pentagon. We rarely agreed on anything. Dave probably saw me as part of the problem, as being out of harmony with the army's new thinking. He was not wrong: much of what transpired at Carson struck me as wrongheaded and as caving in to the permissiveness that marked the 1960s. We did concur on one point. Walking home from a commanders meeting, we discussed the many assignments in the army that required a highly qualified officer. Dave said, "Ralph, the problem is that 90 percent of the jobs in the army need a ten percenter," the term applied to those rare officers promoted below the zone ahead of their contemporaries. Dave's observation was astute: most of the army's requirements proved so demanding that filling them called for truly outstanding officers. The trouble was that many of the best officers and NCOs were leaving the army in droves. In the meantime, they "put in time." Many other career-first officers—the "go-along-to-get-along" types—just went with the flow. Vietnam nearly fractured the army, which was weakened by officer careerism, the rotation/replacement system, atrocities, desertions and "combat refusals," fragging, racial strife and drug abuse. Gen. Creighton Abrams wondered aloud if he commanded an army in Vietnam or a mental hospital. In my view, the root problem rested in a lack of officer leadership, and that problem would worsen before it got better. I stood determined to provide some Old Army leadership in the effort to turn around my brigade.

Swimming against the Tide

Immediately after taking command, I spoke with my commanders and gave them the standard Puckett talk. I could not tell them anything they did not already know. No matter how limited their experience in the brigade, it was more than mine in a mechanized unit. Our primary responsibility was making the brigade combat ready, and my task focused on providing all the support necessary for them to perform their jobs.

Addressing the disciplinary problem ranked as top priority. I spoke with Lieutenant Reed, my "lawyer," laying out my plan to break the backlog in judicial proceedings. Commanders violated regulations by their noncompliance with prescribed time lines for completing investigations, preferring charges, and taking to court the many cases that deserved such actions. Noncompliant commanders not only hurt the command, but they also abused the rights of the soldiers. I instructed the lieutenant to monitor that commanders met all future dates. After appraising the situation in each battalion, he would throw out all nonprosecutable cases and vigorously try all those that went to court. I told him he enjoyed my full confidence and spoke for me in all matters pertaining to judicial and nonjudicial punishments. I gave him a true, mission-oriented order: "Fix this mess!"

Next I briefed the battalion commanders, stating that current conditions were wholly unacceptable and informing them that ignoring procedures would not be tolerated. Our lawyer was my representative and would report directly to me any failures to meet deadlines. They would abide by his instructions, and if anyone had objections, they were to see me, not criticize Reed for carrying out my specific orders. I realized the lieutenant had a daunting job on his hands. I knew he was doing the commanders' jobs, but I wanted immediate action. As a junior officer, he would have to operate outside the chain of command using the cudgel of my rank to bring into line officers several grades superior to him. Unfazed, he went to work with thoroughness and diligence. The initial survey indicated the situation was worse than suspected. After culling the cases that could not be pursued and destroying the records, he took the rest to court. In only a couple of months, all the pending judicial cases were in compliance with regulations. Our "lawyer" proved quite the find. He tried every case in the brigade and won all of them save one.

Interior guard represented one of our biggest problems; malfeasance on guard was the basis for many disciplinary cases. Not only had guards slept on duty or deserted their guard post, but on several occasions prior to my arrival, antiwar dissidents had approached guards and wrested away their weapons. As a precaution, our post interior guard carried ax handles—the local hardware stores obviously benefited from the spike in ax-handle sales—instead of weapons. Wanting to see firsthand, I inspected the guard regularly before reveille. My sergeant major worried about my safety and wanted to accompany me. Such was the state of the U.S. Army in 1970; a commander could not walk his brigade area at night without fear for his safety. I refused the offer. Each inspection found at least one guard asleep or sheltering himself from the wintry cold in the furnace room of a nearby building. I tried to get the word out to the soldiers that if they failed to perform guard properly they might be apprehended and would be punished. I called the brigade duty officer and directed him to report to me when I found any unsatisfactory guard. I hoped that waking this young officer would impress upon him the importance placed on guard duty. I followed up with a report to the battalion commander. Those who breached the rules were invariably tried and found guilty; punishment was swift. Over time, the situation improved significantly.

Physical fitness is one way to combat mental stressors and build unit cohesion. Naturally, the tankers objected to any cross-country foot movement. Since they rode in tanks and armored personnel carriers, why should they train to walk? We instituted quarterly fitness tests patterned after what we had done in the Tenth Special Forces Group. To incentivize personal fitness, the brigade instituted a "Run for Life" program with the slogan "Go the extra mile." T-shirts emblazoned with "25 Miles," "50 Miles," and "100 Miles" were awarded. The post newspaper gave us coverage, including a photo featuring my executive officer presenting a T-shirt to Rogers. The fitness drive produced some beneficial results but made little headway against the tide of apathy.

In addition to punishment, publicity, and physical fitness as means of improving discipline and morale, I appointed a "special assistant" and frequently met with him in a conscientious effort to determine what we could change without hurting combat effectiveness. My sergeant major selected a soldier, an African American, as the special assistant with duties similar to those of an ombudsman. Soldiers contacted the special assistant with their grievances, and he brought the problem to the appropriate staff officer, the sergeant major, or me with a recommended course of action. I viewed the ombudsman as an expedient until I could get commanders to listen to soldiers and get us functioning as we should. I briefed the commanders on what I was doing, emphasizing that the special assistant was expected to conduct himself with the highest decorum and to meet the highest standards. I cautioned the special representative he was not to "wear my eagles" and should be extra respectful to officers and NCOs. His ability to help soldiers would be significantly impacted by the way commanders and staff saw him. While the special assistant did assist in solving several problems that otherwise would never have come to my attention, he failed to keep himself under control. He committed shoplifting in the PX. In the end, the soldier lacked the character needed for the responsibility placed on him.

Rap sessions were scheduled for each month. Any enlisted man could raise any subject to me without fear of retribution from the chain of command. The sergeant major saw to it that at least one representative attended from each company in the brigade. Reluctant at first, the troops found it hard to believe the brigade commander would listen. Over time, they began to open up. The complaints, relatively minor from my viewpoint, held significance to the soldier as it affected his quality of life. The sergeant major investigated and addressed the problem; there was never any reason for me to get involved.

These actions were designed to improve trust and help alleviate the toxic environment in the brigade, but, in my estimation, they seemed not to have changed matters. One exchange I had with two enlisted men highlighted the gulf that existed. The soldiers—one Caucasian, the other African American—asked to speak to me about some of their concerns. I obliged in the hope of improving the climate in the brigade. Almost immediately they became obstreperous and argumentative. In one diatribe, one of them accused my generation of being murderers (Vietnam), subjugating women, and destroying the environment. I responded to each of these accusations. Although I entertained many questions about Vietnam in my own mind, I outlined the American goals in Vietnam and how we had inexorably moved toward an impasse far from acceptable to even the staunchest supporter of our involvement. While my views on appropriate gender roles probably qualified me as a male chauvinist, Jeannie and I inculcated in our daughters the belief they could overcome society's unrealistic restrictions and prejudices and be anything they strove to be. Not mollified, one pronounced that either our generation would change and "come around" or there would be dire results. Taken aback by this attack on the army, my generation, and me personally, I could not let that outburst stand unchallenged. Lowering my voice and looking him straight in the eye, I said, "I will not listen to your threats. You refuse to discuss our differences dispassionately. I am trying to play ball with you. I am not one of those who will take his bat and go home if he does not get his way. You either play ball with me, or I'll take my bat and knock your head off! Get out of my office." Stunned by my reaction, they left. I fully expected they would lodge a complaint with the inspector general claiming I had been not only verbally abusive but also physically threatening—or at least make a stink in one of the many soldiers' councils. In either case, I could expect a rebuke from Rogers or worse, but I never heard from either the inspector general or the commanding general. To me, the division leadership, so eager to avoid strife, had become indulgent. What was needed was firm, fair leadership focused on becoming combat effective while treating the soldiers with the respect they deserved. I felt very few, if any, recognized this gulf existed.

The confrontation with the two enlisted men was symptomatic of the pervasive, palpable tension on post. The celebrated appearance of one of the most divisive figures of the period—"Hanoi Jane" Fonda—certainly raised the temperature. Because Fort Carson appeared so much in the news, Fonda, in search of more publicity, appeared at the main gate one day with a legion of photojournalists in tow. Rogers totally neutralized her. Much to her surprise, the general invited Fonda to his office. He put on the charm offensive. When she claimed the stockade was a "political prison," he offered to escort her to the lock-up. She accepted and was allowed to converse with the detainees. Everyone she encountered was there for, in almost all cases, minor infractions of military law. Rogers then suggested she return to address the troops in one of the "open dialogues" routinely held on the stage of the theater on main post. Totally disarmed by the engaging general, she left and never took Rogers up on his offer.

Although he never gave Ms. Fonda any indication of it, Rogers probably was sizzling inside, as I later discovered at some cost. That night the general and Smith and their spouses, Collier and Ann Ross, and Jeannie's brother Frank came to dinner in our quarters. Over dessert, the topic of the *Pueblo* incident came up. Not knowing any more than what appeared in the press at the time, I ventured the opinion the United States had not gone to bat for Commander Lloyd Bucher and his sailors at the time of the seizure of the ship by the North Koreans and should have taken immediate military action to secure their release. Rogers exploded and bluntly informed me I was completely wrong and ignorant of what actually transpired. The general's outburst—so out of character—shocked us all and certainly put a dimmer on the evening. Rogers soon left. Always the diplomat, Smith told me, "Ralph, I don't know what got into Bernie. He had no cause to say what he did" and apologized in his stead. I smiled and said, "Sir, it doesn't matter. Something ticked off the general and he exploded. I've worked for him before. Once he vents his spleen it's all over." There was no doubt what set Rogers off.

As time-consuming and mentally taxing as the cultural wars proved to be, the most frustrating part of commanding the brigade lay in the failure to improve combat readiness. One-fourth of the manpower turned over each quarter. With even crack troops, this kind of personnel turbulence would have been harmful; with disgruntled short-timers training for a new role on new equipment, meeting combat-ready standards was a forlorn hope. The division was earmarked for Operation Reforger (return forces to Germany), the annual "strategic mobility exercise" testing the movement and deployment of combat-ready forces from bases in the United States to Germany confronting a simulated Soviet breakout from the Fulda Gap. One brigade would proceed directly from Carson to two bases near Kaiserslautern carrying only their duffle bags; in theory they would mount prepositioned armored vehicles and immediately join the NATO order of battle. The other two brigades would follow, complete with all their vehicles and weapons. The U.S. Army in 1970 could not have executed Reforger. Red Army tankers would have been eating spätzle in Kaiserslautern before the Fifth Mech arrived in force. The army rated readiness in four categories—personnel, equipment, training, and supplies—on a scale of 1 (not combat-ready) to 5. At Carson, units routinely scored 1s and 2s across the board.

On the whole, training was not as bad as expected. The mechanized infantry had no "branch home," no Benning, Knox, or Sill where officers and men received specialized training. Most of the officers, NCOs, and soldiers with Vietnam experience had no exposure to M113 tracked vehicles, yet we were handed the mission of preparing to fight a mechanized war in Germany. The brigade held some field exercises and participated in one division-size Command Post Exercise (CPX)—an exercise involving primarily commanders and staff, communications, and some support personnel—that indicated we had made some progress. Maintenance—particularly vital in a mechanized division—was the biggest headache. There were a lot of vehicles (in addition to communications, weapons, and other equipment) that required many hours of hard, skilled work to keep them operating. While a great amount of time and effort was devoted to maintenance, the desired results were never achieved. Trained people were in short supply. Spare parts were difficult if not impossible to obtain. My brigade staff visited subordinate units often so that the more experienced and knowledgeable people at brigade could assist those in the units. Sometimes this approach helped, but just as often it created frictions.

In December 1970, Rogers left Carson for reassignment to Washington to head the Office of Army Congressional Liaison with the task of convincing the lawmakers of the merits of an all-volunteer army. Before he left, Rogers called a meeting of his commanders and heaped praise on his replacement, a classmate, Brig. Gen. John Bennett. While I did not want Rogers to leave, I had a positive feeling about Bennett. Almost immediately after the change of command, Bennett assembled the brigade commanders and General Smith. Bennett spoke briefly, directly, and clearly expressed his complete dissatisfaction with what he had seen—the extremely poor appearance of many of the soldiers, their failure to render the proper military courtesies, and the large number who skipped training. He made it clear he expected the brigade commanders to correct the situation and ensure standards were met together, with the implied threat we would either shape up or ship out. No brigade commander made any comment.

When Bennett withdrew, Smith held us for a short discussion. None of us had much to say. We knew Bennett was right. As tactfully as he could, Smith told us we had to produce immediate results. I returned to my office and, alone with my thoughts, tried to determine the impact the new commanding general would make. I had failed in the most important facet of my job—to prepare the troops under my command for combat. This realization weighed heavily on my mind.

Shortly after Bennett's assumption of command, the division was reflagged the Fourth Infantry Division (Mechanized). The Fourth Division had been reassembled at Carson after the phased withdrawal of its brigades from Vietnam. Other than donning the Ivy Leaf patch, nothing much changed. We brigade commanders sweated out the reflagging ceremony. Would all my vehicles start and make it around the parade ground as the division passed in review? As happened in previous ceremonies, would some soldier hit the "push-to-talk" button on a radio and make disparaging remarks about the army or keep the switch depressed, preempting the radio net and preventing any communications? That those two questions stood foremost in my mind spoke volumes about my lack of confidence in my brigade. As we rolled past the reviewing stand, I asked myself, as I had done so many times before, "Where have I failed? What can I do to improve the combat readiness of my unit?" Those same questions had plagued me almost daily since assuming command of the brigade, but I had never arrived at a satisfactory response. Even though everything went off without a hitch and the division put in a very impressive performance, I felt that an irresistible force was overwhelming me. In the midst of all these men, I felt alone. I wondered if the other commanders entertained the same doubts.

Good-Bye to All That

For three years I had toyed with the idea of leaving the army. At West Point, I was ready to turn in my papers, but the prospects of a brigade command under Rogers and a return to troop duty convinced me otherwise. At the time, I had a hard time envisioning myself being anything but a soldier. But if Vietnam was disheartening and West Point disillusioning, Fort Carson was downright demoralizing. According to the army, I had punched all the right tickets—the Ranger company in Korea, airborne battalion commands in Vietnam, graduation from Leavenworth and the War College, service in the Pentagon on the army staff. On the promotion pyramid, I stood ahead of many of my contemporaries, commanded a brigade, and, although nothing is certain in the army, advancement to brigadier general was not impossible. Curiously, the more I succeeded—in terms of promotions and assignments—the more estranged I felt. West Point and a brigade command represented choice appointments and great opportunities for career enhancement, but both left a very sour taste in my mouth. I felt alone, swimming against the tide as I tried to uphold standards the army seemed no longer interested in maintaining. Disappointed with my performance, in my estimate I had failed. I harkened back to my desire as a first lieutenant to serve in combat as the best regimental commander in the army. I always wanted to be placed in a position that taxed me mentally, physically, and psychologically to the utmost. I experienced that feeling commanding the Rangers in Korea and with the 2/502nd in Vietnam: exercising direct command in intimate contact with my men, forging that special bond that seldom develops in any place other than in combat. After completing my tour at Carson, all that loomed was the prospect of a long stint in staff slots far removed from the men. A return to the Pentagon filled me with dread.

Beyond career considerations, a sense of unease settled over me. Commentators talk of the malaise the United States slipped into in the 1970s. I felt something akin to that, as if I had lost my way. The country was in social upheaval like no time since the Civil War. Every belief I grew up with was being assailed. Never in its history had the army been in worse shape or held in lower regard by the people it served. With the very fabric of American society fraying, it was a difficult time raising teens when the values Jeannie and I tried to instill were questioned by their teachers and peers. Many times Jeannie and I discussed my leaving the army, but she refused to influence my decision, which portended such momentous change in all our lives. She did not want any of the blame if I retired and discovered I had made a mistake. Although her refusal denied me her wise counsel, she was right.

For three years, I had been courting and been courted by Outward Bound. In 1968, I had read a *Life* article about the organization and its mission. It appealed to me as a very worthwhile program that could have a major and positive impact on young people. After all, it offered all the things that attracted me to volunteer for Special Forces, and I would not be cooped up in a windowless garret in the Pentagon pushing papers. After meetings with the executive director and key members of the board, a job offer was definitely in the works. Given the timbre of the times, Outward Board worried about whether a hard-boiled army colonel would be a good fit for their organization. The test came when I took two weeks leave and attended an Outward Bound managers' course in Baja, Mexico. The participants were midcareer managers. I was part assistant instructor and part participant. The Outward Bound staff members would influence the final decision. Many of the younger ones were "free spirits" who subscribed to the philosophy, "if it feels good, do it." Some had been conscientious objectors. I told the director, Murray Durst, that if they wanted to make a specific job offer, I needed at least sixty days' notice so Bennett could find my replacement. Apparently I passed the Baja test: Murray made the offer, and I accepted.

I immediately asked General Bennett for an appointment. After he told me to be seated, we exchanged a few pleasantries, and then I said, "Sir, I am retiring July 1." After a short silence he asked me why I was taking that fateful leap. I had no pat explanation, just that Outward Bound had offered me a job as the national programs coordinator. He expressed his surprise and genuine regret that I was leaving the army. Then he reached into his drawer and extracted a document containing a long roster of colonels under consideration for promotion to brigadier general. He then went down the list and asked whether I thought each officer named was better than I. He expressed his opinion on each of them. At the end, I ranked "ahead" of all but two. While his appraisal was very flattering, I had many doubts. He inquired how I would feel when many of those officers on the list became lieutenant generals and corps commanders. I replied if I served on active duty long enough I hoped that, if deserving, I would make general, but that had never been my goal. The general asked me to hold the paperwork until the last minute—sixty days before the requested effective date. He probably expected that I would be on the next promotions list and see the light. I thanked him for his time, courtesy, and concern. As I saluted and turned to leave, he said, "Ralph, you may be able to accomplish more for our youth and this country in Outward Bound than if you remained in the army."

I worked full bore until the day of my retirement. There were a lot of things I wanted to accomplish before I turned in my suit. Finally the day for the change of command came. Initially I planned for only a minimum number—the battalion commanders and their staffs, the headquarters and headquarters company commander and his first sergeant, and the colors. Bennett "suggested" that I have a full brigade review, saying that the troops would want to say good-bye to me and welcome the new commander, Col. William J. Livesey—who retired with four stars.

A few military and civilian friends attended. Jeannie and our children were there. It became a bigger ceremony than I had imagined. The day was beautiful—bright, clear, cool—as only a day in the Rocky Mountain West can be. Bill Livesey and I rode around the formation in a jeep. General Bennett made some very complimentary remarks about both of us. I expressed my pride in my soldiers and how important they were to our country. Bill made his comments. The troops passed in review. Happily, there were no untoward incidents, and all vehicles were mobile.

What did I feel as Bill and I trooped the line? I bottled up my emotions, refusing to think about the momentous changes about to occur. I would be leaving an institution that had and still meant so much to me, something to which I had dedicated twenty-two years of my life. It was the only life I knew and really cared about. I shut my mind, allowing no doubt to enter my thinking. To paraphrase a famous fictional Georgian, "Tomorrow would be another day."

Bennett lavished more praise on me during the reception in the officers' club and then presented me with an impressive keepsake, an iron horse-head hitch, the type Old West riders tied their mounts to. The inscription read, "To Colonel Ralph Puckett, Jr. Commander Bull Dog Brigade 'He Really Gave a Damn' from the Iron Horsemen." Bennett remarked that I was the first recipient of the memento that he had directed would be presented on similar occasions in the future. I made a very brief statement, again thanking the general and friends for coming to the ceremony. The room quickly emptied. It was over. My retirement became effective on 30 June 1971.

14

Life in Mufti

Outward Bound, Discovery, and MicroBilt

Before heading east, Jeannie and I decided to take a family vacation to the Grand Canyon. We would begin at Lees Ferry in northern Arizona, raft down the Colorado from Lake Powell through Marble Canyon, then hike to the South Rim. An ambitious plan—too ambitious for the teenage girls. They opted out and would spend time with Jeannie's parents in Columbus. We cleared quarters, loaded up the mobile home, and set off.

Descending the river, it was easy to imagine how John Wesley Powell felt when his expedition entered the Grand Canyon in 1869. His account described the canyon walls polished smooth as marble. After five days on the river, we reached Phantom Ranch, the head of Bright Angel Trail. The eleven-mile five-thousand-foot ascent at an average 9 percent grade presented a real physical challenge. Whenever I looked at Jeannie and Tommy, their faces said, "Why did I ever consent to this?" Finally reaching the rim, we made a beeline to the mobile home and cranked up the air conditioning. Later, Tommy and I bought and presented Jeannie with a blue ribbon that read, "I Hiked the Bright Angel Trail."

After a day and night pit stop to recuperate, I cranked up the motor home and started our long journey to Virginia. We spent some time in Columbus with the in-laws and a day with my mother in Tifton and then headed north.

Hard Reentry

Before my retirement, Jeannie and I had visited Reston and selected a suburban home on a cul-de-sac. Equivalent to our quarters at West Point, it was the nicest place we had ever had. Embarking on a new life with the knowledge that major changes confronted us all, we believed the job, the new house, and the pleasant northern Virginia town we would soon call home offered the promise of a soft reentry into civilian life. We had enjoyed the time we spent in Annandale while I worked at the Pentagon. For the first time, Jeannie and I had all our possessions in one place.

Sociologists speak of the army as a "total society," as an internally organized community isolated, both physically and psychologically, from mainstream society. The army has a highly stratified social system where relations are regulated by law, ritual, and custom—even off post. Officers typically came from similar backgrounds—white, Protestant, middle and upper-middle class—and emphasized traditional ways of doing things. The majority espoused political and social conservativism. Military installations were self-contained and offered family, medical, and social services not enjoyed by most civilians; schooling, churchgoing, and leisure activities took place on post. I fit the mold: a small-town boy from the Deep South with entrenched values who had led a cloistered life in the army since entering West Point.

Much had changed in American life since the late 1940s, and none of it was so radical—and foreign to my way of thinking—as that produced by the upheavals of the 1960s. The intense political debates, colored by what seemed like a pervasive opposition to the war, often centered on censure of the army and those who served. If the sociologists were right—hard to say otherwise—then the adjustment to civilian life would be doubly difficult, given the altered atmosphere.

Reston seemed the perfect place for a new start. Reston itself was styled a "New Town." A planned community of fewer than six thousand people founded in 1964, it served as a model for a fundamentally different concept for suburban satellite towns outside major urban centers. Reston balanced mixed-density and mixed-income housing with commercial developments; planners interspaced open spaces, connected by walking and biking paths, all centered on an artificial lake. Thirty miles from the Mall, Reston allowed effortless access to all the educational, social, and cultural attractions of Washington without the stress of living in a deeply fractured city. Plus I had an easy commute to the office. While I immersed myself in the new job, Jeannie looked after placing the children in schools. That appeared to go well: Tommy entered the sixth grade in the Hunter's Woods School, and the girls enrolled in the district's recently constructed high school in neighboring Herndon. After our twenty-two moves in nineteen years, Reston looked like the perfect spot to put down roots.

Murray Durst and wife Sue, a congenial pair, did their best to help us get settled. While the move of the national headquarters to Reston remained a work in progress, Murray began laying the groundwork for his vision of the organization's way forward. As former director of the Outward Bound School in North Carolina, he recognized both the inherent strengths and weaknesses of the program.

Outward Bound used outdoor challenges to assist in the development of teamwork and self-confidence. The individual schools looked upon themselves as self-sufficient entities that required no control or guidance from some meddling national office. Since none of the schools were self-supporting, they wanted fund-raising assistance from Outward Bound International (OBI) and nothing else. In fact, the schools—the directors as well as instructors—saw OBI as a financial drain because they had to contribute to the national headquarters. Until OBI's fund raising exceeded school contributions, this friction could not be removed and the organization could not move forward.

The week I reported for work, Outward Bound had three student deaths: one resulted from an accident in Minnesota, and the two others were caused by hyperthermia in the Pacific Northwest. These deaths provided a wake-up call. Outward Bound stood in significant danger of losing its liability coverage. The insurance representative stressed the importance of the creation of and strict compliance with a uniform safety policy. Although that period was not as litigious-crazy as today, one lawsuit for negligent death could sink the organization. As national programs coordinator, it fell to me to develop and implement safety guidelines and ensure their enforcement. Failure to do so would result in the cancellation of our coverage.

OBI called a meeting of instructor representatives from each school to begin the preparation of this policy. Each school sent two or three of its senior instructors to the host school in Colorado. I went there fully expecting opposition; all these people were technically qualified and highly individualistic and, in the past, had proved highly antagonistic to control from above. Remarkably, however, after reviewing each component of an Outward Bound program— the trek, rock climbing and rappelling, canoeing, sailing, and the solo—we achieved unanimous agreement. Returning to Reston and consulting with Murray, I assembled a policy statement and went out to the schools soliciting feedback. After a series of revisions based on inputs from the schools, we formulated a fixed policy.

Murray directed me to visit, together with school and OBI representatives, each of the schools. The initial focus on safety compliance expanded into all facets of school operations including program content, logistics, and administration. Each "peer review" lasted three to five days, after which I compiled the findings and returned the report to the school under review. Murray and I were pleased that the schools saw the peer review as positive and welcomed it. Over the next two years, I visited all the schools save the one in Oregon.

After about a year, it became apparent the national board wanted to reorganize and strengthen fund-raising efforts. That meant Murray was out. Durst had a sound business sense and the ability to get along with a very diverse group of free spirits, but he lacked what it took as a fund raiser. Both his support and wise counsel helped me over some rough spots. I submitted a résumé and went to see Kent Rhodes, the CEO of *Reader's Digest,* our largest financial supporter, knowing my candidacy was a long shot. I never really wanted the job. Kent was cordial and went through the motions as a matter of courtesy.

The board selected a new executive director who lived in the New York City area. Obviously if the chief drive centered on fund raising, you go to where the money is, and that meant New York. OBI would move. The new national director-designate—a very polished individual—visited Reston and offered all the executive staff an assignment in New York. Jeannie and I invited him to dinner, and again he made a pitch for me to stay in the organization. Neither of us had any desire to pick up again and move to "the city."

I decided to take the Outward Bound philosophy and form my own program. In my view, the organization had lost sight of its educational mission. Several private schools had approached Outward Bound expressing interest in creating joint programs. The Madeira School—an exclusive prep school for girls in Great Falls, Virginia—was one of those schools. I visited the headmistress, Ms. Barbara Keyser, to determine what she wanted. Keyser was all business and clearly stated her objectives and the parameters within which a program must operate. I returned to my office and drew up a proposal.

Outward Bound saw only problems and no real potential in running one-day-a-week hybrid programs. I returned to Madeira and told Keyser that while we appreciated her interest in Outward Bound, we could not accommodate her. In her direct manner she asked, "Why don't you do it for me?" I reminded her, "I work for Outward Bound." She retorted, "Why don't you quit and do it on your own?" I informed her that I was considering doing just that. She said the school had set aside a considerable amount of money for what she had in mind, and if I became a free agent to get back to her.

The bluff headmistress made a significant impact on me. Because of her encouragement and confidence in me, I decided to take the leap and founded a company offering adaptive programs such as the one Madeira desired and called it Discovery. Aside from Madeira, the National Parks Service and the

Washington public schools system offered possibilities. I told Murray and gave him my date for leaving. He wished me well.

Our suburban idyll turned out to be a real disappointment, more stressful than life in the army. After living in the cocoon of the army for nearly two decades, entering civilian life felt like living in an episode of *The Twilight Zone*. The country had changed, but we had not. The people in our Fairfax County neighborhood appeared more transient than military officers. There did not seem to be any social center of gravity. Our neighbors came from all over the country. Government agencies transferred their people as readily as the army. Within two years, the Pucketts had lived longer on the block than anyone else. At least in the army, the officer corps was communal; friendships and family relationships were easily formed. Jeannie and I shared little in common with the people on our street. To add to the problem, sleepy little Reston boomed in the 1970s. Its population increased by more than 500 percent, fundamentally altering the feel of the place.

Even affluent northern Virginia could not escape the culture wars that wracked the country. One of our neighbors, a minister, had a son heavily into drugs. While high one night he badly burned himself. Herndon High had its share of social problems, chiefly widespread drug use and violent clashes between students, often over race. The administration and teachers appeared impotent. It was, after all, the Age of Aquarius, whose creed was "Drugs, Sex, and Rock & Roll" and "Trust nobody over thirty." The girls, who had led cloistered lives, were confronted by all these alien stresses. Jean had a rough senior year. Aside from attending her third school in four years, she was bullied.

At first, Tommy flourished. Hunter's Woods School featured an "open classroom" team-teaching approach. Tommy loved school and made good grades. That changed dramatically when he entered intermediate school. His grades dropped precipitously, and he became morose and uncommunicative. Each night as we settled around the table for supper, he invariably said, "I hate school." Jeannie and I asked for a meeting with the principal and Tommy's teachers. The Hunter's Woods teachers described Tommy as an "exceptional" student, which translated at his new school as "special needs." He ended up in the "slow learners" class. The teachers assigned him small tasks such as distributing papers and work materials. By the time the teachers assessed his intellectual abilities, they decided on keeping him because Tommy was so cooperative and helpful with the other students. Detecting our alarm, the principal promised to move Tommy into the streamed cohort at the beginning of the next grading period.

Jeannie and I left convinced we needed to pull Tommy out of the public school system. He needed a school that valued learning and tried to meet the individual needs of each student. On the advice of Barbara Keyser, we settled on Woodberry Forest, a postcard-perfect prep school about forty minutes north of Charlottesville on the banks of the Rapidan. Sending Tommy there meant his separation from the family and imposed a heavy financial strain, but it was the best thing we could have done. Tommy got back on track and blossomed at Woodbury.

Jean went off to college at the same time. While at West Point, Jeannie and I had made a number of trips, scouting out colleges. Many of these carried us into New England, usually in autumn to take advantage of the beautiful scenery afforded by the leaves changing. The landscape is dotted with small liberal arts schools. Talking to the admissions people, we found these schools a little too liberal for our taste. Eventually Jean settled on St. Lawrence University. As the name suggests, the small private school was located about twenty miles from the river and the Canadian border. The chief attraction was skiing, for which Jean had a passion. Her parents hoped that passion would not be diverted to any of the hockey players. We feared she would marry a hockey player and end up living in Canada. With Jean in school and Tommy at Woodbury, that meant we only had Marty with us. That took some adjustment. We did make plenty of trips to see Tommy at what we came to call Camelot, so perfect was the environment at Woodbury.

Meanwhile, Discovery began to take shape. Totally lacking any business background, I faced plenty of hurdles. First I put in place an administrative structure and designed the program and established safety procedures. Then I worked up a promotional brochure. A commercial artist created a logo that depicted in stylized form our four core activities: canoeing, rappelling, skiing, and backpacking. The next step involved assembling a team. Somehow the word got out among the outdoorsy people in our area, and applicants arrived.

Discovery evolved around our mission statement: "Personal Growth through Safe Adventure." The safety-first approach stood as the pillar tenet. Our first foray presented a real challenge. A local public school experienced a large turnover in staff, and the principal wanted a one-day "team building" exercise. We obtained permission from the Parks Service to run the program in Great Falls Park on the Potomac. We christened it a "Day of Discovery," and that became the company's marketing slogan for the single-day program built around ropes and initiatives, individual and team-building activities. The weather turned out perfect; the activities proceeded without any glitches. All sixty participants completed every event. The discussion session—and the very positive feedback—brought the day to a successful end.

Discovery developed as an organization that planned and conducted wide-ranging programs tailored to a very diverse clientele. Participants over the years included males and females from age five to retirees. We worked with physically, emotionally, and intellectually challenged people and All-American high school athletes. The University of Virginia offered a three-credit doctoral-level course in conjunction with Discovery. In addition to Madeira, the National Parks Service and the Capitol District school system, Discovery ran programs for juvenile delinquents and youths at risk, the deaf and physically challenged, and gifted students. Although each program contained one or more of our basic activities, the exact mix and level of difficulty was adapted to specific requirements. Confronting a steep learning curve, we made constant adjustments, and over time Discovery offered a larger package of diverse experiences than the competition.

The staff was as diverse as the programs. The typical job candidate was a product of the 1960s generation—rebellious young people who had "dropped out." The great outdoors presented an escape from the urban, materialistic society they scorned. At least one visited a psychiatrist; some of the others might have been advised to do likewise. Another instructor who worked for me for a year slept in a jeep and used a restroom in a park. At the onset, the situation reminded me of my first days commanding the Ranger company in Korea. In both cases, I confronted a very eager but inexperienced group of untrained individuals far from acting and thinking as a team. As I had twenty-five years earlier, I established a vision, set requirements, trained and required adherence to standards, and set the example. The training program concentrated on fundamentals. We would repeat each activity until we got it right, no matter the number of repetitions. The initial group consisted of eight. In the first training session, none appeared at the appointed time. Evidently, punctuality was fascist; none of them owned a watch. Creating a team would be a test.

For the first couple years, I personally conducted all the training. If the army taught me anything, it was how to plan, organize, implement, and evaluate training. We went to work on "ropes and initiatives." Rappelling was an example of an individual activity. Not particularly difficult technically, backing over an eighty-foot cliff proffered a definite emotional challenge. Success built confidence. "The wall" was a team builder. The "patrol," usually eight to ten students, had to figure out a way to get every member over the obstacle. All participants had to make it. If one person failed, the team failed. Some of the new instructors possessed some familiarity with our other activities—rock climbing and rappelling, whitewater canoeing, caving, backpacking, and solos. Discovery developed a "repertoire" of approximately twenty-five individual and team events. Together we created the "story" that would be recounted to set the scene for each event, the control exercised by the instructor, and how students would be encouraged to do their best. Instructors and participants observed stringent, realistic rules. First, staff members would comply with the safety policy, a condition of employment. There would be no drugs or tobacco used and no co-ed nudity. Once we achieved a measure of staff stability and the safety ethic had been engrained, appointed instructors acted as course directors. They assumed charge of all aspects of the program: planning; staff briefings; assembling necessary food, equipment, and transportation; implementation; postprogram student discussions; staff critique; and cleaning and stowing equipment.

Obtaining, training, and retaining people presented the biggest headache. The staff included a former army officer and Vietnam veteran, a son of a West Point classmate, and university graduates, but mostly they were in their late teens and early twenties with no real work experience and fell into the general category of "dropouts." Many came from advantaged backgrounds. Typically they led austere, transient lives, staying in one place "for the experience" only long enough to save enough money to move on. All had one thing in common: in varying degrees, they were casualties of the "culture wars" sharing the quest to "find themselves." Tom Hardy, a graduate of the airborne and Ranger schools who had served as an advisor in Vietnam, was a godsend. Hardy stayed with us for three years and proved indispensable in those first struggling years as middleman between me and the staff. Although outwardly "squared away," Tom could relate to the others. Two other instructors deserve mention. Vance Ellis got the sack for violating a safety rule. About a year later he returned and asked for a second chance. Everyone missed his humor and willingness to shoulder tasks; his leaving had left a hole. Vance's forte lay in conducting the three-day rappelling, caving, and backpacking trek, something that became known as the "Ellis Special." Dave Kolb came to me as a seventeen-year-old junior in high school during our first summer in operation. His timing was good; I needed bodies for a week-long program mounted for the Madeira School. Against my better judgment, he got his opportunity and never let me down. He continued working for Discovery after he left high school and entered a local community college.

As the staff matured and turnover diminished, our individual and collective capabilities increased. They fully embraced Discovery's educational mission and commitment to safety. The ratio was usually 60:40 males to females, but on occasion that was reversed. In the beginning they heard my mantra: "You did a great job, but I'm not satisfied. We can always do better!" The instructors responded and suggested steps to improve their performance and safety, learning outcomes, and the satisfaction of their students. Before long I was saying, "You did a great job. I can offer no suggestions for improvement. I'm very proud of you." Our emphasis upon safety paid dividends. Discovery experienced only one serious accident—a fall during an initiative event—and the student recovered completely. Our insurer, the largest carrier of policies of outdoor programs in the country, reported that Discovery boasted the best safety record. Despite being young, inexperienced, and free-spirited, my staff made Discovery a great success.

By 1979, Discovery was in great shape. The organization achieved a degree of stability, all the programs were subscribed, and we had a substantial bottom line. Although the personnel turbulence had subsided, we constantly recruited and trained new people. The root problem rested in my inability to offer high enough pay to retain people. Discovery staff had no difficulty—provided they wanted to continue in outdoor adventure work—finding better pay elsewhere. The apparent success of the company did not translate into any windfall for me. I drew less salary than my underpaid staff, depending mostly on my army pension. To cut costs, the family pitched in: Jeannie handled the secretarial and bookkeeping tasks, Tommy helped hauling equipment, and Marty worked one summer as an assistant instructor. The daily physical and emotional grind took its toll. The backpacking aggravated my Korean War wounds. Trying to hold the staff together and meet payroll elevated the stress. For seven years I had been pounding away, without stint or little downtime, trying to ensure the endeavor succeeded. Weekends, usually the busiest times, were just other workdays. Something had to give; I could not continue at that pace forever. Muscle spasms were a constant source of discomfort, but the break came when, one night, I experienced thirty-three of them. The next morning I told Jeannie that I was either going to sell Discovery or close it down. She empathized with my feelings, having long worried about the emotional and physical drain on me. When not at work, I was so exhausted that I could do nothing but catch a few hours of sleep. Both of us were aware of the strain on our marriage and family life.

Prior to making the decision, I started grooming one of the most mature instructors, Randy Smith, as my number-two man and eventual replacement. Randy wanted his own business and jumped at the chance to acquire Discovery. We made an inventory, and Randy bought the equipment at cut-rate prices. I sold everything except the name. Three of my staff stayed on. I assisted Smith with promotional efforts, helped him put together proposals for Madeira and the Fairfax County Department of Youth Services, and met with the current headmistress of Madeira and the appropriate people in Fairfax County. Subsequently, Randy signed contracts with both, providing the financial bedrock for his first year.

At a small farewell party I made a short but heartfelt speech. I expressed my gratification in what we accomplished, which more than fulfilled my original vision, and then thanked individually my fifteen employees. I was proud of their achievements and would miss them. But I would not miss Reston. Jeannie and I decided to move to Atlanta. We would be close to Jean and Marty, who had settled there after graduating from college.

Georgia Back on Our Minds

Georgia acted like a magnet, drawing the Pucketts, except for Tommy, back to the Peach State. Other than family connections and a stay in Columbus during my year in Vietnam, none of the children had any particular southern roots; they were typical "army brats." Nevertheless, both girls started their adult lives in Atlanta. Jean was the first. After two years in northern New York, she transferred to the University of Georgia (UGA). In 1976, Jean graduated from UGA with a degree in political science, and after paralegal training she joined the staff of a law firm in Atlanta. Marty left for school in 1975, entering Lynchburg College in Virginia, which made Jeannie and me "empty nesters." Four years later, she graduated with a degree in special education. An outgoing and engaged teenager, Marty always wanted a career in education, and at Lynchburg College she discovered her calling teaching special needs children. After completing her practica, Marty decided to move to Atlanta. The same year, 1979, Jeannie and I made a trip to Atlanta to scout out a house and found one in Buckhead, an upscale suburb north of Atlanta. We went back to Reston, packed up our belongings, and made the twenty-third move in our married life.

For the next few months we settled in and tried to decide on what to do next. Jeannie did not wait; she opened her own interior decorating business. Before long, she had plenty of clients as she worked from home and affiliated herself with the nearby Atlanta Decorative Arts Center. I still wanted to remain in the outdoor experiential education field and approached Westminster School, probably the most elite private school in the Southeast. The principal of the boys' high school, Charlie Breithaupt, arranged a meeting; we clicked, and I left with a job. Charlie wanted a program for both the ninth-grade girls and boys. He reminded me of Barbara Keyser of the Madeira School in that he knew exactly what he wanted: a required course that would build teamwork and combat cliques.

Discovery was back in operation but with a different business model. The staff would consist of me and an assistant. The only applicant, Bob Coursen, came aboard and remained for two years. The instructors would come from the student body. We started building our ropes and initiatives course on campus, the core of our afternoon sessions. The program involved attending a two-hour session once a week climaxing in a three-day trek "in the wilds." The region provided plenty of options for three-day weekend jaunts. From its modest start, I operated on the assumption the program would grow. We rotated student leaders for different ropes and initiative events with the view of determining who would act as patrol leaders on the expedition and potential instructors should Westminster decide on expanding the program.

As expected, the first year was a hit with the kids, parents, and the administration, and the school wanted to extend the program. The difficulty in developing leader/instructors was not talent—we had a wide selection of bright, mature for their age, and highly motivated young people—it was finding the time, between vacations, heavy academic loads, and extracurricular and social demands, for properly inculcating in them the skills required of patrol leaders. When properly motivated, youngsters are capable of a lot more than most adults expect. Student leadership never presented a problem. When Coursen left, I brought down Dave Kolb from Virginia. As I knew he would, Dave provided a strong right arm and excelled as a leader-trainer. By the fourth year, Discovery ran co-ed programs from prekindergarten through the senior class as well as for parents and alumni. Breithaupt provided invaluable support from "the front office." By any measure, the program went from strength to strength. And this was all achieved by relying on students as instructors.

The only hiccup occurred one winter weekend on a trek in Cheaha State Park in Alabama. Whether through bad luck or faulty intelligence, we mounted the expedition in what one newspaper reported as the "coldest weekend of the century." Wind chill pushed daytime temperatures into the single digits and below zero at night. Back in Atlanta, parents and school officials were anxious and expected—probably hoped—the trip would be curtailed. When we arrived back on campus at our scheduled time on Sunday, the waiting parents were greeted with tales of derring-do: night camps, climbing a sheer rock face, rappelling over a one-hundred-foot cliff, all without a single cold weather or other injury. The kids—especially our cohort of patrol leaders—faced real challenges and responded like hardened veterans.

Attachment to a school like Westminster provided me with valuable contacts. In 1984, I met Gene Sadler, founder, president, and CEO of MicroBilt, a computer start-up company. Gene and his wife, Dot, invited us to spend a weekend at their beach house. Out of the blue, Gene asked if I would come and work for him. After explaining that I knew nothing about computers, he replied the company had all the computer types it needed. What MicroBilt required was someone to organize the company. Over the ensuing months, we discussed what role I might play. Naturally, the offer of a job as vice president with a very attractive package proved difficult to refuse.

The problem was my commitment to Westminster. The administration, teachers, and parents offered their unqualified support; interacting with the students was a joy. Unlike in northern Virginia, there were no personnel, payroll, or personal liabilities. After accepting Gene's offer, I went to the headmaster. Why not repeat the experience with the first Discovery and hand the program over to the very capable Dave Kolb? It proved a surprisingly hard sell, but Westminster named Kolb interim director on a single-year probationary status.

Jumping from experiential outdoors programming into a corporate boardroom was a big leap. Joining a start-up venture like MicroBilt proved far different than entering an established company with a defined management culture. That was clear from my first staff meeting. Gene never bothered to show up, nor had the specifics of my job description been laid out. Clumsily I introduced myself as the new executive vice president, gave a brief prospectus on my life, and expressed my management philosophy. My immediate task centered on establishing organizational procedures and practices with the overriding goal of creating a supportive environment to enhance the company's performance. They looked at me blankly, and when the meeting concluded they went off to their offices.

At that time, MicroBilt developed software and leased computer terminals to companies. Some programs ran credit checks on clients; others tallied items sold against inventory, which granted companies greater control over purchases and just-on-time distribution. In the mid-1980s, MicroBilt offered cutting-edge technologies. As soon became apparent, MicroBilt provided corporations the wherewithal to enhance their efficiencies and improve cost accounting, yet its own organization was in shambles.

The first task rotated around gaining some appreciation for how things worked. In a pattern probably common to all computer start-ups, Gene was a visionary who found a lucrative market niche and hired talented young computer-wise people who had their own ideas. Many people on staff reminded me of my instructors in northern Virginia except some of them wore suits. Gene's two sons held vice presidencies; one oversaw sales and the other, logistics. A rift existed between the computer development side and those who provided the deliverables. The company paid rock-bottom salaries to the salesmen, who naturally wanted a bigger slice through commissions, and the support staff. Morale obviously suffered.

Taking what passed for the organizational wire chart, I met with each department and section to determine the existing standard operating procedures and what needed changing. After considering the inputs and recommendations, I drafted and circulated for comment a paper matching functions with tasks, proposing organizational and procedural improvements. As a subset of this initiative, I began preparing a job description for each member of the staff using Department of Labor criteria. Again incorporating feedback, I wrote a final draft for Gene's perusal. As always, he agreed with the proposals and distributed the findings to the various vice presidents for implementation.

While undertaking this study, I uncovered a glaring problem in accounts receivable. Many accounts stood months in arrears. Companies entered into contracts containing provisions for penalties for past-due payment. The total added up to a small fortune. I took the problem to Gene, thinking my sleuthing would be a revelation; MicroBilt could increase its income by 25 percent. Gene knew all about this and calmly doubled my figure.

Meeting with the vice president for finance, we agreed to go after the outstanding payments. After compiling a list of delinquents and gaining Gene's approval, the company sent out a carefully crafted form "reminder" letter. In no time at all, we received a torrent of telephone calls from irate clients demanding to talk to Sadler. I told the switchboard to direct the calls to me. In many cases, the complaints proved valid; the problem rested with MicroBilt's faulty billing and maintenance accounting records. I bore the unhappy task of calling our clients with the results of our internal review, apologized for the error, and informed them a revised statement was on the way.

Needless to say, Sadler was less than pleased with the outcome of my initiative, which succeeded primarily in angering our customer base and exposing company mismanagement. He ordered a stop. I argued that if we did not intend to enforce the letter of the contract, the company should delete the penalty proviso. It was just like at West Point; the regulations remained on the books even if obeyed only in their nonenforcement. Gene remained adamant; MicroBilt would let the arrears ride.

Obviously this fiasco did nothing to enhance my standing in the company, which became clear when Sadler handed me the job of policing the appearances of our offices. Gene had a thing about messy desks. I had always been a "clean desk" man, and Sadler wanted that as the standard. Some staff improved the way they left their desks at the end of the business day, but most made little or no effort. Again, Gene never made it an issue, and that policy, too, went observed mostly in the breach. Another issue was the slipshod work of the cleaning and janitorial service. A call from me to the head of the company and a couple of night checks resulted in only incremental improvements in performance. I was now vice president for vacuuming and clean wastebaskets.

After about ten months, the job descriptions and enhanced office procedures manual was completed and issued to the offices of the vice presidents, where it immediately took up residence on the bookshelf unread. The company's senior management liked things precisely as they stood, and Gene preferred a happy shop over an efficient one. The exercise did have one salutary result. Sadler needed capital for expansion and attracted the interest of some British venture capitalists. The prospective investors arrived in Atlanta to look over our operations. They met with the senior managers and appeared impressed with my work on improving the organizational structures and standardizing procedures. Sadler's motivation for bringing me on board to undertake the assignment now made perfect sense.

As time went on, I became more isolated from Gene. As we passed in the hall, I often asked to speak with him about some matter. He would say "later," but later never came. I never worried about getting sacked because that was not Sadler's style. At the same time, I could not in good conscience come to the office, have a cup of coffee, put my feet up on the desk, go through the motions, and go home having accomplished nothing. I was not wired that way. Unlike others, I never just walked into Sadler's office, but finally I did. Citing no reason, I resigned my position, effective in sixty days. Gene appeared surprised but not displeased.

In typical Puckett fashion, I never discussed leaving MicroBilt with Jeannie. She knew my frustrations. I joined the company expecting to use my experience, education, and personal leadership talents to launch a new career. MicroBilt offered me a great opportunity. I envisioned being a significant player, contributing to the growth of the company. Instead, I achieved nothing concrete and now found myself ineffectual and sidelined.

The next two months I finished my projects and wrote a number of memoranda for the record. On my last day I said my good-byes and thanked everybody for their cooperation. Most had no idea I had resigned. "I have been with Gene a long time," a colleague confided in me. "No strong personality has ever stayed with him for long." About six months later, my replacement called and asked where he could find a copy of the procedural manual. I told him to look in his right-hand drawer. Evidently, Gene had reconsidered and wanted the changes implemented but could find no copy of the manual.

When I drove out of the MicroBilt parking lot, I felt as if a weight had been lifted from my shoulders. Jeannie continued doing well with her business. We had the financial resources for me to retire, but I was not sure I was ready for that. I knew I would never work for anyone again or start any business that required any employees other than a secretary. That did not leave many options. An obvious benefit of being unemployed was the ability to spend more time with the family.

By the summer of 1985—when I left MicroBilt—Jean was married and would soon present us with our first grandchild. By this time, she had left the law firm and opened her own wedding consultancy and planning business. Marty began at a private school teaching special education sections and working with children with behavioral issues. Later she moved to a public school as a resource person for problem students. In 1987, she married Bob Kinnett from Columbus.

Tommy never joined us in Georgia. After graduating from the University of Virginia (UVA) in 1982, he moved to New York. Like Frank Sinatra sang, "If you can make it there, you can make it anywhere," and that challenge drew Tommy to the "big city." During spring break his first year at UVA, Tommy decided school was a waste of his time and talents and that he would leave Charlottesville for the bright lights of the metropolis. One summer of looking for a job in New York convinced him that school was a better course of action. He returned to school, graduated with honors in English, and set off again for New York. After many rejections he finally landed a job as a copywriter. Once he got his foot in the door, there was no stopping him. He finally got his big break in advertising with a prestigious firm. Tommy's flair for creativity—which he inherited from his mother—and the skills he learned in English expression at Woodbury Forest and UVA made him a natural.

As for me, I became a man of leisure but still remained active. Shortly after leaving MicroBilt, a friend, Bob Valentine, approached me with a request. Bob was head of the administrative board of the Northside Methodist Church, where Jeannie and I were members. The church had plans for a major expansion. Fund raising did not loom as the major obstacle; what worried Bob was that all the attendant stress would splinter the already fractious church leadership, staff, and congregant volunteers. I offered my services gratis and embarked on a project that in many ways resembled what I had just completed for MicroBilt. Bob was right about the fractiousness. Trying to hammer out an agreed common approach was like herding cats, and it took a deft hand not to alienate anyone. After much commotion, we finalized a business and organizational plan, the central component of which was hiring a professional lay manager. Pleased with the results, I decided full retirement was now in the cards.

Retirement permitted space for some self-indulgence in the way of traveling. In October 1985, the commandant of the Escuela de Lanceros invited me to return to Colombia for the thirtieth anniversary of the founding of the school. The offer held a second enticement. I had always wanted to see Machu Picchu, the Inca citadel in Peru. I could make the trek into the high Andes if Tommy went along. Plus the expedition would provide the opportunity for spending some real "quality time" with him. Trekking in the mountains of Peru would act as a bookend to the South Rim hike.

Tommy jumped at the chance. We flew to Lima and spent three days taking in the sights and visiting museums. Our travels took us to Cuzco, the capital of the Incan empire and "gateway" to Machu Picchu. Incan military engineers really knew their stuff, as evidenced by the superb planning and workmanship that went into the construction of the fortifications. The train ride through a massive gorge to the base of Machu Picchu must be one of the most impressive in the world. Instead of doing the usual four-hour tourist "drive-by" tour, Tommy and I spent three days and nights there and much of the time had the magnificent site pretty much to ourselves. One day we climbed Huayna Picchu, a nearby peak that towered above the ruins of Machu Picchu. No trip to Peru would be complete without a visit to the tropical forests at the headwaters of the Amazon. Tommy had never seen a rainforest, and we both marveled at the amazing variety of flora and fauna.

We continued on to Bogotá, Colombia. The day we arrived, terrorists attacked a city bus and killed several Colombians. Our Colombian hosts escorted us to Melgar. Gen. Jack Galvin, head of Southern Command in Panama, was the guest of honor. Jack had risen far in the army since taking over for me as *asesor* (advisor) to the school. Jack very graciously insisted that Tommy and I accompany him and share in the VIP treatment. Like Jack, the Escuela had come a long way from its near-foundling beginning, and I felt a blush of pride remembering thirty years before. The ceremonies complete, we flew back to Atlanta.

One winter Tommy and I took a ski trip to Jackson Hole, Wyoming. On the final leg from Denver, I told him about a ski instruction book I was reading, *How to Break Out of the Intermediate Rut*. On the first run on our first day I took a nasty spill. I did everything right, pulled my arms and elbows to my side and tucked my head for the jolt to come. I hit with a thud and immediately knew I had done some real damage. A ski patrolman arrived and asked if I needed a sled to get down. The "James Bowen Effect" kicked in, and although the pain was excruciating, I would "be a man" and make my own way down. The medic at the aid station wrapped my chest in a snug bandage on the assumption I had a couple broken ribs. When I returned to my room I spotted two pillows stacked in the middle of the bed propping up my book with a note: "Dad, you better read the book again."

After reviewing the X-rays taken by the medic, the doctor in the local hospital telephoned to advise that I come in immediately. When I arrived by taxi, I spotted a sign on a clinic bearing the name Dr. John Feagin. Was it the same doctor who had treated my knee at West Point? The X-ray indicated five broken ribs, with others cracked, and I was admitted to the hospital. Later they discovered a punctured left lung that was filling with fluid. The hospital hooked me up to some sort of fluid evacuator that required an incision under my left arm. There I remained for a week.

Tommy came to visit each evening after his day on the slopes. He called Jeannie every night but always made excuses why I could not come to the phone. Eventually she suspected something was amiss and made Tommy come clean. He handed me the phone, and I assured her there was no reason for her to fly out to minister to me. Finally I was released but instructed not to fly for another week. John Feagin came to see me a couple times and invited me to his house for dinner. Finally I made it back to Atlanta but continued the regime of inhalation exercises the therapist taught me in the hospital. Months passed before the pain in my chest subsided.

Broken ribs just added to the long list of injuries I had sustained over the years. They would mend. To that point, the family defied medical actuary charts. That was about to change. Nothing could prepare us for the scourge about to ravage the family. The first casualty was Jeannie's mother, who died of lung cancer. A heavy smoker, we saw her condition as a clear case of cause and effect.

The Admiral, Jeannie's father, experienced his own health problems. He stayed with us in Atlanta before moving into a small apartment back in Columbus. He was battling pancreatic cancer. The deaths of parents who have lived normal life spans, while intensely dismaying for family members, are expected as a natural rite of passage. After heart disease, cancer claimed the most victims. But cancer hits irrespective of age or lifestyle. If life is a crap shoot, it appeared the dice were loaded, because in 1990 Jeannie was diagnosed with breast cancer.

After the lumpectomy, three physicians—the surgeon, an oncologist, and our family doctor—arrived in Jeannie's hospital room. The remedies required invasive procedures—a mastectomy followed by a round of chemotherapy. I experienced a kind of numbing dread never felt in the worst of circumstances on any battlefield. In a firefight, you fall back on your training, and, guided by intuition, you regain control of the situation. Nothing prepared me for this. Jeannie took the news entirely in stride, never wavered, and agreed immediately to take the most aggressive measures to fight the cancer. Later, the oncologist confided to me Jeannie's probability of winning that fight stood low, perhaps 30 percent. I had had better odds on that hill in Korea.

The surgery complete, we settled into the routine of treatments every three weeks over the next six months. The rotation never varied: the chemo totally zapped Jeannie, leaving her as weak as a kitten; once home she experienced waves of debilitating nausea that lessened over time until the next treatment, when the cycle started anew. At each step you wondered if the treatment was worse than the cure and struggled with doubts that the chemo regimen was having any positive effect. In the midst of all this, word arrived the Admiral had succumbed.

One morning, Jeannie walked into the living room and without so much as a "Good morning," announced, "I am moving to Columbus. You can come if you want." What could I say? That would be the best, and only, offer I would get. We had been thinking about moving back to Columbus for some time. Atlanta was getting more and more congested, and the cost of living continued to rise. When you lead a peripatetic life in the army, nowhere is really home. Sure, you have strong attachments to your childhood home where so much of your personality was formed, but as the title of one of Thomas Wolfe's novels correctly warned, "You can't go home again." Jeannie put a different twist on that. "You can go home again," she told me, "if you don't expect to find the furniture arranged the same way!"

15

Not All Old Soldiers Fade Away

Fort Benning Redux

Jeannie and I knew the move of the wandering Pucketts to Columbus might represent the last chapter in our lives together, but we went with the fervent hope that it would not begin with a tragedy. Jeannie finished her last chemo round. Within a week, we had a buyer for our house in Atlanta. We had already selected a home in Columbus. While it underwent renovations, we settled into the same apartment the Admiral had lived in before he died. Perhaps it was not the best choice under the circumstances, but the arrangement worked. All this transpired over the Christmas season. It was quite natural that Jeannie wanted to return to Columbus. The city was her hometown, she had a brother and longtime friends there, and Fort Benning was ten miles away. She reasoned that, in the event she did not make it, I would have a support network already in place. As usual, she was thinking about me.

After retirement, I lost any real contact with the army. People are incredulous when they ask—and they frequently do—if I regret leaving the army when I did, forfeiting a shot at flag rank, and I tell them no. Although disheartened, I left with no chip on my shoulder. After all, my case was not unique. I remained interested and informed on security issues and developments in the armed services, but my busy life had steered me in other directions. Back in Columbus, I decided to reach out to Fort Benning. It seemed like the natural thing to do. Little did I know that would open a second coming of sorts for me in the army, a longer one in some ways as challenging as—and certainly more rewarding than—my time on active duty.

The first step was extending a dinner invitation to the current commander of the Ranger Training Brigade (RTB), Col. John Maher, and his wife. Maher stepped right out of central casting; he was the perfect representation of a Ranger. We hit it off and became fast friends. Soon, my RTB circle expanded. Neal Wickham, an old buddy, told the brigade executive officer, Maj. Bernie

Champoux, about me. Champoux invited me to speak at a Ranger graduation ceremony. One contact led to another, and soon I was giving talks to the officer basic and advanced courses, other graduations, and dining-ins. Maher upped the ante and asked me if I would act as an honorary instructor. Forty years after my hitch in the Ranger Department, here I was, once again, an instructor at Fort Benning.

"The Ranger" Returns to Benning

The timing of my "return" to the army proved propitious. The end of February 1991 saw the conclusion of Operation Desert Storm. The unexpectedly easy triumph of American-led coalition arms in the first Gulf War lifted, in the words of President George H. W. Bush, the veil of the "Vietnam Syndrome." In a real sense, my reconnection with the army removed any residual disillusionment I harbored from the Vietnam era. In many respects, the army had reinvented itself in the intervening two decades. Those social experiments that brought convulsions to Fort Carson produced, from the wreckage of Vietnam, the all-volunteer army that executed those rapid and decisive operations in the Gulf.

The collapse of the Soviet Union and the Warsaw bloc left the United States as the sole remaining superpower. The end of the Cold War and the dissolution of the Soviet Union in 1991 raised questions about the army's future missions in the "new world order." The immediate peace dividend resulted in the reduction in forces of 35 percent. Desert Storm proved the army retained plenty of its teeth, but many wondered about the need for retaining heavy divisions and the LandAir doctrine developed to fight the Warsaw Pact forces in the Fulda Gap—although those force structures and that doctrine proved the perfect fit to fight a "Soviet mirror-image" Iraqi army. In the decade between the two Gulf Wars, many came to believe the solution rested in technology—air power and precision-guided ordnance that made its debut in the Gulf. Where would the ground army fit in this IT-driven revolution in military affairs and the "frictionless" war of the future? As in the 1950s, the army had to reimagine itself, and the burden fell upon the army schools to recognize and adapt to the uncertain but changing conditions of war.

My appointment as honorary instructor and frequent invitations to speak to Ranger and other classes opened up other opportunities; like a rock tossed into a mill pond, it caused a ripple effect. In many ways, Columbus was too big to be a typical post town like Junction City, Kansas, or Lawton, Oklahoma. That is not to say Columbus was not a pro-army town; many soldiers find Columbus army-friendly enough to remain in the area when their service is over. Despite that, the majority of the city's residents had no personal contact with Benning or the army. When civic groups asked me to speak, I jumped at the chance. Some of the talks centered on leadership embodied by historical figures like my hero, George Washington, and Abraham Lincoln; others centered on current security issues; all focused on fortifying a sense of active patriotism and educating the public on the role played by the U.S. Army.

In tandem with public speaking, I began writing columns for the local paper, the *Ledger-Enquirer*. Reasoning that writing would reach a wider audience and make a greater impact, I received plenty of support and encouragement from the editorial page editor, William Winn. My connection with the *Ledger-Enquirer* continued for several years. While continuing deployments overseas—Somalia, Panama, Haiti, Yugoslavia and Kosovo, Iraq and Afghanistan—produced plenty of fodder for my pen, Winn and his successor, Dusty Nix, urged me to weigh in on issues confronting the community ranging from education and economic developments to race relations and the environment.

An annual news flashpoint occurred every November starting in 1990—the protest demonstrations organized by the School of the Americas Watch group led by a since defrocked Catholic priest, Father Roy Bourgeois. The first protest, held at Fort Benning's main gate, involved ten protestors; by 2005, their numbers approached twenty thousand. Cold War anticommunism obliged the United States to partner with some unsavory Latin American and Caribbean regimes, most of them military or military-backed juntas with not a few senior officers affiliated with the School of the Americas (SOA). The SOA's mission—the school had been relocated to Fort Benning from Panama after the United States ceded control of the Canal Zone—was dedicated to improving the military efficiencies of hemispheric sister republics, including an emphasis on counterinsurgency operations. Iran-Contragate and atrocities committed by death squads, such as the murder of six Jesuits in El Salvador in November 1989 that prompted the first protests, elevated the heat. Having experienced life in Colombia during the height of *la Violencia* and given my experience in the special operations directorate in the Pentagon, I possessed a pretty good understanding of the complexity of the problem. Latin American countries remained more feudal than modern; land and wealth remained in the hands of small oligarchies, military *caudillos* guaranteed order, which meant the status quo, and often organized extralegal death squads to repress opposition, more often than not directed against the vast majority of the population, composed of landless *campesinos* working the plantations. While it was never American policy to train and support officers and men who committed human rights violations, some SOA-trained officers were implicated. SOA exercised no control over trainees once they returned to their countries, but all this produced a public relations disaster for the army. Each year a small number of protestors breached the law, provoking their arrest by illegally entering the post and becoming judicial martyrs for the cause.

I took part in a variety of SOA projects, spoke at graduations, gave in-class lectures, and attended training. On five or six occasions I attended the protests for my self-education and to gather material for my articles. Always careful to identify myself as a former officer and supporter of SOA, I engaged in exchanges with some of the protesters. Many protesters, mostly students, were there for the event; those who were informed received their catechisms from SOA Watch or their professors. I had my own fixed views. I do not think my proselytizing made any converts. Except for one ugly scene—a college student called me a murderer—the encounters were always good-natured and provided grist for my *Ledger-Enquirer* articles. With the demise of the Cold War, the focus of SOA changed to the war on drugs with emphasis on the rule of law, human rights, and democracy. The school's name also changed to the Western Hemisphere Institute for Security Cooperation (WHINSEC). The protests continue each November, but they are muted compared to those of the mid-1990s. In 2015, the number of protesters fell to about two thousand, and SOA Watch announced that it would shift its activities to some unnamed site in the Southwest.

Another long-term educative commitment developed at this juncture. In Atlanta, I participated in a program sponsored by the Foreign Policy Association (FPA) called "Great Decisions." The mission—to expand public knowledge of and interest in foreign relations—dovetailed with my speaking and writing projects. Soon after arriving in Columbus, at that point merely wishing to continue my participation in the program, I visited Columbus College (now Columbus State University) and inquired if the school had any affiliation with "Great Decisions." When the answer was no, I wondered why not. That question evolved into me acting as instructor for the course, an offering of the college's continuing education office. Each year the FPA selected eight subjects with significant foreign policy implications and furnished a workbook consisting of brief, unbiased readings, a set of "talking point" questions, and a select bibliography for each subject. The old adage, "You do not really know any subject until you teach it" certainly proved true. I put in probably twenty hours of prep time for each session that included a prepared overview lecture and a guided discussion. The adult students—mostly professional people from the community—kept me on my toes. My affiliation with "Great Decisions" and Columbus College lasted nine years. During this time I joined the local chapter of the Military Order of World Wars and served as a member of the National Security Committee. As with all my efforts, the organization was dedicated to fostering patriotism and awareness of security issues, especially among the youth.

Why did I immerse myself with all these time- and energy-demanding activities? One reason is that I have a hard time saying no—especially to any request that promises to build support for the army and its missions. Another reason stems from being raised to believe you always have to give back. Personally, I gained a great deal—the demands of going behind the podium, whether giving a public talk or conducting a class, and writing editorial thought-pieces required a good deal of hard intellectual work. For me, it was a period of growth. Another reason, at least in the beginning, probably grew out of anxiety, my dread of losing Jeannie.

At first, her prognosis remained uncertain. Having finished the chemo protocols before leaving Atlanta, Jeannie made the monthly trip to her oncologist, Dr. Perry Ballard, in Atlanta. Each checkup produced no result, the best possible news for cancer patients. Over time, Jeannie's strength and vitality returned. She reopened her interior design business in Columbus and made frequent treks back to the decorative arts center in Atlanta searching for the "just right" fabrics and furnishings. Her business grew and occupied a good deal of her time and energies. Her full recovery—including from reconstructive surgery—was a restorative elixir for both of us. Jeannie's full engagement with Jean Puckett Interiors freed up guiltless time for me to pursue my many and varied projects.

Although speaking, writing, and teaching remained important elements of the "new" Ralph Puckett, my responsibilities as honorary instructor at Fort Benning always took precedence. During John Maher's tenure as Ranger Training Brigade (RTB) commander, those commissions continued to grow. Ranger training placed a high premium on approximating the emotional, psychological, and physical stresses experienced in combat. A component of the training involved the deprivation of food and sleep. Observing Ranger training, especially during the Mountain Camp phase in north Georgia, Maher grew concerned that the regimen of starving troops of food and sleep had deleterious effects on learning and health. Maher brought in Natick Laboratories from Massachusetts to evaluate trainees' nutrition levels and how that impacted decision making. He asked me to serve as a member of the team.

Testing took place the day before the course began and at the end of each of the three training phases. After crunching the numbers, Natick reported the average Ranger burnt 50 percent more calories than he consumed. As Maher expected, cognitive skills progressively declined at each stage of the course. Without hesitation but knowing he would come under attack by "old" Rangers for going soft, Maher increased the rations. He asked me to conduct a historical assessment of Ranger nutrition. I contacted all previous directors of Ranger training, asking them to complete a questionnaire. The results proved unavailing. While food intake went from regular to increased rations to food deprivation, all the commanders and instructors responded that the food allocation was always "just about right." As an outcome of the research, Natick would present their findings at a meeting of the National Academy of Sciences in Washington. My study would be included in the presentation.

Based upon my experience as an instructor in the Ranger Department and in command of Special Forces field training exercises in Europe and airborne battalions in Vietnam, the question of combat load was a thorny one. Back in the early 1950s, three "C" rations—a ration is food for one soldier for one day—weighed eighteen pounds. When loads approached or exceeded eighty pounds, a soldier had to think long and hard before adding anything to his pack. I never thought the solution in Ranger School lay with administratively determining food intake. The problem of sustenance in the field should be determined by realistic tactical considerations. The tactical play should involve a resupply component, forcing the patrol to locate and secure the drop zone or contact point. If the patrol does its job, its members will eat. If it fails, they go hungry. The command should not tinker with caloric deficits as a training tool. Let the tactical play determine that. The same applies for sleep deprivation. Rangers must discover and draw upon inner strengths they never knew they possessed. But snatching four hours of sleep each night over a nine-week course may produce automatons, not resourceful fighters. These questions remain unresolved to this day.

Jeannie and I flew up to Washington in typical Puckett fashion, a day early. That night a blizzard hammered the East Coast, closing airports. I ended up being the lone representative from the RTB. Never in my wildest dreams did I think I would deliver a paper and field questions before a panel of the National Academy of Sciences (NAS). The NAS approved Natick's findings—nutritional deficiencies incrementally degraded physical and cognitive performance.

Another enjoyable task Maher asked me to perform involved addressing the officers and NCOs of an airborne battalion that had just completed a special three-week training course. Several battalions from the division had cycled through the program. There was considerable buzz about one battalion commander, by all accounts a real "comer"—a leader destined for great things. One look at his 201 File proved that: a 1974 West Pointer who had served with airborne and mechanized infantry units, the holder of the prestigious George C. Marshall Award as the top Leavenworth graduate, he went on to earn a graduate degree in public administration and a Ph.D. from Princeton before acting as aide-de-camp to the chief of staff of the army. There was more to him than brains. While the other battalion commanders put in an appearance at the beginning of the training and just as quickly returned to Fort Campbell, this officer stayed in the field the entire time. He exemplified the type of officer I always aspired to be—one who leads by example. Word was he could outrun and out-push-up anybody in his battalion. In other words, he was not the usual "operator" so often encountered in the officer ranks, somebody who just worked the system without challenging its inertia and moved on to the next billet to do the same. Upon meeting him, I saw that he possessed personal shine that was no artifice. I thought back to my distant West Point days to a subcourse entitled "Great Captains" and remembered the story of Napoleon taking his first command, of the army of Italy. Napoleon had that unmistakable but not easily defined "something." This young officer had it too. His name was David Petraeus.

My association with John Maher paid many dividends. He and his friend Col. David Grange, who commanded the Seventy-Fifth Ranger Regiment, came up with the idea of creating a Ranger Hall of Fame. Just like Cooperstown, the hall would enshrine "the greatest Rangers of all time." The seven extant Ranger associations would tender recommendations. Rumors floated that a hall of fame was in the works, but I did not give it too much thought. I was amazed when told Ralph Puckett's name would be included among the first twenty-one inductees along with the likes of Robert Rogers, John Mosby, Bill Darby, and Frank Merrill. The ceremony took place on 18 June 1992 on Malvesti Field, the site of the RTB obstacle course. Emotions gripped me after being presented with a medallion. I wished Daddy could have been there. Of all the honors bestowed upon me, being included in the Ranger Hall of Fame in the inaugural class certainly ranks among the top.

Before Maher left, he engineered another accolade for me. He decided to initiate special awards for Ranger School graduates and approached Jeannie about naming one for me. Naturally, Jeannie embraced the idea, and after exchanges with our children they decided to fund a plaque to be presented at each graduation ceremony. Ranger graduation is a big event for the soldiers who have endured great physical and emotional stress for sixty-one days, slogging through the piney scrubs of Fort Benning, the mountains of north Georgia, and the swamps of Florida. Those who are required to repeat one or more phases in the course have a much longer program. The Puckett Award goes to the selected officer honor graduate. The first recipient was 2nd Lt. Stephen J. Roach, who graduated on 13 November 1992. The distinguished honor graduate receives the William O. Darby Award.

Honorary Colonel

In 1996, Col. William Leszczynski, a cadet when I commanded the regiment at the Academy, assumed command of the Seventy-Fifth Ranger Regiment. Bill asked me if I would serve as honorary colonel. Honorary colonels act as a link with the rich history, customs, and traditions of the Rangers and help build esprit de corps through speeches and informal chats with members of the unit. Frank Dawson, another inaugural inductee into the Ranger Hall of Fame, who had won fame on Omaha Beach, was stepping down owing to health problems. Bill did not have to ask me twice; I was delighted and honored to accept. Leszczynski looked for more from the honorary colonel than morale building; he wanted me to act as a mentor to the leadership and fully participate in training. Acting as honorary colonel would require some traveling. While the headquarters and the Third Battalion were at Benning, the First Battalion was stationed outside Savannah and the Second Battalion on the other side of the continent at Fort Lewis, Washington. The chief of Infantry endorsed Leszczynski's recommendation, and the secretary of the army designated me as honorary colonel. Since tours lasted two years, I expected to leave the assignment when Bill's replacement arrived. That speculation proved wrong; I remained honorary colonel of the Seventy-Fifth Rangers for a dozen years.

Being the honorary colonel provided a perfect vantage point to observe army training. The Gulf War provided a distorted road map for the future. The army understood it would be called upon to fight large-unit operations and at the same time develop capabilities to conduct unconventional warfare. Somalia exposed the flaws in post–Cold War doctrine where elements of the Third Ranger Battalion confronted an entirely new threat: the chaos of fighting a nonstate opponent that used asymmetrical techniques devised to exploit American vulnerabilities by taxing the political decision-making process. Ranger training needed to meet the new challenge, but the senior leadership and doctrine writers appeared slow to grasp the changing conditions of warfare. As honorary colonel, I often discussed my ideas with the regimental commander and his S3 and the battalion commanders and staff. Training exercises needed to be tougher and more realistic. In training, the Rangers always won because the mock opposition force (OPFOR) possessed inferior capabilities. Succeeding when the cards are stacked in your favor and everything goes according to the script is a poor indicator of combat-readiness status. Mogadishu proved that tactical commanders and their units must react to unforeseen eventualities. The old adage that "the plan does not survive first contact with the enemy" should always be part of training. Only units that perform when everything goes wrong can consider themselves well trained. I used historical examples— some personal—to buttress my case. They listened, and though my arguments made some headway, change in the army is always incremental.

Over the years, I participated in a broad assortment of Ranger training activities at Benning and the continental United States, Alaska, and Korea—the indoctrination phase, the initial testing of the lower-ranking enlisted volunteers to the regiment, battalion training for team leaders, and unit training for the squads through battalion-level exercises. Ranger indoctrinations, graduations, changes of command, memorials, or return-from-combat-mission ceremonies provided a forum for sharing my views on leadership to successive cohorts of captains, lieutenants, and NCOs. I observed live-fire exercises in New Mexico, Fort Bragg, Fort Knox, and Fort Benning. Another responsibility involved sitting on the Ranger assessment and selection board evaluating prospective commissioned and noncommissioned officers for assignment to the regiment. The honorary colonel position came with a number of added extras: three trips to France and Normandy for D-Day commemorations, and participation in conferences, seminars, and symposiums on leadership at places like the Air Force Academy in Colorado Springs and at headquarters, U.S. Army in Europe, in Heidelberg, Germany.

What drove me was the belief my suggestions might help a young officer be a better leader or that something that I said might save a life of a Ranger in combat. I was never happier than when out in the field with the men, imparting my experience-taught lessons. Rain or shine, heat or cold, I walked the ranges, discussing fundamentals of leadership, and striving, by example, to impart the "Be all you can be" value system the army espoused. Rangers who watched a seventy-something-year-old man with gimpy feet hump up hills and trudge through swamps, rivers, and dense forests on patrols lasting over a day would think twice about giving up. Several times a year I visited the Florida and Mountain Ranger camps to assess the training programs: cadre adeptness and leadership, tactical relevance, the realism of the scenario, and overall management proficiency. I also worked with the company grade officers of the Seventy-Fifth during the grueling three-day Mungadai officer development program, named for Mongol special force warriors. When it was solicited, I offered feedback in the form of suggested actions for consideration followed with a written memorandum. The message never varied, derived mostly from my experience with the Eighth Army Ranger Company in Korea: train the fundamentals and, drawing from the legendary coach Vince Lombardi, run the "blocking and tackling" drills and retrain each task—all centered on mastering individual and small-unit skills and techniques—until it was done right. Only then will a unit be combat ready. If each Ranger leader incorporates this philosophy, the net effect will positively impact the combat efficiency of the entire regiment.

One story came out of training that made the rounds. During a Mungadai in the mountains of north Georgia, the exercise controller, Lt. Col. Luke Green, asked me to observe an ambush while attached to the opposing force (OPFOR). Luke affixed white bands around my arm and helmet, designating me as "administrative," and radioed the observer controller with the eight-man patrol telling him about my presence, expecting he would pass the word on to the Rangers. As OPFOR moved along a trail, suddenly bursts of machine-gun and rifle fire broke out. The drill was for OPFOR to return twenty rounds of fire and then fall dead so the Rangers could search them and retrieve anything of intelligence value. Knowing my input would be asked for later, I did not hit the ground but went to my knees. A member of the Ranger patrol yelled, "Get down." I crouched down but kept my head up. I ignored a second command to get down, so the soldier called to his leader, "Hey, this guy won't get down." The reply came, "Put your knee in his back!" He did as ordered. I turned to the Ranger and speaking very quietly told him I was administrative. "Who are you?" he yelled. "Colonel Puckett," I replied. With that, he jumped up and ran away yelling, "Oh my God! It's Colonel Puckett." The story made it into the press, with much embellishment, which included a wrestling match and me proclaiming, "C'mon, I can take you guys."

The next night, the regimental commander, Col. Stanley McChrystal, addressed the Rangers. When he and I entered and the captains came to attention and then took their seats, they yelled, "Colonel Puckett, it was Captain Gray," pointing out the culprit. Everybody had a big laugh. Thereafter, whenever I showed up at the 3rd Battalion headquarters, some Ranger would tell Jim

Gray, the battalion intelligence officer, there was somebody in the front office he needed to see. Once I joked that as soon as I got back into shape, I would challenge him to a showdown in front of the entire regiment.

One of the most memorable trips took me back to the "Land of the Morning Calm" in autumn 2000. Korea was not calm during my last visit. A company from the First Ranger Battalion staged out of Hunter Army Airfield, Georgia, for the exercise, and Lt. Col. Joe Votel asked me to come along. One thing that did not change about Korea is the weather extremes. Although outfitted with snivel gear (designed to keep the wearer warm, dry, and comfortable), I was still cold. The company performed a night helicopter assault into a rugged and mountainous training area. The Rangers executed a difficult cross-country approach and seized and attacked from the high ground. Amid artillery simulators, smoke grenades, and blank automatic weapons rounds, the company took and cleared their objective—a bunker and trench complex—reorganized and exfiltrated with their designated casualties. The next day we held a thorough after-action review, including my observations related to specific training remedies for shortfalls observed.

While in Korea, we toured the site of the mid-February 1951 Battle of Chipyong-ni, the "high-water mark" of the Chinese New Year's Offensive. Ron Miller, a historian from the UN Command staff, vividly described how the three battalions of a Twenty-Third Regimental Combat Team, the First Ranger Company, and other units denied vastly superior Chinese forces the vital transportation link. The fight at Chipyong-ni reminded us that American troops sometimes fight outnumbered and surrounded against very determined adversaries. The lesson is always the same: the ultimate weapon in war remains ground soldiers tougher, smarter, and better trained than their enemy.

Sadly, the Rangers would not have to wait very long before the regiment faced that test: the 9/11 attacks ushered in fourteen years (and counting) of near-continuous overseas deployments of elements of the Seventy-Fifth Ranger Regiment in support of operations in Afghanistan and Iraq. In less than two months after the terrorist attacks, components of two Third Battalion companies conducted an audacious low-level parachute assault on a desert airfield in southwestern Afghanistan. Over the course of 2002–2003, all three battalions had been deployed—in whole or in part—in both Afghanistan (Operation Enduring Freedom) and Iraq (Operation Iraqi Freedom). In the War on Terror that followed, elements of the regiment conducted airborne and air assaults, special operations infiltrations behind enemy lines, direct-action raids against heavily defended enemy positions, and mounted patrols in major population centers stretching from the sands of Anbar Province in western Iraq to the Hindu Kush Mountains along the Afghan-Pakistani border.

When not deployed, units underwent training. Gone were the pro forma exercises. Training took on a greater urgency colored by operational experience. By autumn 2002, the difference was clear. In an exercise in Alaska, a company practiced fighting its way off a "hot" landing zone, in part a product of my inputs stemming from experience with a 502nd company in August 1967. In New Mexico a couple of weeks later, I observed a company conduct a sequence of four "cold hits," two live-fire exercises without any reconnaissance or much intelligence and with incomplete plans. The chemical play proved a little too realistic; the honorary colonel had to beat a quick five-hundred-yard retreat, coughing, choking, and crying. In the after-action report, one lesson learned was "sustain and improve gassing of HCOR [honorary colonel]."

The 9/11 attacks produced a palpable change in attitudes of recruits. About a year before the assaults, I helped put together an outreach program sponsored by St. Luke United Methodist church for enlistees in the noncombat arms undergoing initial-entry training. I always elicited reasons why recruits had joined the army. Before 9/11, the majority saw the army as an avenue for opening up civilian opportunities—a trade or money for school. Unsettling to me, many of them agreed they received insufficient field training; once they went to their Advanced Individual Training centers, they would train for their specific military occupational specialty (MOS). After the events in Manhattan, Washington, and Pennsylvania, I noticed a sea change: a majority expressed the keen desire to "give something back" to their country.

Focusing increasingly on my honorary colonel role, by the end of the 1990s, I sharply curtailed my army liaison activities with the Columbus community. I still had the family to think about. From 1999, many of those thoughts took on a dark hue. Jeannie had beat cancer—a true blessing—but the disease then hit another Puckett, daughter Jean. For two years, everyone expected a good outcome. Jean's breast cancer appeared to take the same trajectory as had her mother's: the apparently successful operation followed by the six-month regimen of chemotherapy and then reconstructive surgery. Then, in 2002, she began to experience shoulder pain, which she first dismissed as a result of overdoing her exercise. When Jean finally returned to Dr. Ballard, the diagnosis could not have been worse. One day she called when I was home alone. After apologizing for having to tell me without Jeannie being there, she stoically informed me the cancer had metastasized in her liver. The news was like a hard blow to the solar plexus; I was devastated. The doctors combated the disease with astringent drugs but without result; Jean decided to end the treatments. Now on palliative care, Jean grew progressively weaker.

Jean's condition put a pall on what otherwise would have been a very happy occasion: my being named a West Point Distinguished Graduate. For over a year I knew my nomination was under consideration by the association of graduates. Much to my surprise, the affirmative notification arrived. The ceremony would take place during June Week 2004. Tommy met Jeannie and me at the airport and drove us to the Academy. For five years, Tommy had lived and worked in Paris before returning to the same advertising firm in New York but with a nicer package. We attended a gala reception and spent the night in the Thayer Hotel on post. The scene the next day could not be improved upon: the weather was perfect as the ceremony took place on the historic Plain. The thought that I shared the award with Dwight D. Eisenhower, George Patton, Omar Bradley, and Matt Ridgway filled me with awe and not a little humble pleasure. Afterward we attended a gathering in a corner of the mess hall. Among the other six inductees were Dr. John Feagin, who had treated me after two of my skiing accidents; Denis F. Mullan, who had been a plebe in my Beast Barracks squad; Dave Hughes, with whom I had served in the Pentagon and at Fort Carson; Gen. William F. Knowlton, superintendent when I was assigned as a regimental commander; and Robert M. Shoemaker, an Army War College classmate. I had not had the pleasure of serving with the sixth, Glenn K. Otis. Ted Swett, who engineered my appointment, presented me with a commemorative watch from our class. Jeannie, Tommy, and I cut short our participation in the festivities, explaining we had to return to Georgia to tend to Jean.

Any relief from the sadness that awaited us soon evaporated. The day after we returned home a call came from Tommy. The news cut me off at the knees. He had been diagnosed with leukemia. Many thoughts—none of them good—flooded over me. Jeannie and I faced a terrible choice: we could not both stand vigil over Jean and render any real comfort to Tommy. Jeannie decided to stay with Jean, and I flew to New York.

At the time, Tommy was at Beth Israel already undergoing treatment. I remained a week, spending each day with Tommy. As I sat there, my thoughts revolved around him. Was I going to lose him? He meant so much to me and his mother. I said very little as these questions twirled around in my head, but I listened intently to the conferences with the doctors as they made their rounds. The following week, on 30 June, Jean succumbed. Jeannie had no time to grieve; she immediately went up to be with our son. After about a month, Tommy transferred to Sloan Kettering. After rejecting bone marrow replacement as an option, the doctors continued with chemotherapy. Tommy's partner, Ralph "Chip" Whitman, stood by his side throughout the entire ordeal. A mountain of support to Tommy and to us, Chip conducted his own research, kept an exact diary of all the treatments, and held the doctors' feet to the fire at every turn. Chip's mother, Daphne, acted as backup. An account executive for a stock brokerage firm, Chip is a bright, personable, and honorable young man, one of the best things that could have happened to us. Chip is family.

When first learning Tommy was gay, I had reacted with dismay—more for him than for me. I felt he might get discounted as a person and in his career because of his sexual orientation. I need not have worried. Tommy and Chip are wildly successful and happy; parents could not ask for anything more.

After six months, Tommy was cleared to return to work part-time. Over time, his "numbers" reached satisfactory level; then the emphasis turned to maintenance and improvement. After five years of tri-monthly blood work and semi-annual bone marrow checks, Tommy regained his full health. However, the gut-wrenching anguish we felt during Jean's decline and death could not completely offset the boon of our son's recovery.

In December 2005, I took my fourth trip to Colombia to celebrate the fiftieth anniversary of the founding of the Escuela de Lanceros. Four years earlier, at the invitation of the chief of the military group in Colombia and the just-departed commander of the Seventy-Fifth Rangers, Col. Ken Keen, I had toured a number of installations. A long-serving Ranger and Special Forces specialist with a master's degree in Latin American studies, Ken provided a wealth of knowledge and leadership. We visited the Escuela Militar, Colombia's West Point; the NCO academy; a basic training center; and naturally, the Escuela de Lanceros—as well as an active unit in the field at base area Tres Esquinas, in the southern part of the country in the heart of the coca-growing region. The highlight was returning to the Lancero school. Lt. Col. Alberto José Mejía, an acquaintance from Benning, saw to it that a Lancero instructor patch was sewn onto my battle dress uniform.

The return visit during the first week of February 2003 proved far livelier. Accompanied by Ken Leuer, a retired major general and president of the National Ranger Memorial Foundation, and Ken Keen, I met with the American ambassador, Anne Patterson, toured the same three schools plus the Colombian helicopter school, and went into the field, again to the coca belt on the Ecuadorian border and to Arauca Department on the Venezuela-Colombia frontier. In Arauca, we visited Saravena, called "Little Sarajevo" because of the level of violence in the district. There we met a Special Forces captain,

Ben Tucker, then on his fourth tour, this time with a fifty-man insertion team. The FARC (Fuerzas Armadas Revolucionarios de Colombia) and the Colombian National Liberation Army (ELN) used safe havens in Venezuela to launch cross-border incursions. The night before I left, FARC conducted a high-profile terrorist attack, a car bombing of a Bogotá nightclub about three blocks from where we were having dinner, killing thirty-four and wounding 164. Later that month, FARC captured and held hostage three American contractors. Following these attacks, the United States stepped up its support of Colombian operations against the narco-terrorists.

Each time I returned to Colombia, I was hailed as the founder of the Escuela de Lanceros; and each time I reminded them of the Colombian names on the commemorative plaque at the gates of the school. In 2001 and 2003, the Colombians awarded me a medal; in 2003, with the Lancero Order of the Red Cross, they presented me with an impressive sculpture of an original lancer, a citizen-soldier who fought with Simón Bolívar for the nation's independence. Later, in 2008, I purchased a stone with the names of Lieutenants Fernandez, Negret, Moros, and Patino inscribed and placed it on the Ranger Walk at Fort Benning.

The family calamities had taken a toll. In 2006, I turned eighty. Although I still looked okay in uniform and felt fine, my feet and knees were giving out on me. Between getting wounded in Korea and 2006, I had twenty foot operations. Infections were chronic. Fifty-six years of walking funny to relieve the pain damaged my knees, requiring arthroscopic surgery and finally joint replacements. I asked Col. Richard Clarke, the new regimental commander, to replace me. I said that although I greatly appreciated the honor and would have liked to continue, my immobility precluded me moving across country during night exercises. Clarke tried to talk me out of leaving and pointed out there was no need for me to go to training. "All or Nothing" Puckett thanked him but declined. On 16 January 2008, the regiment held a change-of-responsibility ceremony; Gen. William "Buck" Kernan (Ret.) replaced me. A week later I went in for the first of two knee-joint replacement surgeries.

Another suggestion I made to Colonel Clarke had a pleasing, if unintended, consequence for me. The army has instituted a competition for soldier and noncommissioned officer of the year awards. Since the regiment already held an internal selection process to determine who would go on to the army-wide competition, why not hold a parallel contest for lieutenants and captains and incentivize it by creating an award? Clarke liked the idea and named it the Colonel Ralph Puckett Leadership Award. The contest is a great motivational tool; participants are graded on physical fitness, technical military proficiencies, and writing skills. That some of the best junior leaders in the army compete for an award bearing my name remains a source of great gratification.

As the honorary colonel, the biggest thrill sprang from my association with a succession of some of the best officers produced by the U.S. Army who commanded the regiment. I served with seven regimental commanders, all eventually general officers, many going on to hold key commands in Iraq and Afghanistan. McChrystal and Joe Votel earned four stars, and Ken Keen, three. I expect others still on active duty will continue progressing. Colonels who rotated in command of the regiment became generals because they had performed exceptionally well before being selected as the regimental commander and were tabbed for greater things. I just hoped that my support proved helpful. Although not certain of my influence, I confined my efforts to nudging them beyond the limits of their experiences. After deployments to Afghanistan and Iraq began, I was included in the planning briefs and offered insights whenever I considered them cogent. I saw the troops off and welcomed them home, on occasion with tears in my eyes.

General McChrystal's retirement from the army was a significant loss to our country. He is extremely bright, a great leader and soldier, a fine physical specimen—a role model for military and civilians alike. I saw all of those qualities in him when I worked with him for two years as honorary colonel. I remember him taking the time to discuss with me the coming activities for the regiment and training that I might enjoy seeing. I remember the field training exercises and the Mungadais. On both, McChrystal invariably threw in a surprise activity that added a significant physical and tactical challenge. His Rangers always expected a surprise but never knew what or when. He is another officer I would have loved to have served under.

Colonel Keen was another regimental commander who, like Colonel McChrystal, supported many of my initiatives. He was particularly sharp, invariably able to recognize shortcomings in briefings by staff members. He saw through smokescreens and elicited the omitted information. I observed him as he accompanied the Mungadais. His critiques were always simple and to the point. He used a questioning technique that was particularly effective. Rather than criticize or state what he thought should have been done, he used questions to keep his Rangers thinking: "When you were at Point 'B,' what was your plan? Did you do what you planned and rehearsed? If you had to do it again, would you do the same thing? What would you do differently?" Every question was a teaching point; the answer required thought.

In May 2001, I was sitting in the briefing room at Hunter Army Airfield, the home of the First Battalion, waiting for the start of a commander's training conference. Much to my surprise, in walked Jeannie and Mary Ellen Keen followed by Maj. Gen. Dell Dailey, commanding general, Joint Special Operations Command. Dailey asked me to come forward, and he presented me with the United States Special Operations Command Medal "for exceptional and distinctive contributions . . . during . . . peacetime." Keen clearly had petitioned for the award and stage-managed the event.

During my time as the honorary colonel, I made three trips to the war zones—two to Afghanistan and one to Iraq—visiting many of the teams in the operational areas. Several things impressed me favorably. Many outposts were manned by a small task force composed of Rangers and members of other agencies. The commanders were junior officers discharging responsibilities—and fulfilling them—that in previous wars would have been held by more senior officers. Called upon to exercise their own judgment and initiative, these younger Rangers reacted immediately to new information. Morale, physical fitness and resilience, and high levels of military skills and leadership were everywhere evident. On one of the trips to Afghanistan I celebrated my eightieth birthday. The Rangers surprised me with a birthday cake.

Those twelve years as honorary colonel were the best tour of duty I had in the army; they were not limited to the Ranger Regiment but included many other commands at Fort Benning. The officers and men always showed me more deference than deserved, but I considered my inputs had relevance. Being honorary colonel reconnected me with the army and brought home how much I missed being with soldiers.

In 2004, I prepared a study on ways and means to better prepare graduates of the Infantry Basic Officer Leader Course (IBOLC) to succeed in Ranger School. Infantry lieutenants are expected to progress to Ranger as the capstone of their preparation for platoon combat commands. Almost all of my practical suggestions were approved by Maj. Gen. Ben Freakley, Benning's commanding general. Unfortunately, some pertaining to assigning only Ranger-qualified officers and NCOs to training positions could not be implemented because the army was short hundreds of personnel with that qualification. General Freakley's immediate decisions impressed me; he needed no staff study before deciding and directing action.

Another program of particular interest to me was the Basic Officer Leadership Course (BOLC II). BOLC II was part of a test program that included newly minted second lieutenants from almost all branches in a basic orientation program before proceeding to their appropriate branch schools. After observing and talking to many of these lieutenants during the course, I recommended making the training more challenging and less programmed. In my periodic observation memoranda forwarded to Maj. Gen. Walter Wojdakowski, the commanding general, I stressed that a stated objective of the program—the graduates would be warriors—was not achievable. I defined "warrior" and discussed the training required to develop that quality. Shortly thereafter, the course objective was changed. I also commented on other shortcomings. Wojdakowski raised these concerns at a conference with the commanders of the BOLC III TRADOC (Training and Doctrine Command) branch-material schools.

One thing that pleased me was that my initial assessment of David Petraeus proved on target. Over the years we saw each other occasionally when he came to Benning or at leadership forums. He always made time for a personal chat. Just as he had shown in that battalion leadership program in 1992, Petraeus never proved satisfied with his own performance or those under his command. He was the outstanding division commander in the first phase of the Iraq War, and his counterinsurgency operations in Mosul in 2003 set the standard for what followed with his reconceptualization of doctrine as commandant of Leavenworth. As commander of the Multinational Force–Iraq and Central Command (CENTCOM), he executed the "new thinking" in the "Surge." Two things most impressed me about David Petraeus. First, as a scholar-soldier, he has the mental penetration to understand security problems at their existential level. Policymakers and generals cannot engineer outcomes, nor can overwhelming conventional force impose the national will on unconventional opponents. Petraeus understands this and is not afraid to "tell it like it is," even when hectored by politicians who want assurances of quick and decisive results. Second, he genuinely cares for his people. A young soldier lost an eye in combat with the 101st Airborne Division. Petraeus helped him get into Officer Candidate School at Fort Benning and followed his progress. I met the soldier and invited him to speak at a Rotary Club gathering. Petraeus sent me comments to use in my introduction of the soldier. Petraeus later spoke at that young soldier's graduation and pinned on his second lieutenant bars. I know of other examples of his looking after soldiers. To my way of thinking, General Petraeus belongs in the pantheon of great American generals because, as an officer and leader, he personifies the ideal I always held out—but never achieved—for myself.

The current army is far and away better than the one that fought in Vietnam. Unlike in Vietnam, the army demonstrated a capacity to change in response to the altered battle space—not easy to achieve in the midst of a war. The vertical command structures "flattened"; instead of the micromanaging of Vietnam, the command climate encouraged initiative and entrusted junior leaders with increased responsibilities. General McChrystal was one who was instrumental in bringing about the change. The multiple deployments not only indicated the willingness of our men to sacrifice, but they also proved—probably beyond the expectations of the brass—the high quality of the army's junior leadership.

Still in There Pitching

Colonel Clarke was right on one score: I did not have to go into the field to continue my association with Fort Benning. People complain that when they call me on the phone, more often than not Jeannie tells them, "Ralph is not here. He is out with the Rangers." When I stepped down as honorary colonel, I lost my slot in the starting rotation but probably got more work out of the bullpen. Senior leadership at Benning continued to include me in some of the study groups, probably in deference to my age.

In a bold move, the army amalgamated the armor and infantry schools at Fort Benning; the resultant Maneuver Center of Excellence was tasked with forging a new level of combined arms operational art. The army selected the crème de la crème of young general officers to command the Maneuver Center. The last two commanders—Maj. Gen. H. R. McMaster and Maj. Gen. Austin "Scott" Miller—met and surpassed all expectations. McMaster, a Petraeus protégé, is a true scholar-warrior out of the same mold. From my perspective, Miller emphasized a mastery of basic soldier skills and leadership. Since basic soldier skills training has long been a special interest of mine, I am always pleased when asked to participate in discussions of relevant issues. One was the incorporation of women into Ranger training. Miller calmly insisted standards would remain in place. If females met the test, they would get the Ranger tab. Miller defused what could have been a contentious issue.

For years, I labored collating leadership lessons garnered from eclectic reading, writing, and speaking as well as from my army experiences. I worked on putting together a book intended to serve as a guide, particularly for young soldiers. Writing a book is a daunting and lonely enterprise. As Mark Twain observed, writing is 1 percent inspiration and 99 percent perspiration. Often I lagged, the project languished, only to get kick-started by Jeannie saying, "Get on with it." A recipient of plenty of help from external readers, I am indebted in particular to John Lock, a retired lieutenant colonel and Ranger, who mentored me throughout the process. A collection of mini-essays and vignettes, the book chiefly centered on training, mentoring, military mores and ethics, and personal growth. Finally, in 2007, *Words for Warriors: A Professional Soldier's Notebook* came off the presses. I was both relieved to finish the book and pleased with its reception. I attended a variety of ceremonies but rarely missed those involving awards bearing my name. In addition to the medals and plaques, the winner always received a signed copy of my book. Other awardees also receive copies. The total donated so far stands at more than one thousand.

Gen. Edward Meyer, former chief of staff of the army, opined in his letter recommending me as a West Point distinguished graduate that my activities after retirement, more than my uniformed service, qualified me for induction. Be that as it may, I have been showered with honors over the years and include them here not as self-promotion but to acknowledge those responsible.

In 1998, the Korean War veterans' association of Ranger Infantry Companies Airborne named me Airborne Ranger of the Year. The following year, I was selected for membership in the Gathering of Eagles society, centered at Maxwell Air Force Base in Montgomery. Rather taken aback when nominated—my career had hardly been "closely associated with aviation"—I received assurance my ten Air Medals more than certified me for membership. I was the ninth army man inducted.

Over the years on visits to Tifton, I always sought out my two old high school buddies, Charles Kent and Charles Massey, for a chat over coffee. They worked for my inclusion on the Wall of Fame for distinguished Tiftonites. That became a reality in April 2004. While pleased to receive the acknowledgment of my hometown, I received an honor in 2007 that floored me. Every year since 1980, the National Infantry Association presents the Doughboy Award—a chrome replica of a helmet worn during World War I—for outstanding contributions to the Infantry. The highest award the chief of Infantry can bestow, it usually goes to a general officer, and occasionally to a politician (such as Senator Robert Dole) or civilian (like Bob Hope). Beginning in 1996, a similar award was initiated for enlisted soldiers. At the ceremony held in Freedom Hall, at Lawson Airfield, Fort Benning, not only did I receive the chrome helmet, but the Infantry Association presented Jeannie with the Shield of Sparta, Infantry's way of commemorating the selfless sacrifices and courage of army wives. For me, Jeannie's pleased and surprised reaction was the best part of the event. She said it was the first medal she had ever received.

Honors still flowed in after I stepped down as honorary colonel. I received the Mary Reed Award for "service above self" from the Rotary Club of Columbus, Georgia, and the distinguished citizen award from the Boy Scouts of the Chattahoochee Valley. Then, at the end of 2015, came another deluge of tributes. In October, at a black-tie affair in Columbus, the Pastoral Institute presented Jeannie and me with the Sue Marie and Bill Turner Servant Leadership Award. Then, a month later, the National Infantry Museum and Soldiers' Center honored me for lifetime service with the opening of an exhibit in the Ranger Hall of Fame. Made possible by a generous donation from the Pezold family and the hard work of many, chief among them Phyllis Aaron, the "wall" displays my service memorabilia and a photo collage. The event and exhibit also features a video with tributes from Generals Petraeus and McChrystal and three Ranger command sergeants major, Chris Hardy, Dennis Smith, and Matt Walker. All of this is humbling, and to say the least, Jeannie and I were overwhelmed. In December, I made my sixth, and probably last, trip to Colombia. Joined by my old friend Ken Keen and the new commander of U.S. Army South, Maj. Gen. K. K. Chinn, we helped celebrate the sixtieth anniversary of the founding of the Escuela de Lanceros. Once again fending off claims that I had founded the school, I reflected back on how we started with nothing. Since then the Colombians have created one of the finest special operations training programs in Latin America. Given all the fanfare, some friends joked that they grew tired seeing my face in the local media.

As the years rolled by, the days when I was 165 pounds of "romping, stomping, airborne hell" seemed a long way off. Now when I am in the field, I labor to "take a knee" and wear nothing more than a protective vest during live-fire exercises. General MacArthur knew a thing or two about old soldiers. He believed people grew old only when they deserted the ideals of their youth. The years may wrinkle the skin "but to give up . . . wrinkles the soul." Those youthful ideals planted by my father became the bedrock of my being, and I always strove to live up to them in my day-to-day life.

As we grow older we marvel at how time sped by. Napoleon once observed that he could always regain lost ground but never time. Although we learn from history, the past cannot be changed. Life is not a crapshoot; it consists of chance but also skill. We determine what we become by what we do each day. The present impacts—either positively or negatively—the future. Every decision and action has a knock-on effect. Countless times I have met soldiers of all ranks who reported that something I had said or done in training had profoundly impacted them. I seldom remember the occasion, but for them it was significant. Because we never know our influence over others, we must always live each day according to the highest standards. I believe that I left my commands more combat ready than I found them. I have always thought if I helped save a soldier's life, then I more than earned my pay; that knowledge—and I am told it is so—is greater than all the honors and awards accumulated over the years.

Other than my father, George Washington influenced me most. Washington remains a timeless national icon because of his republican rectitude and for always keeping his word. As a battlefield commander, he had a losing record. His greatness as a general rested in his personal intangibles; and he was at his best when the chips were down. His bold riposte across the Delaware kept alive the flickering embers of American hopes in the war. After the drubbings at Brandywine and Germantown, with his beaten and demoralized army wintering in Valley Forge, he did not return to Mount Vernon and the comforts of home. He stayed with his men, endured the privations, and with the help of General von Steuben, trained his troops and restored their morale and combat efficiency as proven the next time the Continental Army faced the British at Monmouth. It was a different army. He established his reputation based entirely on the way he conducted his life. Earlier, in a conference with Native Americans, he said, "Brothers, I am a warrior. My words are few and plain; but I will make good what I say."

I would like to be remembered that way.

Afterword

When once asked by a friend in uniform to describe Col. Ralph Puckett in one word, I replied with emphasis, "Inspirational!" That word best captures what "Ranger" Puckett was to countless soldiers over his decades in uniform and best captures what he has been during his subsequent decades supporting those in uniform, especially those in the U.S. Army's Ranger Regiment, Ranger School, and Infantry School. Indeed, Ranger Puckett has given countless hours of service—even after taking off the uniform following some twenty-two years of active duty—as the honorary colonel of the Ranger Regiment (for some twelve years), as an honorary instructor for a variety of courses at the Infantry School, and as a member of the boards of various organizations supporting the Rangers and the Infantry School, as well as in a variety of positions with the Boy Scouts and other civic organizations. In each capacity, he invariably inspired those with whom he had contact to strive to be the very best soldier and leader they could be.

The leaders of the battalion I was privileged to command in the 101st Airborne Division (Air Assault) and I were among those inspired by Colonel Puckett when we first encountered him in the early 1990s. He gave the graduation address during the ceremony marking our completion of a superb several-week Infantry Leader Course conducted by cadre members of the Ranger School. We'd all heard a great deal about him already, and he more than lived up to his billing: in truth, he was extraordinarily impressive, and that event marked the beginning of a relationship between the two of us that continues to this day and now has extended to our son, an army captain. I was subsequently inspired by Colonel Puckett on numerous additional occasions in subsequent encounters during my own thirty-seven-year career that culminated with service as commander of U.S. Central Command and as the coalition commander during the Surges in Iraq and Afghanistan. Ranger Puckett was, in fact, a consistent source of energy, example, and inspiration to me and many others throughout the wars of the post-9/11 period, during which time he made multiple trips to Afghanistan, Iraq, and other far-flung locations to visit and encourage Rangers and others deployed in those war zones and during which he sent us countless letters and e-mails that inevitably contained meaningful messages.

In getting to know Ralph Puckett well after he retired from the military, it was no surprise to me to learn that he was one of those individuals who, from an early age, was never "proud to be average." Rather, he was one who always sought the highest achievements in whatever endeavor he pursued, and he typically sought leadership positions in those endeavors, as well. As a Boy Scout, for example, he not only earned Eagle Scout rank with gold palm, but he was also a senior patrol leader, two very coveted and hard-earned accomplishments. He was so intent on being a fighter pilot in World War II (which ultimately ended before he was old enough to join the military) that he took flying lessons at age fifteen, before he ever got behind the wheel of a car, and soloed at sixteen. With the war ended, he then attended the U.S. Military Academy at West Point, where he was not only a star boxer but captain of the boxing team. And then, as a newly commissioned Infantry officer, and after attending the Infantry officer basic course, jump school, and glider school, he volunteered to serve in the Korean War.

In Korea in 1950, as a young second lieutenant without a day of troop duty, he was given the mission of forming, training, and commanding the Eighth Army Ranger Company. And it was in that assignment that Ralph Puckett's association with Rangers began—and where the legend of Ranger Puckett began as well. The company was small—just three officers (the two others were Ralph's classmates from West Point and had no more troop experience than he did) and seventy-three enlisted men, the latter all good soldiers but not Infantrymen. They all had their work cut out for them.

Second Lieutenant Puckett established a clear vision for the soldiers in the Ranger Company—placing enormous emphasis on physical fitness and mental toughness ("every Ranger to be a tiger"), on competence as an individual soldier, on teamwork within each element and among the team of teams that comprised the company, and on faith in oneself, one's Ranger buddies, and the leaders of the unit. Not coincidentally, each of these qualities was embodied in the vision that later guided development of the U.S. Army's Ranger School and, subsequently, in the stanzas of the Ranger Creed written several decades later.

The training of the Eighth Army Ranger Company was extremely demanding, with every aspect of it focused on enabling the soldiers and the unit to achieve the qualities in their commander's vision. Lieutenant Puckett and his fellow leaders put particular emphasis on forthright assessments and after-action reviews following every activity in order to improve with each iteration of training. While never reluctant to praise his troopers, Ranger Puckett never conveyed full satisfaction with their performance or with his own; rather, his emphasis was on always doing better. And they did, demonstrating exceptional capability when the company entered combat in October 1950, successfully conducting combat day and night patrols and ambushes.

Years later, at unit reunions, those who served in that unit remained fiercely proud of the extraordinarily tough training they underwent before entering combat. And many of Puckett's soldiers subsequently credited that training with their survival in the fierce fighting that ensued when the Chinese entered the war in late 1950.

On 25 November, in one of the toughest battles of that period of the war, Lieutenant Puckett led from the front as his troopers seized and then fought to hold the strategically important Hill 205 overlooking the Ch'ongch'on River in the face of a massive Chinese offensive. Surrounded by hundreds of Chinese, who launched six waves of attacks, the fifty-one-man company fought fiercely, with Puckett calling in numerous "danger close" artillery missions. Though a mile from the nearest friendly unit, the company held on; however, nearly 60 percent of its soldiers sustained casualties, and Puckett himself was wounded three times and had to be evacuated to the United States, where he would be hospitalized for a year for the wounds he sustained in the battle—and where he would receive our nation's second-highest award for courage on the battlefield, the Distinguished Service Cross. It was with that service that the Ranger Puckett legend began to take shape.

It was during his yearlong recovery that Ralph met Jeannie Martin, whom he would marry in 1952 and with whom he was to share the sixty-four years since then, with her supporting him and him supporting her throughout the decades of their marriage, the birth of their two daughters and one son, and the subsequent births of their six grandchildren.

Following his lengthy recovery from the wounds he sustained in Korea, Ranger Puckett joined the newly established U.S. Army Ranger Department, serving as an instructor and tactical officer, and commanding companies at Fort Benning and in the mountain Ranger camp in north Georgia. He then served as a rifle company commander and staff officer in the Sixty-Fifth Regimental Combat Team, before beginning another significant chapter of the Ranger Puckett legend.

In 1955, Puckett was sent to Colombia, where he served as a Ranger Advisor to the Colombian Army and helped it form the Lancero Course, essentially the Colombian Army's Ranger School. He is still remembered—and respected—some sixty years later in Colombia for the enormous contribution he made during the formation of the course that is now the premiere small-unit leadership course in Latin America.

Upon return from Colombia, Ranger Puckett attended the Infantry Officer Advanced Course, had various additional assignments, and completed the Command and General Staff College, before joining the Tenth Special Forces Group in Germany, where he commanded two units and solidified his reputation as a leader committed to the toughest, most realistic training conceivable.

That training would stand him in good stead when he deployed to Vietnam to command a battalion and serve as a brigade executive officer. Leading from the front once again, he was wounded twice more. And, once again, he earned a Distinguished Service Cross during a night-long defense, this time in a fierce battle near Chu Lai, inspiring his soldiers to rally and repel a significant North Vietnamese Army force. Indeed, his very presence helped galvanize the unit's paratroopers, for after he linked up with the unit, one of them recalled later, "We all stiffened . . . and felt that nothing bad could happen now, because 'the Ranger' was with us." Yet another chapter was added to the Ranger Puckett legend.

After returning to the States in 1968, having received additional awards for valor in Vietnam, Colonel Puckett served as a regimental commander at West Point and then a brigade commander in the Fourth Infantry Division (Mechanized). In each assignment, he is still remembered for his commitment to exacting standards and emphasis on physical toughness and demanding training.

Colonel Puckett's retirement at the end of June 1971 marked the end of his time in uniform, and the beginning of an important chapter of his life. He decided to retire because he had been invited to take a position that appealed enormously to him, that of national programs coordinator for Outward Bound. As always, he threw himself into the new endeavor, giving energy and direction to an extraordinary organization, and spurring a number of initiatives that made a superb organization even better. Following that experience, he became the executive vice president of MicroBilt, a soft- and hardware computer company, learning considerably about the revolution beginning in the IT sector and enjoying the new challenges immensely. In each of his civilian capacities, he brought what he'd always provided to the military units he had led: clear vision, dedication, integrity, and inspirational leadership.

But at heart, retired Colonel Puckett was still a Ranger and an Infantryman, and he thus sought to help the organizations in which he had enjoyed serving in uniform. And, as the years passed, he inevitably gravitated to the further service he would render to the Ranger Regiment, the Ranger School, and the Infantry School, as well as to an array of civic organizations. As always, he brought impressive qualities—humility, energy, vision, and support for the highest of standards. And he touched—and inspired—tens of thousands of soldiers, boy scouts, and fellow citizens.

Ralph Puckett was, in my experience, truly unique in his commitment to serve those in the ranks of the organizations he treasured. He was also unique in the way in which he inspired each of us he touched to truly strive to be all that we could be. Despite the praise and compliments that he frequently offered, he was, at heart, a leader who was never fully satisfied with anyone's level of performance, including his own, no matter how exceptional; rather, his approach could best be characterized by a phrase familiar to many of us who served: "One more, Ranger"—whether it was one more push-up, one more pull-up, one more iteration of a tough training exercise, or better performance in any aspect of our profession as soldiers and leaders. But he managed to provide his exhortation in such a positive, encouraging manner that we did everything humanly possible not to fail him; indeed, we did all that we could to live up to his expectations, to enable him to "confirm our excellence," as he put it. And when some of us did stumble or fail him, his response was supportive, encouraging us to recognize our mistake, learn from it, and take action to avoid it in the future. He truly cared about people and genuinely sought to help them achieve their fullest potential.

That technique of leadership—affirmative, positive, motivating—is what truly set Ranger Puckett apart, and that is what made him such a tremendous addition to any organization he led or supported. He truly embraced the greeting Rangers render to superior officers, "Rangers lead the way!" And he wanted to be sure that every Ranger would, indeed, do just that.

All of this is chronicled in this book; Ranger Puckett's experiences and those of others with whom he was associated during a lifetime of exceptional service. I hope you found his story as inspirational as Ranger Puckett has been for so many of us over the years.

General David H. Petraeus (Ret.)
Arlington, Virginia
January 2016

Acknowledgments

This book had an unusual genesis. Probably two decades ago—at the insistence of family members—I began work on a memoir. For a number of reasons, the project never gained much traction. For starters, I thought only real historical players wrote memoirs. I never subscribed to the idea that every life has a story; my story had no real historical significance. Jeannie, my wife, constantly prodded me. My children—Jean, Marty, and Thomas—urged me to "Do it, Dad!" They pointed out that my experiences would be of real value to young soldiers. The book slowly took form but the manuscript read like a set of reminiscences, which was fine—it was intended as a chronicle for present and future generations of Pucketts, revealing how one of their forbears played a small role in events that helped shape American history. Progress was slow and haphazard before it was overtaken by other concerns.

The September 11, 2001, attacks and the opening of operations in Afghanistan a month later and in Iraq in March 2003 rechanneled my energies. As honorary colonel of the Seventy-Fifth Ranger Regiment, I had access to its training and began compiling my observations. Hoping to improve the combat effectiveness of the Rangers, I assembled a series of essays and thought pieces written for junior grade officers and senior company noncommissioned officers that evolved into *Words for Warriors: A Professional Soldier's Notebook* (2007).

Work on the autobiography languished. My many other activities impinged on all my available time. In 2012, my son invited Jeannie and me to spend nine days in his cottage in the Hamptons—time I used to kick-start the project. That autumn, I offered an overview of my experiences as a battalion commander in Vietnam to faculty and students at Columbus State University. One of the listeners, a professor in the history department, asked me to make a similar presentation to his class. Several months later, the same professor, Dan Crosswell, approached me with a request that we do an oral history. Not terribly enthused with that idea, I told Dan about my memoir. He asked if he could read it and perhaps provide some editorial advice. He later volunteered to take the lead on the project under the condition that the manuscript would receive a total rewrite. From that point, our partnership grew.

We followed a time-tested procedure. The production cycle ran monthly.

Dan ran my text through his filter, reorganized and reworked extraneous elements into a chapter, removed my homilies, and presented the first draft in the middle of the month. We would get together for a couple of hours and Dan would probe for personal insights while clarifying the narrative. Armed with his notes, he made additions and changes, and at the end of the month, we repeated the process. When one chapter was complete, we proceeded to the next. The sequence did not go as smoothly as we had envisioned. The Vietnam chapters proved problematic. Even as I experienced it, my time in Vietnam—running near-consecutive operations under the operational command of different parent organizations in three different war zones—was all a blur. Trying to reconstruct places and events all these years later presented real challenges. That said, the project was complete in a remarkably short time. Our method guaranteed that while Dan wrote the text, the words were all mine. We sought accuracy and honesty in the telling of the story and any errors or omissions are wholly the responsibility of the authors.

A shout of appreciation goes out to the many people who aided in making this book a finished product. The very discerning director of the Association of the US Army Book Program, Roger Cirillo, nominated the book for inclusion in the excellent American Warriors series published in conjunction with the University Press of Kentucky. The people in Lexington sent it out for peer review; the reviewers gave it a "thumbs-up" and offered cogent recommendations for how the manuscript could be improved. The unnamed commentators were right so the additions were made, and the text is better as a result. The very patient Allison Webster, executive assistant to the director of the press, acted as the project manager. Ila McEntire, the senior editing supervisor, did just that. The always pleasant and extremely efficient Susan Murray, a freelance editor, executed the copyediting, and Grant Hackett relieved us of the tedious task of indexing. The affability and professionalism of the University Press of Kentucky is of the highest order. Thanks also to Phyllis Aaron who, in addition to her day job as the project manager of the National Infantry Foundation, provided emergency technical support for the photographs and maps. Thanks also to the graphics and production staff at the press.

I am deeply indebted to all the soldiers with whom I have been affiliated in the sixty-eight years since my commissioning on the Plain at West Point. This story is as much theirs as it is mine. Recounting events that occurred five and six decades ago presents difficulties and inevitably, the names of men who should appear in these pages and do not were lost in the mists of memory. That is a regret.

Gen. David Petraeus kindly consented to take time from his packed schedule to write the afterword. My heartfelt gratitude is extended to the general, a man and soldier for whom I harbor the deepest respect.

The person most responsible for keeping this project on the rails is Jeannie. She continued insisting I needed to interject some emotion and personal insights into the story but mostly Jeannie badgered me to get on with it. Dan may have received some of the same. While I sometimes expressed my irritation with her constant reminders, I knew she was right. (She always is.) I often use the overused and now cliché "wind beneath my wings" analogy, but it expresses my genuine feelings.

Ranger is one man's story, and in its recounting is manifest the hope that in some small way, this account will contribute to making the extant and future U.S. Army a better and more effective force.

Index